The Internet

Made Simple

The Internet Made Simple

P.K.McBride

MADE SIMPLE
BOOKS

Made Simple
An imprint of Butterworth-Heinemann
Linacre House, Jordan Hill, Oxford OX2 8DP
225 Wildwood Avenue, Woburn MA 01801-2041
A division of Reed Educational and Professional Publishing Ltd

Ɽ   A member of the Reed Elsevier plc group

OXFORD   BOSTON   JOHANNESBURG
MELBOURNE   NEW DELHI   SINGAPORE

First published 1998

British Library Cataloguing in Publication Data
A catalogue record for this book is available from the British Library

ISBN 0 7506 3944 X

 Typeset by P.K.McBride, Southampton

Archtype, Bash Casual, Cotswold and Gravity fonts from Advanced Graphics Ltd
Icons designed by Sarah Ward © 1994
Printed and bound in Italy

FOR EVERY TITLE THAT WE PUBLISH, BUTTERWORTH-HEINEMANN
WILL PAY FOR BTCV TO PLANT AND CARE FOR A TREE.

Contents

Preface

The Internet is vast, varied and changing fast. Some parts of it are designed for very specialist audiences, some of its facilities are complex to use. Other parts are of general interest and some services are simple to access. This book concentrates on those aspects that will be of interest to most people – browsing and searching the World Wide Web, using electronic mail, reading newsgroups, downloading files and creating Web pages.

The best way to get to grips with the Internet is to explore it. But exploration, Livingstone-style, can take you into a lot of dead ends, or round in circles. While this is fascinating, it can also be frustrating – I speak from experience. This book aims to provide you with a map, and some of the basic tools that you need, so that you don't get (too) lost.

The first four chapters cover the preparations to be made while at the base camp. They provide a crash course in the native language of the Internet, its key concepts and jargon, and setting up the equipment that you will need for your expedition.

The next four chapters explore the World Wide Web, trying out a number of routes into it and seeing what you can do while you are there.

From the Web, we strike out into other areas of the Internet – e-mail, newsgroups and the stores of files for downloading.

Towards the end of the book, we take a brief look at creating Web pages, introducing the basics of HTML – HyperText Markup Language – and sampling the

Tip

If you are new to computers and need an introduction to Windows 95, you might like to try the companion book *Windows 95 Made Simple*.

possibilities of the HTML editors that can be found in the Netscape and Internet Explorer packages.

The final chapter contains some practical advice on finding Internet access providers, and lists some useful sources of shareware and other files. For those of you who like to know these things, there is an introduction to some of the technicalities of data communications.

This book brings together the best of *The Internet for Windows 95 Made Simple* and *Searching the Internet Made Simple* – thoroughly updated, with a lot of new material and all in full colour.

Many thanks to my Internet access providers, Total Connectivity Providers for their excellent service over these last three years; to co-authors Sam Kennington and Nat McBride for sharing their enthusiasms; to Rebecca Hammersley at Butterworth-Heinemann and Ian Wilcox at Ace Pre-Press, for help in sorting out the colour design; and to Catherine Fear, my copy-editor, for going over it with her fine-tooth comb!

Enjoy your travels around the Internet!

P.K.McBride

1 Internet FAQs

What is it?

The Internet is not a single network, but a collection of thousands of computer networks, throughout the world. These vary greatly in size and in the number of computers that are connected to them. These linked networks are of two types:

- **LAN** (Local Area Network), covering an office or perhaps a campus;

- **WAN** (Wide Area Network), joining distant sites. A WAN may extend over the whole country, or even over many countries.

All LANs and most WANs are owned by individual organisations. Some WANs act as **Access Providers**. Members of the public and/or businesses can join these networks – usually in return for a modest charge.

The computers likewise vary from giant supercomputers down to desktop computers – PCs, Macintoshes, Amigas, Archimedes or whatever. They are owned and run by thousands of separate universities, government agencies, businesses and individuals.

There is no central authority or governing body, though there is an Internet Society, established a couple of years ago to co-ordinate and standardise rules of operation. The Internet relies on co-operation, driven by goodwill and enlightened self-interest. And it works!

Definitions

FAQ (Frequently Asked Questions) – at almost every place on the Internet where you can ask for help, you will find a FAQ list – a set of common questions, and their answers. Do check the FAQ first, before asking your own question.

Network – a collection of linked computers. On a LAN, users can share printers and other networked resources. On any network – including the Internet – users can communicate and share data with each other.

Access provider – an organisation offering access to some or all of the services available over the Internet.

Who's on-line?

Take note

The information in this book was up to date as it went to press, but anything you read anywhere about the Internet may be out of date. It changes so rapidly, and there are so many people creating new services and devising new uses for it, that by the time anything gets printed, it may well have been overtaken by events.

If you want to know what's happening NOW get onto the Net and watch the changes from the inside.

Some would say 'Everybody who's anybody', but that's not true – yet! So who is on-line on the Internet?

- **Academics**: Students and staff at universities, colleges – and some schools – throughout the world. These form the largest and most active group of users. Apart from the fact that they use the Internet for their studies, they will also not normally have to pay the phone bills!

- **Business users**: many multinational companies have discovered that the Internet provides the most efficient and cheapest way of communicating with colleagues around the world. An increasing number of companies are also realising that it is a viable way to sell goods and services.

- **Government organisations**: some use the Internet for their own communications; some to make information available to the public. The US government has been actively on-line since the early days of the Internet; in the UK, 10 Downing Street, the Treasury and many other departments are now on-line – even the Queen has a home page!

- **Individuals**: anyone with a reasonably modern computer, modem and phone line can join the Internet through one of the public access providers. Millions have already linked up. In the UK at the present, around 20,000 new subscribers are coming on-line each month, and the rate of growth is increasing.

What's in it for me?

If you have access to the Internet, you have access to:

- **16 million host computers**, all of which are possible sources of information that could be useful to you in your work, your travelling, your academic research or your hobbies.

- **40+ million people**, any of whom could be future friends, customers, fellow enthusiasts, problem-solvers. There may well even be a few old friends out there already.

- **gigabytes of files** containing programs – including the software that you need for working on the Internet – books, news articles, pictures – still and video – sounds and much else.

- **a whole raft of services**, such as financial advice, stock market information, airline times and reservations, weather reports, small-ads and electronic shopping malls.

Where do I start?

Here, of course. Read on to get an idea of what's going on out there, then learn how to set up your hardware and get on-line with an access providers. You can then start to explore the World Wide Web, e-mail and the other services available through the Internet.

Definitions

Host computer – one that provides a service for Internet users. The service may be simple pages of information, access to files for downloading, a place to meet and chat with other users, or a complex interactive service.

Gigabyte – a thousand megabytes or 1,000,000,000 bytes. Taking each byte as a letter, this is the equivalent of around 2,000 thick paperback books.

Definitions

Hypertext – documents linked so that clicking on a button, icon or keyword takes you into the related document – wherever it may be. Web pages are written in HTML (HyperText Markup Language) which handles links in a standardised way.

Web browser – program that lets you leap between hypertext links to read text, view graphics and videos, and hear sounds. The two leading browsers are **Netscape Navigator** and **Microsoft's** Internet Explorer.

The World Wide Web

This is the most active and fastest-growing aspect of the Internet. It consists of many countless numbers of pages, held in over a million computers scattered across the world, and all joined together by **hypertext** links and accessed through a **Web browser**. Web directories (Chapter 6) have organised sets of links to pages, and many pages will have links to others on related topics.

Most pages are illustrated with still or animated graphics, though some keep to simple – but fast – text-only displays. Some have video or sound clips that you can enjoy on-line; other have links to files – programs, documents, pictures or multimedia clips – that you can download into your computer. Some pages work interactively with the reader, or act as places where users can meet and 'chat' – usually by typing though voice communication is coming.

E-mail

Though less glamourous than the Web, electronic mail is arguably more useful. E-mail allows you to communicate and exchange files quickly and cheaply with other Internet users. You can send a message half way round the world in a matter of minutes, and all it costs is a few seconds of telephone time.

Newsgroups and mailing lists

They are a combination of bulletin boards and newsletters, with each dedicated to a specific interest, topic, hobby, profession or obsession. At the last count there were over 20,000 different newsgroups, plus a smaller set of mailing lists.

Mailing lists and news groups are organised in slightly different ways.

- A mailing list is a direct extension of e-mail. Messages to the list are sent individually to all the people whose names are on it. You have to join the list to get the messages.

- Newsgroups are more centralised. The messages – here called articles – are initially sent to the computer that hosts the group. News servers collect new articles from the groups several times a day and hold them in store. If you want to read the news, you connect to your **news server** and download articles from there. If you subscribe to a newsgroup, the news server will pass incoming articles on to you, but you can read articles without subscribing.

FTP

FTP stands for File Transfer Protocol and is the standard method for copying files across the Internet. FTP hosts hold archives that are (usually) open to anyone to search and download files from. Some hosts have directories into which you can upload files, so that other people can share them.

You can download files through a Web browser, but to upload you normally need a dedicated FTP program.

Gopher

This menu-driven system was a first attempt to make the Internet more accessible. It has now been overtaken by the far friendlier Web, though you will still meet some Gopher menus – mainly in academic sites.

Definitions

News server – a computer at an Internet access provider's site that collects newsgroup articles for the benefit of its users.

Download – copy a file from an Internet host to your own computer.

Upload – copy a file onto an Internet host computer.

Take note

There are other ways of working on the Internet, e.g. Telnet, which lets you run programs on a remote computer. These are not simple to use, and are beyond the scope of this book.

Definitions

Usenet – still a significant name on the Internet. The Usenet news groups make up the greater part of all the Internet's meeting places.

NSFnet – the (US) National Science Foundation's internetwork. The high-speed cables between its sites formed the backbone of the Internet in North America.

Appropriate Use rules – most of us are grateful for these, as they help to reduce the amount of junk e-mail in our mailboxes. It's a shame that they cannot be more strictly enforced!

How did it start?

The history of the Internet is interesting, but there is no room here to go into any details, and you want to use the Internet, not write essays on its history. However, there are a few things you should know, as they help to explain aspects of the present.

The Internet story starts with ARPAnet, a long-distance computer network devised by the US Government's Advanced Research Projects Agency. From an initial four computers in 1969, this grew over the next 10 years to connect 200 computers in military and research establishments throughout the US, with a few overseas links. It proved, beyond doubt, the practicality and the value of internetworking. By the mid 1980s several academic 'inter-networks', including **Usenet**, BITnet, CSnet and **NSFnet** had been set up. These combined with the research part of ARPAnet, to form the Internet.

The crucial point is that the core of the Internet was – and still is – government-funded research or academic organisations. It was not set up as a commercial proposition, and commercial activities on the Internet are a recent innovation. There are still **Appropriate Use** rules that restrict the use of the Internet for profit.

The second historical fact is that the Internet originally linked mainframe computers, most of which ran the Unix operating system. PCs, Macintoshes and other personal computers only came onto the Internet later. As a result, the Internet has a distinct Unix flavour about it. You can see this in directory and file names – the slashes go the 'wrong' way / not \ as in Windows. And if you go beyond surfing the Web with a browser, you may start having to use some Unix commands.

How big?!

As there are so many organisations involved, with no single controlling body, and as it is constantly growing, no one really knows how big the Internet is. These figures are based on sampling, trends and earlier counts.

How many people?

The best guess is that there are over 1 million people in the UK and 40 million worldwide who link into the Internet, either from their home or office, with more joining every day. If the number of users continues to grow at its current rate, everyone in the World will be on the Internet in about eight years. I don't quite think so...

How many computers?

In 1989 there were around 100,000 host computers connected to the Internet. It reached 500,000 by mid-1991 and has been doubling every year since. At the time of writing the total is well over 16 million – and these are just the *host* computers, those that provide services to the Internet.

How many sites?

There has been an exponential growth in domains (page 10). The number rose steadily to 70,000 by 1995, but has shot up to over 1,000,000 by the end of 1997. This illustrates one of the problems of estimating size – what are you counting? Until recently, only large organisations had domain names. Now, many individuals and small businesses also have their own domain names.

Tip

At first sight, the sheer scale of things can be overwhelming, but take heart. There are plenty of good directories and search facilities to help you find your way around.

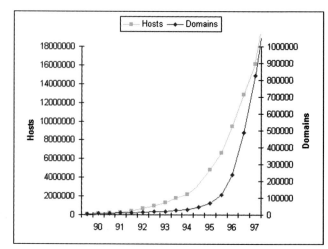

The Growth of the Internet

What will it cost me?

Setting up costs

Of course, if you do not have a computer and a modem, you must buy those before you can do anything. Bottom of the range multimedia PCs – fine for Internet use – are selling for around £750 at the time of writing, and could well be cheaper by the time you read this. A good fast modem (see page 15) should cost under £150, though you can pick up an adequate one for less than half that price. We'll return to modems in the next chapter.

Most software is either free or low-priced shareware – £100 should cover all you will need.

Running costs

You must sign up with an Internet access provider. Expect to pay around £15 a month for unlimited access, so that you can spend all night surfing, playing on-line games or chatting with your mates around the world, or around £6 for a set number of hours – with extra time charged by the minute. Some providers insist on a minimum of 6 or 12 month subscription. See pages 18 and 292 for more on acess providers.

All the time you are on-line, you are clocking up telephone charges. Most providers have local rate connections, so you are looking at about 1p a minute, evenings and weekends.

Overall, if you spent 1 hour on-line every day – and that's probably more than you will do once the novelty has worn off – the total cost would be around £30 a month.

Tip

E-mail is cheaper than snail mail (i.e. the post), and finding information on the Web is cheaper than travelling down to the library, so you could even save money!!

How is it organised?

With something as large as the Internet, it is clear that you need a well-organised naming system to find your way round. Every host computer and network has its own unique name – it also has a number, but on the rare occasions that you need it, someone will tell you what it is. Computers and smaller networks within larger ones may also have their own names, and every user has an address.

Organisations

Names have several parts to them, separated by dots. The parts are sometimes referred to as **domains**, and they are nested. The last part, or outermost domain, is the zone, which identifies either the country (outside the USA) or the type of organisation. The rest of the name is usually derived directly from the name of the organisation. For example:

   vnet.ibm.com

The **vnet** network within **IBM**, a **com**mercial organisation.

   repp.co.uk

Reed **E**ducational and **P**rofessional **P**ublishing, a **co**mmercial organisation based in the **UK**.

   gn.apc.org

GreenNet, a member of the **A**ssociation for **P**rogressive **C**ommunications **org**anisation.

   sussex.ac.uk

Sussex University (**ac**ademic) in the **UK**.

   oregon.uoregon.edu

The main **Oregon** site in the University of **Oregon** (USA).

Zone name examples

com	commercial (US)
co	commercial (elsewhere)
edu	educational (US)
ac	academic (educational outside the US)
net	network provider
org	non-commercial organisation
gov	government depart-ment
uk	United Kingdom
au	Australia
ca	Canada
fr	France
de	Germany
hk	Hong Kong

People

These follow the host name conventions, but with the user's name at the start, separated by an @ sign. For example, this is one of my names:

macbride@tcp.co.uk

tcp.co.uk is the domain name of **Total Connectivity Providers**, a **co**mpany in the **UK**, and **macbride** is my user name with them.

URLs

Every page on the World Wide Web and every file on the Internet has its own URL – Uniform Resource Locator – which tells you what it is called, where to find it and how to get it. For example, the URL of Microsoft's site on the World Wide Web is:

http://www.microsoft.com

The URL for the Made Simple page in my area is rather longer, as it has to locate a file within the site:

http://www.tcp.co.uk/~macbride/msbooks.htm

www.tcp.co.uk is the site, **~macbride** takes you to my Web storage area and **msbooks.htm** is the file for that page.

The first part of the URL defines the nature of the address. The main types are:

http: World Wide Web page (see page 70)

ftp: file in an FTP archive (see page 214)

news: newsgroup (see page 182)

mailto: e-mail address (see page 149)

Take note

As the Internet links up many other networks which have their own addressing systems, some addresses are more complicated than the simple pattern shown here. If you come across an address that you need to use, copy it *very* carefully.

Summary

- The Internet is a collection of **interlinked networks**, working together co-operatively.

- You can often find the answers to your problems in the **FAQ** (Frequently Asked Questions) lists maintained for most aspects of the Internet.

- You may be able **get into the Internet** either through your business or academic network, but if not, anyone can get a connection through an **access provider**.

- The Internet gives you access to people, information, files and a vast range of services.

- **Estimates of the numbers** of networks, computers and people joined by the Internet can never be accurate, as it is growing faster than anyone can count.

- Every network, computer and individual on the Internet has a unique **address**.

- Files are identified by **URLs** (Uniform Resource Locators). These show where the files are, what they are called, and what method to use to find them.

2 Getting on-line

Hardware

To get on-line, you need:

● Hardware – a computer, modem and telephone connection;

● An access provider – to connect you to the Internet;

● Software – for surfing the Web, downloading files and handling the mail and news. (A good browser will take care of all of these!)

Let's start with the hardware.

The computer

Almost any type of machine is suitable. People are using everything from massive mainframes down to ancient Commodore 64s. For the individual user, life is simplest from a PC or Apple Macintosh, as there is the greatest choice of software for these. Business users and students and staff in schools and colleges, will probably find themselves working with networked PCs or terminals of a large computer. Suitable software is available for all major networks and large computer systems.

This book is aimed primarily at Windows 95 users. As with any Windows 95 applications, to run Internet software well you need a fast 486 or Pentium PC, with at least 8Mb of memory. You should have at least 50Mb of free space on your hard drive, some for the software, some for temporary storage while you are on-line and lots for all those files that you can download free from the Internet!

Windows 95 make Internet working easier, just as it makes most jobs easier. The connectivity tools built into Windows 95 can make some things even simpler.

Phone connection

❑ You connect to your access provider through the normal phone system. The only extra kit you may need is an extension kit and wall-mounted socket to put a socket within reach of your desktop.

Take note

New PC's are often sold as 'Internet-ready'. They will have a modem and a browser (probably Internet Explorer – see chapter 4). They will also have a free trial membership offer with one of the big access providers. You can change providers when the free trial expires!

If you have an Internet-ready PC, you can ignore the rest of this chapter and only come back to it if things go wrong.

Definitions

Modem – MOdulator/DEModulator. A device that converts digital signals from a computer into analogue ones for transmission over the phone lines (and *vice versa*).

Take note

For the faster Internet connections, you need an ISDN line. Though these are too expensive for home use, at only a few hundred pounds a year they are within reach of small businesses, schools and other organisations. ISDN could even prove to be cheaper than a standard phone line if there is very heavy use of the Internet.

The modem

The type of modem dictates the speed with which you can transfer data to and from the Internet. The faster it is, the lower your phone bills will be, and its speed is depends on its baud rate and data compression.

Baud rate

This is the number of *bits* per second (bps) that can be pushed down the line. The newest modems now run at 56K – 56,000 bps, though 32K modems are in common use.

There are 8 bits to a byte, but all transmissions have extra addressing and error-checking information attached to them, so divide by 10 to get an idea of the *bytes* per second speed, or by 10,000 to get the Kilobyte rate.

Data compression

There are several methods of data compression (see page 294) but all modern modems can handle one or other of them. Data compressioncan push the effective transfer rate up to over 10Kb per second.

Tip

If there are other extensions to your phone, check that no-one is using one before you try to go on-line. (The modem makes an awful racket.) And ask them not to use the phone while you are on-line, as it can break the connection.

Buying a modem

- Faster modems may cost more, but will be cheaper in the end. A 1Mb file will take up to 10 minutes to download with a 28,800 baud modem, or around 3 minutes with a 56Kb modem. How much a minute do your phone calls cost?

- Card modems are easy to install, need no desk space and leave the serial port free.

- If you want an external modem, you must have an unused serial port.

- If the modem is Hayes-compatible it will work with almost all comms software.

- If you are connecting to the public telephone lines – i.e. normal ones – you can only legally use BABT approved modems.

- Most modems now are fax modems. They will connect you to the Internet and let you send and receive faxes from your PC. If you get one of these, make sure that it has fax software bundled with it.

Take note

No matter how fast your modem, you may still find that data trickles in from busy sites at busy times of day. When it's really bad, the rate can drop below 500 bytes per second.

Take note

With Windows 95's Plug-and-Play technology installing a modem be a breeze. As long as the modem is of a type that Windows 95 can recognise – and that means just about all the current ones – the system will configure itself. It really should be just a matter of plugging it in and turning on the PC (and the modem).

Definitions

Port – connection between the PC and other hardware. Normally a socket on the back of the PC, but expansion slots can also be ports.

Serial port – transmits data one bit after another down a single line. Data communications are almost always done via a serial port.

Parallel port – transmits data one byte (8 bits) at a time, down a set of wires. Faster than serial transmission, but not suitable for phone lines. Printers are normally linked through a parallel port.

All computers have one or more serial ports that can be used for getting data into and out of the machine. On a PC there are four, called COM1, COM2, COM3 and COM4. (COM is short for COMunications.)

A port may be a socket at the back of the main case, or reached through an expansion slot inside the case. If your modem is on a card, plugging it into any slot will give it access to the port. You may have to tell it which one.

● Most PCs have a serial port at the back of the machine. This is COM1, and the chances are it has a mouse plugged into it.

● Some PCs have two serial ports on their case. These are COM1 and COM2.

● A few have no external serial ports.

An external modem must, of course, be allocated the port number that it is plugged into; a card modem can be allocated any internal port that is not already in use.

Take note

You will probably find that the modem's pre-set configuration will work with your machine. If it does, you will only have to worry about COM ports when setting up the software.

If you do have to change the COM port, you will also have to change the IRQ (Interrupt ReQuest) setting. See the modem's manual for details.

Internet access providers

Access providers and service providers

Internet access providers come in two flavours – those who just provide access, and those that also offer their own on-line services for their members.

The two biggest service providers in the world used to be CompuServe and AOL (America On-Line). AOL has recently bought up CompuServe, but for the time being, the two are continuing to operate as separate services. We will look at what CompuServe has to offer in the next pages, but first let's turn to the pure access providers.

Access only

These providers vary from national organisations such as Demon Internet and Pipex, to small firms operating within one town – though many of these also offer a national network of local dial-in points.

Costs are currently (early 1998) around £10 to £15 per month for a **dial-up account**. This normally gives you:

- unlimited time on-line;
- 2 to 5Mb of storage space on their computer for your home page;
- a free pack of software for the Internet.

Some firms charge less per month, but restrict you to 10 or 20 hours free usage, with extra on-line time charged by the minute. These can be a good deal for light users.

Tip

CompuServe and AOL both offer a free trial membership and often put their software on the disks and CD-ROMs of computing magazines. Take up the offers and explore their services and the Internet beyond. See which works best, and whether you want any member services.

For more about selecting an access provider, see page 292.

Dial-up account – one where you connect to your provider (and through them to the Internet) through the public phone lines. This is the way most home and small business users get onto the Net.

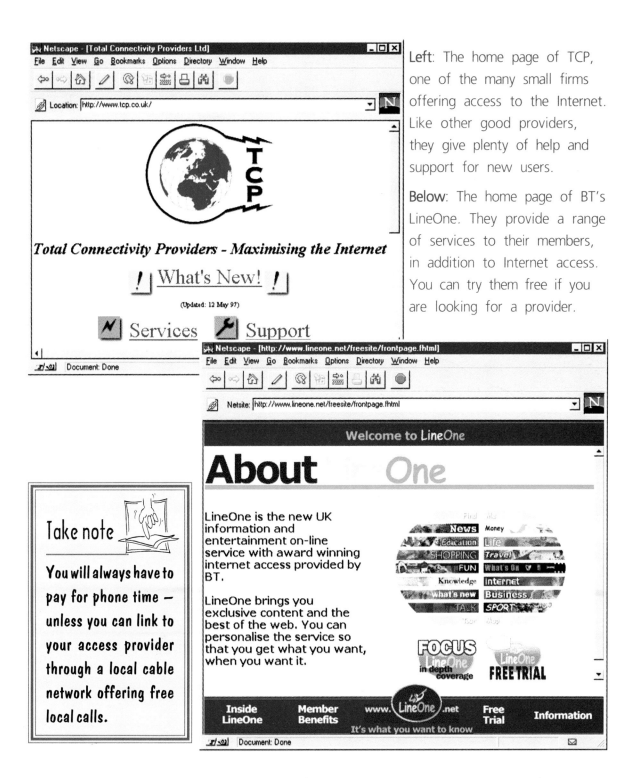

Left: The home page of TCP, one of the many small firms offering access to the Internet. Like other good providers, they give plenty of help and support for new users.

Below: The home page of BT's LineOne. They provide a range of services to their members, in addition to Internet access. You can try them free if you are looking for a provider.

Take note

You will always have to pay for phone time — unless you can link to your access provider through a local cable network offering free local calls.

CompuServe

CompuServe is one of the longest established on-line service provider – they were running before the Internet! It is also one of the largest, with around 500,000 members in the UK alone.

This is a highly graphical system, but each new image is only loaded once. It is then stored ready for next time it is needed. All of CompuServe's own extensive range of services can be reached by working through its menu system, or directly through the **Go** button (as long as you know the name).

Internet Explorer (Chapter 4) is incorporated in the latest issue of their software, and is called up when needed for Internet work.

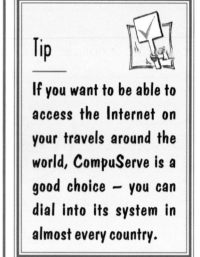

Tip

If you want to be able to access the Internet on your travels around the world, CompuServe is a good choice – you can dial into its system in almost every country.

You can keep an eye on how much time you are spending on-line.

There's lots going on in every area, with CompuServe's own forums and file stores backed by contributions from retailers, magazines and the computing industry.

The mail system is efficient and easy to use. Mail can be composed and read off-line, to keep down the phone bills.

Software

When you first start to explore the Internet, the only software that you really need is a good browser. With either Netscape Navigator (Chapter 3) or Internet Explorer (Chapter 4) you can handle your e-mail and access the newsgroups, as well as surf the Web. Your access provider should supply you with one or other of these – though not necessarily the latest version. At the time of writing, both Netscape and Internet Explorer have reached version 4.0, though earlier versions of both will do the job.

Netscape have led the way in the development of browsers and of HTML – the system for creating Web pages (see Chapter 14). **Netscape Navigator**, seen below, is the leading browser, though **Internet Explorer** now offers much the same capabilities.

Navigation buttons

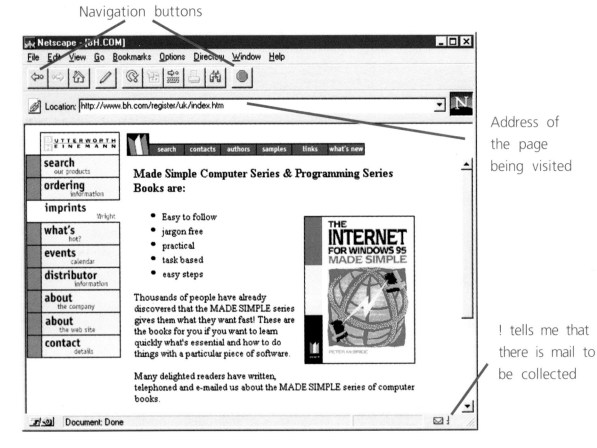

Address of the page being visited

! tells me that there is mail to be collected

This screenshot is from the publisher's Web site. For more information on the Made Simple computer books, stockists and how to order, visit: **http://www.bh.com**

Winsock and Winsock applications

Take note

Most access providers offer software packages to their subscribers. Some, like **CompuServe** and **AOL**, supply software that is specially written for the service; others supply a browser, usually bundled with a program to install it all for you.

Beneath the surface of your browser, there is a piece of software called *Winsock* that handles the links and the data transfer between your PC and the remote computers. Windows 95 has a built-in Winsock as part of its Dial-Up Networking software (see the next pages) and most of us can leave Winsock to do its job quite happily by itself.

Browsers are not the only applications that you can use to work on the Internet. There are many others, often referred to as *Winsock applications*, because they all rely on Winsock for managing the links to the Internet. These are dedicated programs for e-mail, news reading, file transfer, file-finding, people-finding, working on remote computers and other jobs. Most of these jobs can be done equally well – and often simpler – through a browser.

As you get deeper into the Internet, you may decide you would like to use some of these other applications. For example, if you want to upload files to a remote computer, you will need WS_FTP (see page 218) – you can only *download* with a browser. Newer versions of these applications will work happily with Windows 95's Winsock, though if you try to run Windows 3.1 applications you may need Trumpet Winsock.

Take note

Using Windows 95 to connect to the Microsoft Network is very simple – but to connect to any other service you might have to configure the Dial-Up Networking software. See page 26.

Dial-Up Networking

If you have not installed yet Dial-Up Networking, open the Control Panel and use Add/Remove Programs to do so before starting these steps

There are two aspects to configuring a new connection:

● the network software within your computer.

● the connection to the service provider.

1 Open the **Control Panel** and select **Network**.

2 Click **Add**.

3 Select **Protocol** and click **Add**.

4 Select **Microsoft** and **TCP/IP**, then click **OK**. Wait while it is loaded.

5 Select the new **TCP/IP** component and click **Properties**.

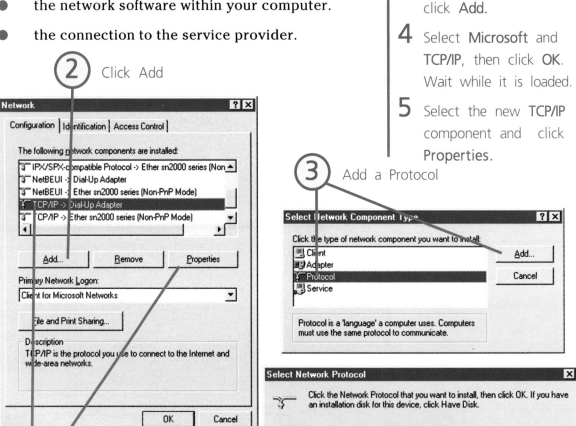

② Click Add

③ Add a Protocol

⑤ Select the new entry

④ Select Microsoft and TCP/IP

24

6 Work through the tabs.

  IP address: select *Obtain IP address automatically*

  WINS Configuration: select *Disable WINS resolution*

  Advanced: select *Set this protocol as default*

  Bindings: check *Client for Microsoft networks*

Either

7 Gateway: leave it blank

  DNS Configuration: select *Disable DNS*

Or

8 Gateway: type in the address

  DNS Configuration: type your e-mail name as the *Host* and your provider's name as the *Domain*, then type their address in the *DNS Server Search Order* and click **Add**.

I've seen two approaches to setting up the connection – one specifies the servers at this point, the other does it in the Dial-Up configuration. Either way you must know your provider's DNS (Domain Names Server) addresses – they should be in the paperwork that your provider sent when you signed up.

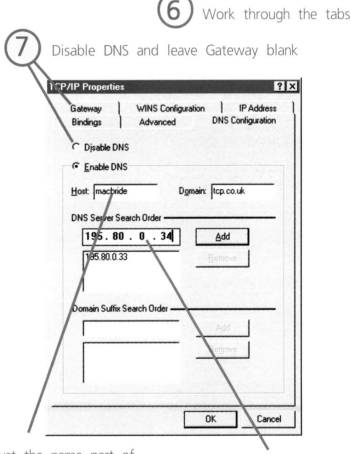

⑥ Work through the tabs

⑦ Disable DNS and leave Gateway blank

Just the name part of your e-mail address

The gateway and DNS IP addresses will be different, but of the same form – 4 sets of digits

⑧ Enter DNS and Gateway details

The Dial-Up connection

Once the Network software is in place, you can set up the connection. A Wizard handles the donkey work, leaving it to you to set the Properties.

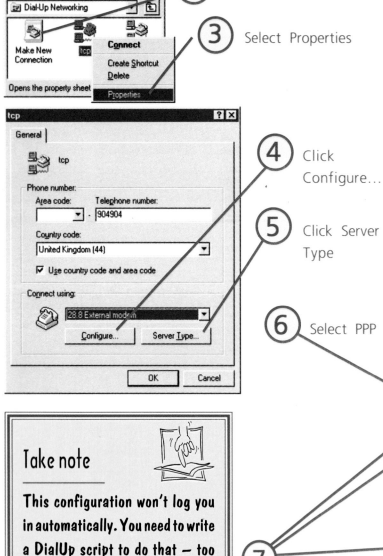

Make a new connection

Select Properties

Click Configure...

Click Server Type

Select PPP

Basic steps

1 Open the **Dial-Up** folder and click **Make New Connection**.

2 Go through the **Wizard** entering a name and the phone details.

3 At the folder right click on the new connection and select **Properties**.

4 Click **Configure** and on the **Options** select *Bring up terminal window after dialling*.

5 Click **Server Type**.

6 For the **Type**, select *PPP:Windows 95...*

7 Check *Log on* , *Enable compression* and *TCP/IP*.

8 Click **TCP/IP Settings**.

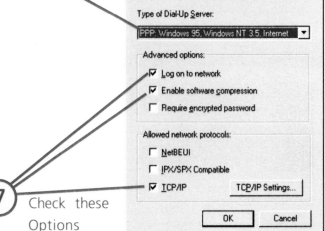

Check these Options

9 Set **Server assigned IP address**

10 *If you selected Disable DNS* (page 25) set **Specify name server** and enter the addresses.

11 *If you selected Enable DNS* set **Server assigned name server addresses.**

❏ **Logging in**

1 Double click the connection's icon.

2 Click **Connect.**

3 At the **Terminal Screen**, enter your *login name*, and *password* .

4 After the *Enabled* message and some garbage, click **Continue.**

❏ Run your applications.

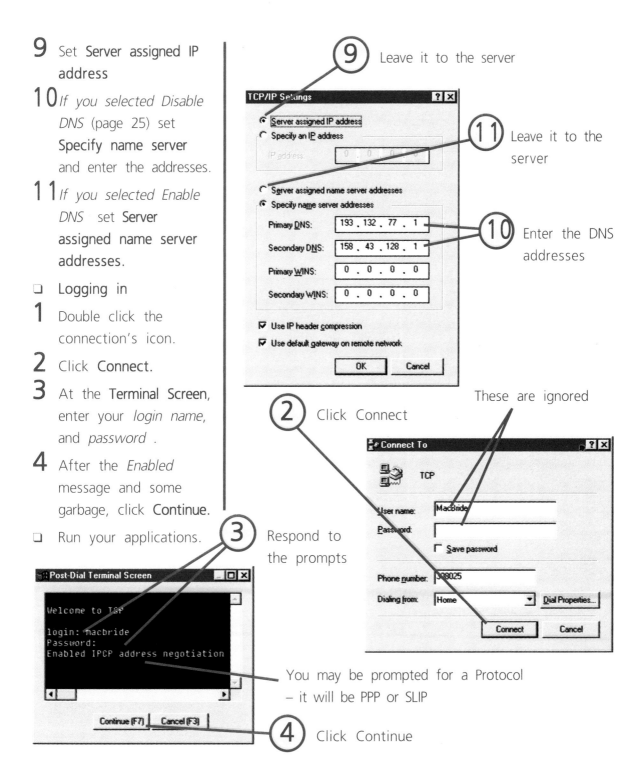

⑨ Leave it to the server

⑪ Leave it to the server

⑩ Enter the DNS addresses

These are ignored

② Click Connect

③ Respond to the prompts

You may be prompted for a Protocol – it will be PPP or SLIP

④ Click Continue

27

Modem settings

With the modem, as with much else in Windows 95, you can generally leave it to the system to find the best settings for it. However, it doesn't always get things right, so it might be as well to check the modem settings.

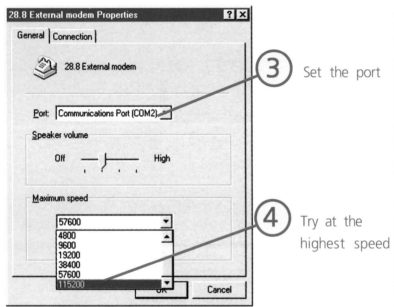

Set the port ③

Try at the highest speed ④

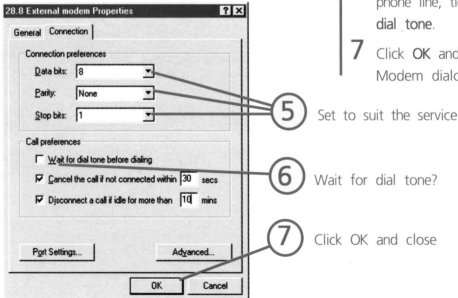

Set to suit the service ⑤

Wait for dial tone? ⑥

Click OK and close ⑦

Basic steps

1 Open the **Control Panel** and double click **Modems**.

2 Click the **Properties** button.

3 On the **General** panel, check the **COM port** – normally COM 2.

4 Set the **Speed** to the fastest – reduce it later if this doesn't work.

5 Switch to **Connection** and set the **Preferences** to suit the service. If in doubt, try **8 - None - 1**.

6 If other people use the phone line, tick **Wait for dial tone**.

7 Click **OK** and close the Modem dialog box.

Basic steps

1 Open the **Modem Properties/ Connection** panel and click on **Port Settings...**.

2 Move the **Buffers** sliders down a notch.

3 Click **OK**.

4 Back at the **Properties** panel click **Advanced...**.

5 Tick **Record a log file**.

6 Click **OK** then close the **Properties** panel.

Tip

The **Error and Flow control settings** shown here are standard, but check with your access provider if you have difficulty in connecting.

Trouble shooting

If you find that you have difficulty in making the connection to your service – or in keeping the connection intact – these things might help:

● Take the maximum speed down a notch;

● Reduce the Buffer sizes on the Port Settings panel;

● Turn on the Record Log file option on the Advanced Connections Setting panel – this won't cure anything, but when you ring your provider for help, you will be able to tell them what has been happening.

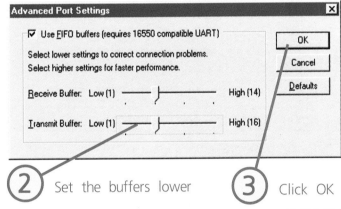

② Set the buffers lower ③ Click OK

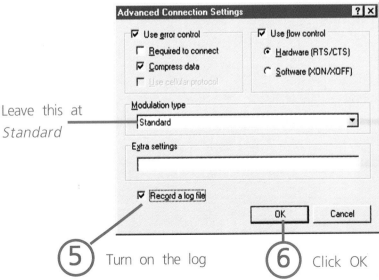

Leave this at *Standard*

⑤ Turn on the log ⑥ Click OK

29

Modem commands

AT commands

With a standard modem, a mainstream access provider, decent software and a bit of luck, you won't have to bother much about these. So, these pages are for those of you who lack one or more of these, and for those who would like to understand a little more about what the system is doing for them.

Most modems will obey the AT command set. This was developed by the Hayes company and is found in all Hayes-compatible modems. It is a large and comprehensive set, but the few listed on the right will probably be all you ever need. They are used to dial the comms service, initialise the settings, and hang up at the end of the session.

● All start with AT – for ATtention!

● Several commands can be written on the same line.

● Some commands have a symbol (& % or \) before the letter.

Examples:

ATDT 0345 0800 1000

Dial this number using Tone dial.

AT Q0 V1 \N3 %C3

Typical setup string telling the modem to:

enable verbose error messages (Q0 V1),

use error correction if possible (\N3)

select a suitable compression method (%C3).

D	Dial, followed by T or P and the phone number
T	Tone dialling (used on all modern exchanges)
P	Pulse dialling
H0	On Hook (Hang-up)
Q0	Enable error messages (Q1 to disable them)
V1	Verbose (full text) error messages
&D2	Hang up if DTR signal lost (connection fails)
\N0	No error-correction
\N3	Try error-correction, but link anyway if distant modem can't handle it
%C0	No data compression
%C3	Automatic selection of V.42bis or MNP data compression
+++	Escape (end session)

Definitions

Carrier – continuous signal to which a second, data signal can be attached. Data Carrier Detect checks that the underlying signal is still present

DCE – Data Communications Equipment, the modem

DTE – Data Terminal Equipment, a terminal or computer running terminal emulator software

DTR – Data Terminal Ready, signal from computer to modem to say that it is ready to receive.

Tip

Always try with the default settings of the modem and your comms software before attempting to set them yourself.

Enable error messages

Error messages as words, not numbers

Hang up if the computer to modem link fails

End of line

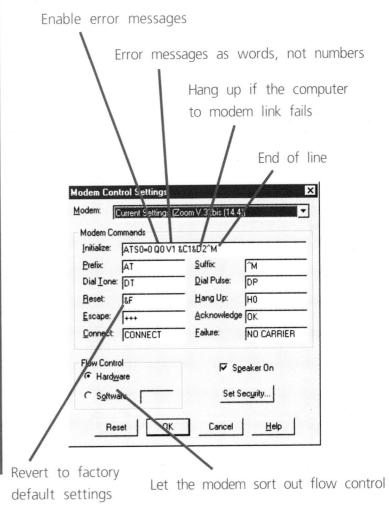

Revert to factory default settings

Let the modem sort out flow control

This screenshot is of the Define Modem dialog box from Compuserve's WinCIM package. Most of these settings were made by selecting the modem from the (long) drop-down list in the top slot; only for a few was it necessary to read the modem's manual! If you use Dial-Up Networking for the CompuServe connection, you cannot reach this panel – Windows 95 takes total responsibility for setting up the modem.

Summary

- **To get on-line**, you need a computer, a modem and a telephone socket.

- **Modems** may be fitted internally or externally, and must be connected to a COM port. Most will simply plug in and go; some may need configuring to your machine.

- The **Baud rate** describes the speed of a modem. The faster your modem, the lower your phone bills!

- If your modem can handle **data compression**, it will speed up transfer times.

- To connect to the Internet, you must have an account with an **access provider**.

- Some access providers, such as **CompuServe** and **AOL**, offer services to their members in addition to Internet access.

- A **Web browser** is essential – though there is plenty of other software that you might like to explore later.

- Some access providers supply their customers with special software packages to install themselves and handle all the details of setting up the connection. However, you may have to configure the **Dial-Up Networking** software yourself.

- Most modems are Hayes-compatible, and respond to **AT commands**. You may have to learn a few of these.

3 Netscape

Netscape 3.0

Netscape 3.0 has several windows, but this is the one that you start in – and the one that you will spend most time in. The main part of the window is used for the display of Web pages. Above this are the control elements.

- The **Menu bar** is always present. Commonly used commands are duplicated in the next three bars.

- The **Toolbar** should be kept visible. Its buttons make browsing much simpler.

- The **Location** shows you where you are. You can type a URL (page 70) here to go to a chosen site. The last 10 URLs that you typed are stored here, for ease of revisiting.

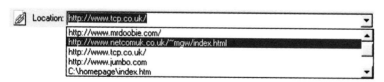

- The **Directory** buttons link to pages on Netscape's site and can be good places to start from. These are also on the Directory menu.

⇦o	Previous page
o⇨	Next page (if you have visited it, then returned to a previous page)
🏠	Home page
🔄	Reload current page
🖼	Load the images on the current page
⇨	Open a location
🖨	Print – wait until the page is fully loaded before printing
🔍	Find text within the current page
⬤	Stop loading

Options

The Toolbar, Location and Directory buttons displays are optional. Use the **Options** menu to turn off those that you do not use much to give yourself a larger viewing area.

The settings can be changed at any point, and hold for future sessions until you change them again.

Turn off the **Auto Load Images** option for faster browsing. If you want to see the pictures on a page, you can always click the 🖼 button.

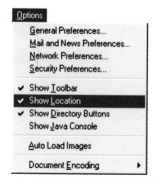

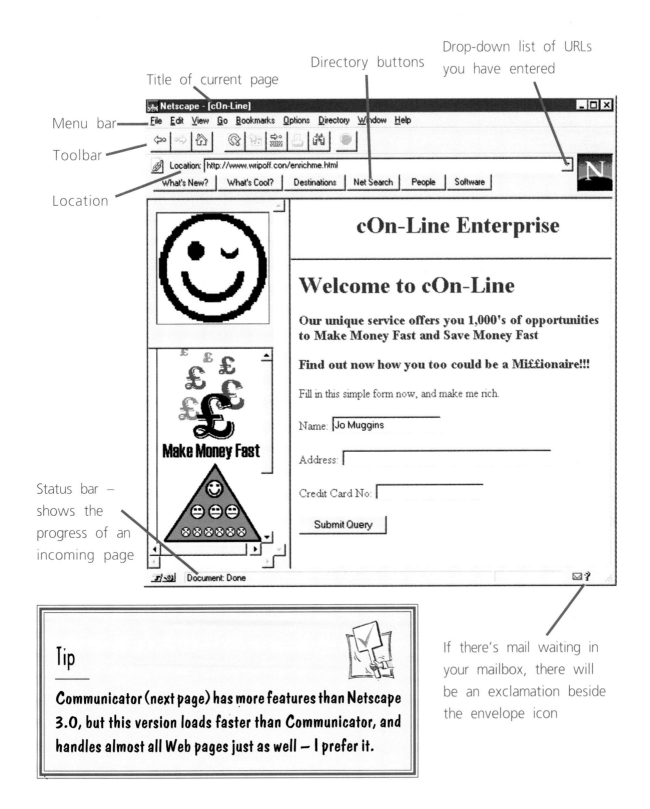

Title of current page

Drop-down list of URLs you have entered

Directory buttons

Menu bar

Toolbar

Location

Netscape - [cOn-Line]

File Edit View Go Bookmarks Options Directory Window Help

Location: http://www.wripoff.con/enrichme.html

What's New? What's Cool? Destinations Net Search People Software

cOn-Line Enterprise

Welcome to cOn-Line

Our unique service offers you 1,000's of opportunities to Make Money Fast and Save Money Fast

Find out now how you too could be a Millionaire!!!

Fill in this simple form now, and make me rich.

Name: Jo Muggins

Address:

Credit Card No:

Submit Query

Make Money Fast

Status bar – shows the progress of an incoming page

Document: Done

If there's mail waiting in your mailbox, there will be an exclamation beside the envelope icon

Tip

Communicator (next page) has more features than Netscape 3.0, but this version loads faster than Communicator, and handles almost all Web pages just as well – I prefer it.

Navigator 4.0

At the time of writing, Netscape Corporation has just launched the new **Communicator** suite. The software has undergone a major reorganisation, with the Mail, News and Editor windows being split off from Navigator to form distinct programs.

- **Messenger** handles e-mail, and has a built-in HTML editor so that 'rich' pages can be created and mailed.

- **Collabra** replaces the News window, and again has access to the HTML editor.

- The HTML Editor becomes **Composer** and CoolTalk (for voice communication over the Net) becomes **Conference.** Both of these are slightly improved.

- **Navigator** remains essentially the same.

The browser window

The toolbars have been redesigned for greater ease of use.

- Right-clicking **Back** and **Forwards** brings up a list of pages, so you can reach them directly.

- The Directory button bar has been replaced by a Custom bar where you can add your own links, and the Directory links are reached through **Places**.

- **Stop** and **Reload** are alternative faces of the same button, switching as appropriate.

Tip

The other Communicator programs can be called up from the Taskbar. This can be 'floated' to anywhere on screen, or docked in the status line.

Take note

Navigator 4.0 is significantly larger and slower to load than Netscape Navigator 3.0, and at present very few Web sites make use of its extra capabilities. As the earlier version is just as good for all practical purposes, you may prefer — as I do — to stay with this for the time being.

There are fewer menus, but they are busier!

Click to close toolbar

You can select which page to go Back or Forward to

Becomes Stop when a page is loading

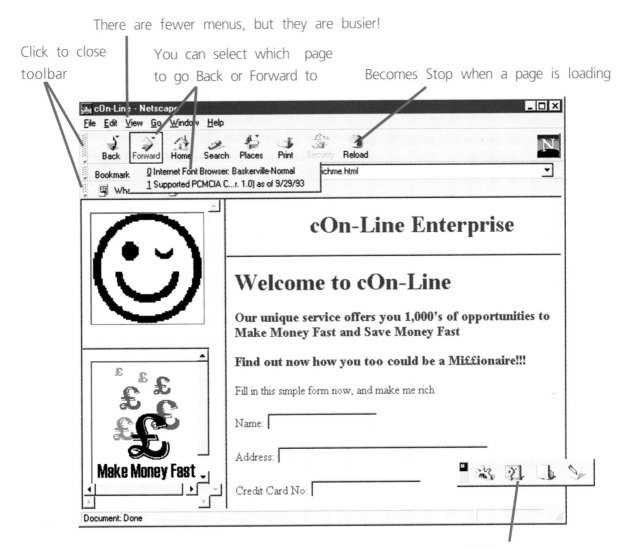

Taskbar to open other Communicator applications

Take note

If you want to change to Netscape 3.0 or upgrade to Communicator, the software can be downloaded free from Netscape's home site at:

http://www.netscape.com

Preferences

There are four sets of Preferences controlling different aspects of Netscape 3.0. Most can be left at their defaults at the start, and changed as and when you feel the need. Start with the General Preferences – these control the appearance of the Browser window.

Basic steps

1 Click on **Options**.

2 Select **General Preferences**.

3 Set the style for the Toolbar buttons.

4 Click on the tabs to change to the Colors, Fonts and other panels.

5 Click **OK** to save.

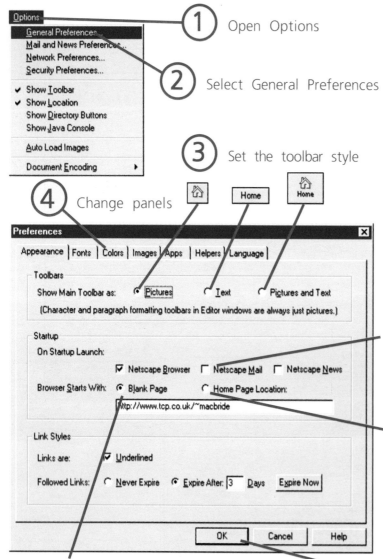

① Open Options

② Select General Preferences

③ Set the toolbar style

④ Change panels

Take note

The Helpers panel is covered in Chapter 9.

If you use the Internet mainly for e-mailing, you might prefer to start with the Mail window

Set a **Home Page Location** if you have a preferred starting place – perhaps your own home page, holding your favourite links

Select **Blank Page** if each session will be a new voyage

⑤ OK saves your settings

Basic steps

1 From **Options** select **Network Preferences**.

2 On the **Cache** panel, set the **Cache** sizes as recommended in the text on the right.

3 On the **Languages** panel, check **Enable Java** and **JavaScript** if you want to run applets (see below).

4 **Proxies** are relevant only if you are on a local area network. Check with your LAN manager if relevant.

Take note

Applets are programs embedded in Web pages. Some are decorative, some are for navigating round sites, some are games. Though a potential source of danger, they should not be able to access or corrupt your files when running in Netscape.

Network Preferences

The Network Preferences control how data comes into your system, and what happens to it when it arrives.

When you revisit a page, Netscape first checks the **caches**, and if it finds an up-to-date copy of the page will load from there rather than over the Internet. Large caches can speed up your surfing, or just be a waste of space – it depends on how you use the Web.

● The **Memory cache** stores pages visited during a session. Set this to 1Mb or more if you like to return to pages to follow up leads – and have plenty of RAM.

● The **Disk cache** stores pages from one session to the next. Set this high if you like to go regularly to the same sites, and their contents do not change much.

(2) Set Cache sizes   (3) Enable Java if wanted

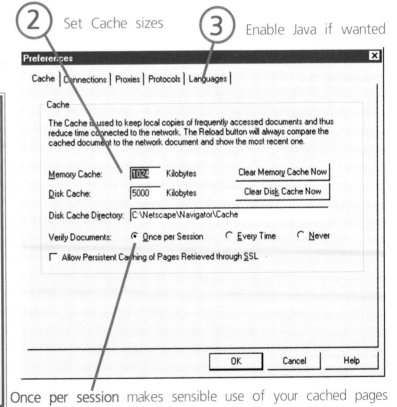

Once per session makes sensible use of your cached pages

Mail and News Preferences

If you are setting up Netscape for the first time, you will need to fill in your e-mail details here. If you are upgrading, the setup routine should have picked up the information from your system.

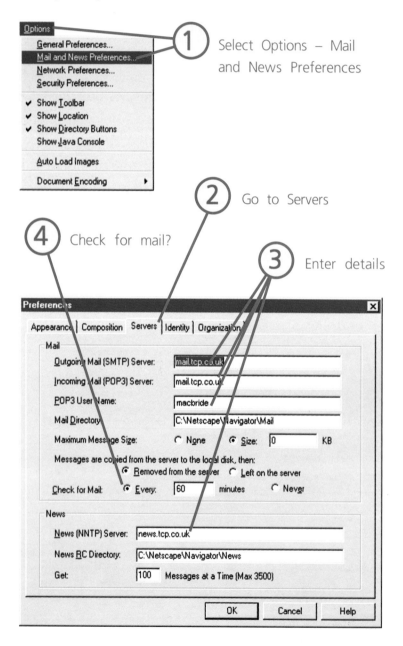

Select Options – Mail and News Preferences

Go to Servers

Check for mail?

Enter details

Options

General Preferences...
Mail and News Preferences...
Network Preferences...
Security Preferences...

✔ Show Toolbar
✔ Show Location
✔ Show Directory Buttons
  Show Java Console

Auto Load Images

Document Encoding   ▶

Preferences

Appearance | Composition | Servers | Identity | Organization

Mail

Outgoing Mail (SMTP) Server: mail.tcp.co.uk
Incoming Mail (POP3) Server: mail.tcp.co.uk
POP3 User Name: macbride
Mail Directory: C:\Netscape\Navigator\Mail
Maximum Message Size: ○ None   ● Size: 0   KB
Messages are copied from the server to the local disk, then:
                               ● Removed from the server   ○ Left on the server
Check for Mail: ● Every: 60   minutes   ○ Never

News

News (NNTP) Server: news.tcp.co.uk
News RC Directory: C:\Netscape\Navigator\News
Get: 100 Messages at a Time (Max 3500)

OK   Cancel   Help

- ❏ Essentials
1 Pull down the **Options** menu and select **Mail and News Preferences**.
2 Go to the **Servers** panel.
3 Enter your **User Name** and the names of your **servers** – ask your service provider if you do not know these.
4 Set how often you want the system to check for mail – select **Never** if you prefer to check by opening the Mail window when you are ready.
5 Go to the **Identity** panel.
6 Enter your (real) **Name** and your **E-mail name**. These will be used in your message headers.
7 If you have a **Signature File** (page 159), **Browse** for it now.

❑ **Optional Mail settings**

8 Go to the **Composition** panel.

9 Select **Allow 8-bit** if you will be receiving mail and news from a variety of systems.

❑ Leave the **Appearance** and **Organization** options until you have been using the Mail and News for a while, then tweak the settings to suit yourself.

⑤ Go to Identity

⑥ Enter your details

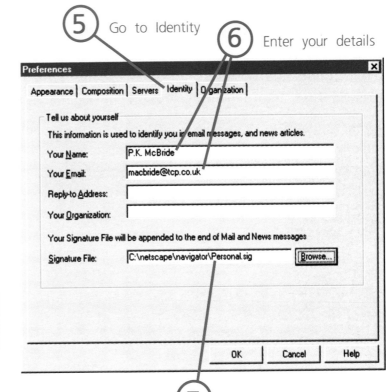

⑦ Do you have a signature?

⑧ Go to Composition

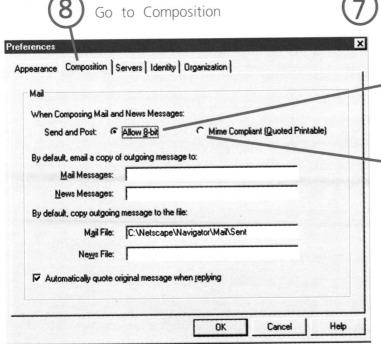

⑨ Allow 8-bit

MIME Compliant text is formatted – prettier, but not all systems can read and write it. See page 198 for more on MIME.

41

Security Preferences

Security on the Internet has not been a problem for most people, though some organisations have suffered from on-line theft and fraud. Netscape incorporates a number of measures to improve the security of your connections.

The settings are probably best left at their secure defaults, but check them just in case. If other people have access to your system, you may also like to set a password to prevent unauthorised access through your Internet account.

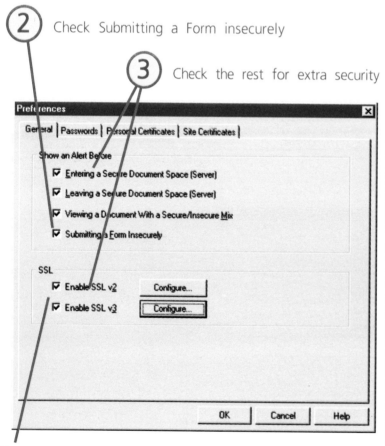

② Check Submitting a Form insecurely

③ Check the rest for extra security

SSL security must be enabled if you intend making credit card payments over the Internet (page 139).

1 Open **Options** (Edit – **Preferences** in Communicator) and select **Security Preferences**.

2 On the **General** panel, make sure that **Submitting a Form Insecurely** is checked – it will allow you to change your mind before sending a form.

3 Set **Show Alert** for all other modes if you want to know when you are entering or leaving secure areas.

❑ **To secure your system**

4 Go to the **Passwords** panel.

5 Click **Set Password**, then enter your chosen password.

6 If you leave your machine unattended while on-line, set the **Ask for Password** to *After* a few minutes, otherwise *Once per session* will do.

42

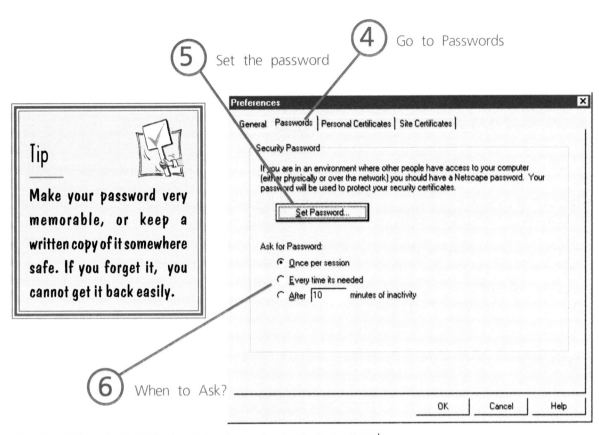

④ Go to Passwords

⑤ Set the password

⑥ When to Ask?

Tip

Make your password very memorable, or keep a written copy of it somewhere safe. If you forget it, you cannot get it back easily.

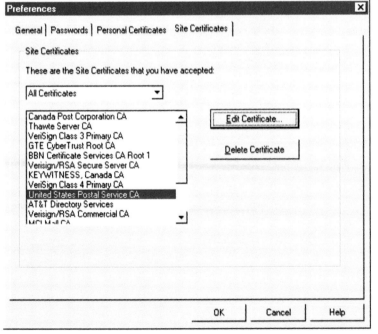

Certificates

Some sites issue their own certificates. These ensure that any traffic between you and the site is not diverted at either end.

Some sites can issue (or will insist on issuing) a personal certificate to identify you when you are dealing with them.

Navigator 4.0 Preferences

In Navigator 4.0, the Preferences are handled through one multi-panel dialog box. Within this, they are organised in much the same way as in the Netscape 3.0 panels, though with two new tabs – for Composer and Working Offline.

Automatic image loading

Images may be pretty, but they can take a long time to download. For fast, efficient browsing, you need to be able to turn off the automatic loading, only getting the images when they are essential. In Netscape 3.0, **Auto Load Images** is an item on the Options menu, where it can be easily accessed to switch on or off as needed. In Navigator 4.0, it is hidden on the Advanced tab of the Preferences.

1 Open the **Edit** menu.

2 Select **Preferences**.

3 Click ⊞ beside the folders to open them.

4 Select a tab.

5 Set options as required.

❑ Image loading

6 Switch to the **Advanced** tab.

7 Turn off automatic loading for faster browsing.

8 Click **OK** to save.

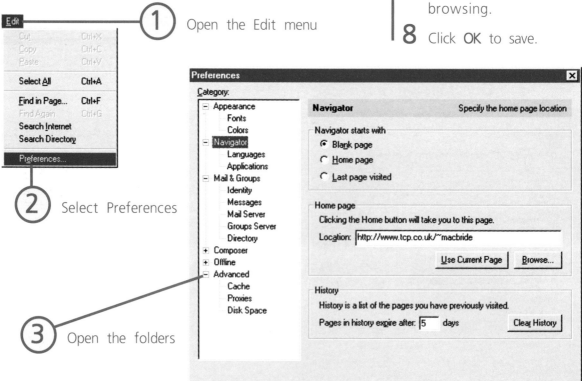

① Open the Edit menu

② Select Preferences

③ Open the folders

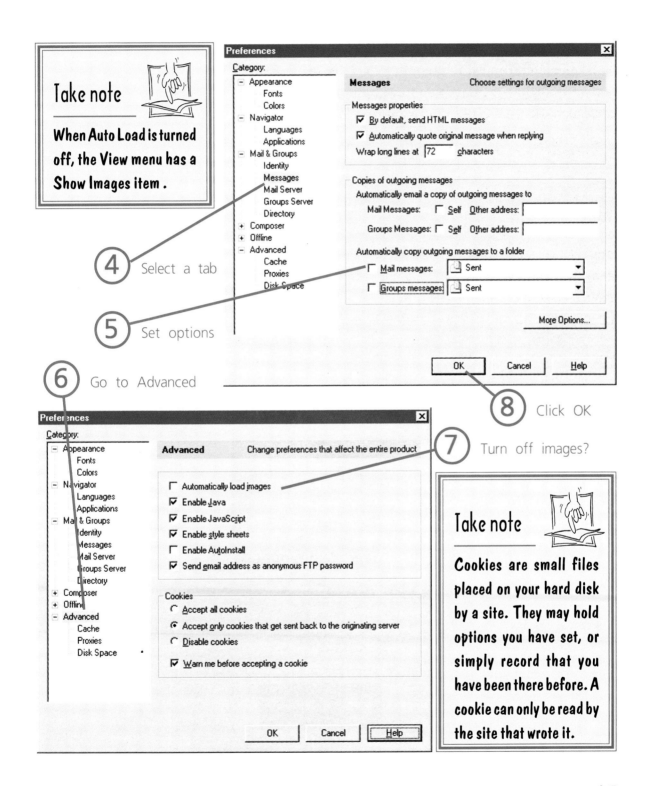

Take note

When Auto Load is turned off, the View menu has a Show Images item.

④ Select a tab

⑤ Set options

⑥ Go to Advanced

⑧ Click OK

⑦ Turn off images?

Preferences

Category:

- Appearance
  - Fonts
  - Colors
- Navigator
  - Languages
  - Applications
- Mail & Groups
  - Identity
  - Messages
  - Mail Server
  - Groups Server
  - Directory
- + Composer
- + Offline
- Advanced
  - Cache
  - Proxies
  - Disk Space

Messages   Choose settings for outgoing messages

Messages properties

☑ By default, send HTML messages

☑ Automatically quote original message when replying

Wrap long lines at [72] characters

Copies of outgoing messages

Automatically email a copy of outgoing messages to

Mail Messages: ☐ Self Other address: [   ]

Groups Messages: ☐ Self Other address: [   ]

Automatically copy outgoing messages to a folder

☐ Mail messages: [Sent ▼]

☐ Groups messages: [Sent ▼]

More Options...

OK   Cancel   Help

Preferences

Category:

- Appearance
  - Fonts
  - Colors
- Navigator
  - Languages
  - Applications
- Mail & Groups
  - Identity
  - Messages
  - Mail Server
  - Groups Server
  - Directory
- + Composer
- + Offline
- Advanced
  - Cache
  - Proxies
  - Disk Space

Advanced   Change preferences that affect the entire product

☐ Automatically load images

☑ Enable Java

☑ Enable JavaScript

☑ Enable style sheets

☐ Enable AutoInstall

☑ Send email address as anonymous FTP password

Cookies

○ Accept all cookies

● Accept only cookies that get sent back to the originating server

○ Disable cookies

☑ Warn me before accepting a cookie

OK   Cancel   Help

Take note

Cookies are small files placed on your hard disk by a site. They may hold options you have set, or simply record that you have been there before. A cookie can only be read by the site that wrote it.

45

Netscape's Home

Netscape has a Directory menu with links to places on the Netscape site, from which to start your browsing. These are well worth using until you have built up your own set of bookmarks (page 72), and some are worth revisiting regularly.

(page 72)

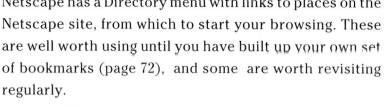

② Select Directory – Netscape's Home

③ Get the images

④ Click the buttons or the hypertext links

1 If you are not on-line, run Netscape and connect now.

2 Open the **Directory** menu and select **Netscape's Home**.

3 If **Auto Load Images** is off, use **View – Load Images** now.

4 Click on the image buttons, or underlined links to surf the site.

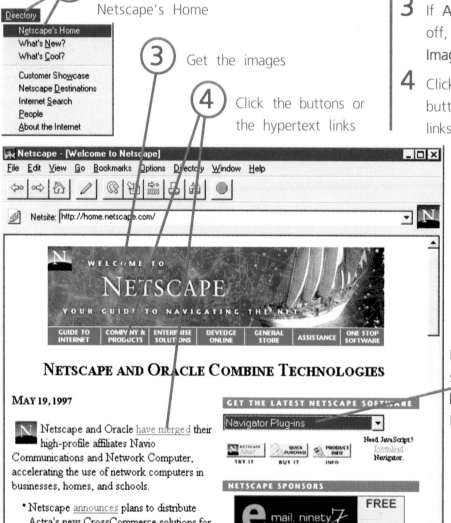

If you want Live 3D, select **Navigator Plug-ins** from the list and click **TRY IT**

46

In-Box Direct

Take note

Web pages can be viewed just as well in the Mail window as they can in the main browser.

One of the services run by Netscape is In-Box Direct, offering Web pages by e-mail. The pages are produced by news, sports and business information providers, other developers and Netscape itself, and are mailed out regularly – some daily.

In-Box Direct can be reached from Netscape's Home. Once there, browse through and subscribe to the services that seem interesting – you can cancel subscriptions later if you decide they are not worth the downloading time.

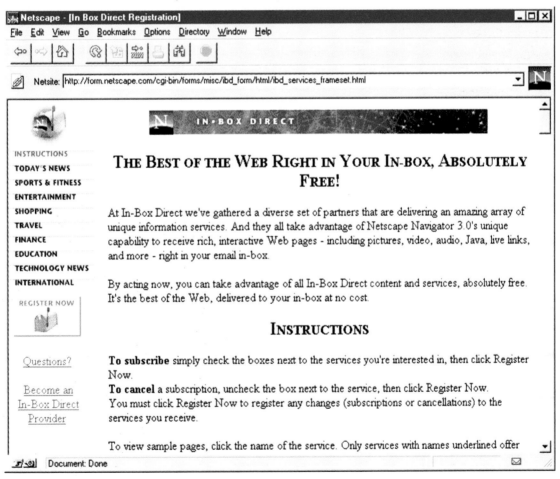

Keep on scrolling to see all the services on offer

Summary

- Netscape software is available in several versions. **Communicator** is the latest, but **Netscape 3.0** is smaller and sufficent for most purposes.

- The software can be **downloaded** from Netscape's Home Page, or wherever you see a download button.

- Netscape is largely **self-installing** and does most of the necessary configuration for you.

- The **toolbar, location bar** and other controls can be removed, to create a larger viewing area.

- To get Netscape working the way you want it, spend some time on the **Preferences panels**.

- The **Mail and News Preferences** must be checked and details entered if they have not been found by the system.

- **Java** and **JavaScript** applets can fun and useful. There is a very slight danger that they could carry viruses or otherwise attack your system. Netscape is more secure than Explorer in this respect.

- **Navigator 4.0 Preferences** are set in almost the same way as the earlier version, but working from one compound panel.

- The Directory button takes you to **Netscape's Home Page** – a good place to start your browsing.

- If you sign up to **In-Box Direct**, you can have news and reports e-mailed to you from selected organisations.

4 Internet Explorer

Introducing Explorer

At the time of writing, the latest Internet Explorer is 4.0. It is equal to Communicator or Netscape 3.0 in is speed and range of features – though better in some respects, and worse in others.

Explorer gives you:

- an excellent screen layout – you can display the Favorites and History lists, Search engines or Channels in a panel down the left of the screen. Pages selected from here are displayed in the main window. This is particularly useful when searching (see page 132).

- safer surfing for families – you can restrict browsing to rated sites, setting your own acceptable levels of sex and violence (see page 56).

The chief disadvantages are:

- Explorer's version of Java is non-standard, nor can it handle all aspects of JavaScript (Microsoft would prefer you to use ActiveX), so the Java applets and JavaScript routines that you meet on Web pages may not run properly.

- It is a large program and relatively slow to get up and running.

- Explorer tends to take control of your system. It installs files in many places – mainly in the Windows folder – and replaces some core Windows 95 files. It also checks selected Web sites and automatically downloads new drivers and other updates, unless you stop it doing so. This is not a disadvantage if you are happy to let Microsoft root around in your hard drive so that it can optimise your system.

Tip

Internet Explorer 4.0 can be downloaded from Microsoft's site at www.microsoft.com, but it is very large (over 60Mb with all the trimmings) and will take ages to download. You would do better to look for it on the CDs that grace the front covers of most PC magazines.

The Explorer browser

The buttons of the **Standard** toolbar are all you really need while browsing. The **Address** and **Links** toolbars can be resized or turned off if not wanted, using the View menu.

The left-hand panel – the **Explorer bar** – displays the Search, Favorites, History or Channels lists. It can be opened or closed as needed.

Close Explorer bar

Drag to move or resize the bars

Open list in Explorer bar

Previous page

Next page

Reload

Remove the frame

Stop loading

Start page

Mail and News

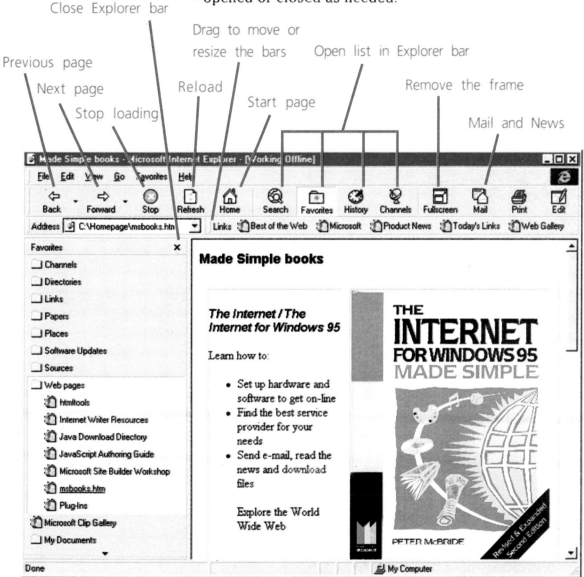

General options

The Internet Options control many aspects of Explorer's display and of how it works. Start on the General panel:

● Choose your **Home page**. This can be left blank or you can always start your browsing at the same place (such as a Web directory – see Chapter 6).

● Set the disk space for storing files of visited pages. When you revisit, Explorer will use these and only download new files if the pages have changed – allocate as much as you can spare for faster browsing.

● Set the **Accessibility** options and choose your own **Colors** and **Fonts** for maximum visiblity, if needed.

Basic steps

1 Open the **View** menu and select **Internet Options...**

2 Go to **General**.

3 For the **Home page**, type the URL (or click **Use Current** if you are on that page), or click **Use Blank**.

4 Click **Settings**.

5 Select when to check that stored pages for new versions.

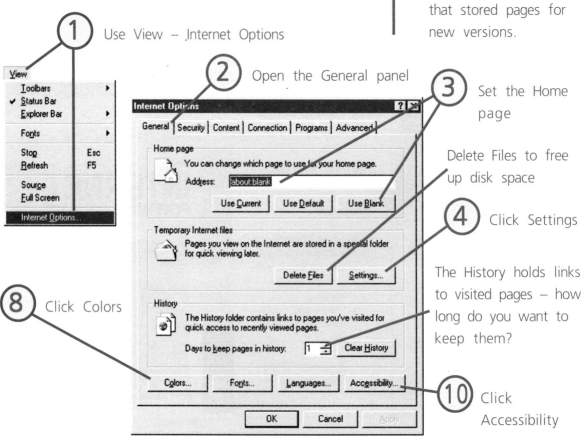

Use View – Internet Options

Open the General panel

Set the Home page

Delete Files to free up disk space

Click Settings

The History holds links to visited pages – how long do you want to keep them?

Click Colors

Click Accessibility

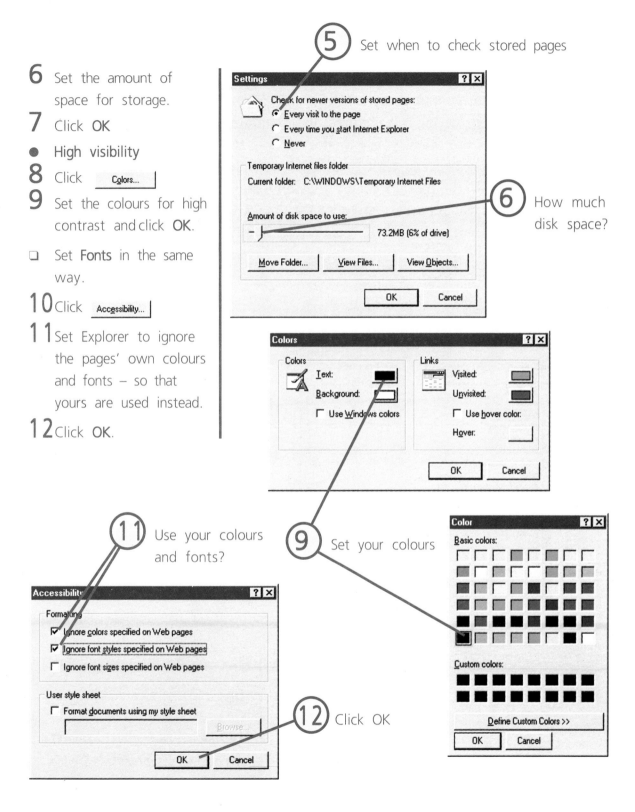

6 Set the amount of space for storage.

7 Click **OK**

● **High visibility**

8 Click [Colors...]

9 Set the colours for high contrast and click **OK**.

❑ Set **Fonts** in the same way.

10 Click [Accessibility...]

11 Set Explorer to ignore the pages' own colours and fonts – so that yours are used instead.

12 Click **OK**.

⑤ Set when to check stored pages

⑥ How much disk space?

⑪ Use your colours and fonts?

⑨ Set your colours

⑫ Click OK

53

Multimedia options

Pictures, audio and video files are sometimes essential, often merely decorative and always slow to load. Turn them off for faster browsing but pictures often contain links – if you can't see them, you may not be able to navigate some sites. You can turn them back on and reload a page to view the files, or simply click on a non-displayed image (it will appear as ⚊) to load it.

Basic steps

1 Open the **View** menu and select **Internet Options...**

2 Go to **Advanced**.

3 Scroll down to the **Multimedia** section.

4 Click to turn the options on or off as required.

5 Click **OK**.

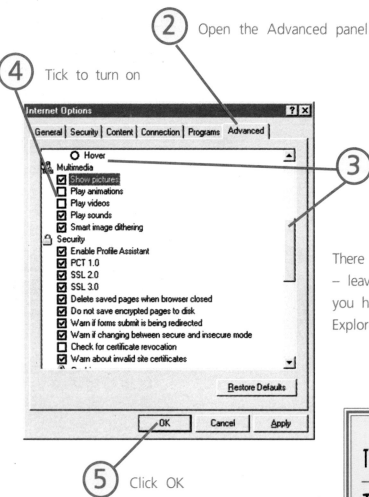

④ Tick to turn on

② Open the Advanced panel

③ Scroll down to Multimedia

There are lots of other options here – leave these at their defaults until you have more experience of Explorer and the Web

⑤ Click OK

Tip

To find out more about Explorer, see *Internet Explorer Made Simple*.

Basic steps

1 Go to the Security panel.

2 Pick the Internet zone.

3 Select High security.

or

4 Select Custom and click **Settings...**

5 Tell Explorer how to deal with each type.

Many Web pages have **active content**, i.e. they contain multimedia files or applets (small applications) written in Java, JavaScript or ActiveX. These should not be able to mess with your hard disks or access your data, but some hackers have found a way round the restrictions – and anti-virus software is no help here. Active content makes browsing more interesting, and if you stick to major sites, should create no problems. (You can also create your own set of Trusted sites by adding their URLs to the list.)

At first, select the Internet zone (i.e. all Web sites), with the security set to **High**. Use the **Custom** option to fine-tune the settings later, when you have more experience.

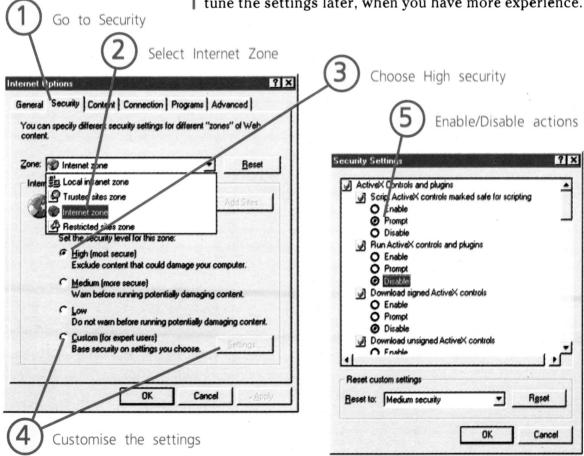

① Go to Security

② Select Internet Zone

③ Choose High security

⑤ Enable/Disable actions

④ Customise the settings

Safe Exploring

With Explorer you can protect younger users – or anyone else who might be offended – from the unacceptable material that lurks in various corners of the Net

The settings on the Content panel allows you to restrict the browser to sites rated by the (RSAC) Recreational Standards Advisory Council – over 50,000 at the time of writing – and to control the levels of sex'n'violence that can be viewed.

If a site's ratings are beyond the limits you have set, access is denied. This can be overriden by the use of the password, should you decide a site has been overrated and is suitable for viewing.

Basic steps

1 Go to the **Content** panel.

2 Click **Enable**...

3 Decide on a **Password** and enter it – twice.

4 On the **Ratings** panel, set the limit for each Category – moving the slider to the right permits higher levels of sex'n'violence.

5 On the **General** panel, tick the options if you want to allow people to see unrated sites, or to use the password to view restricted sites.

6 Click **OK**.

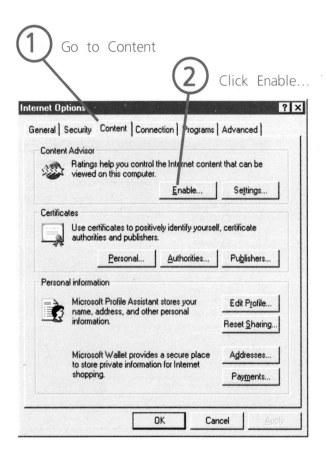

1 Go to Content

2 Click Enable...

Tip

With Content Advisor enabled, the Net is a safer place for kids, but for even greater control over their activities on the Net, you should use access control software. See page 86 for more on safe surfing.

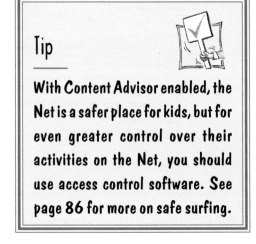

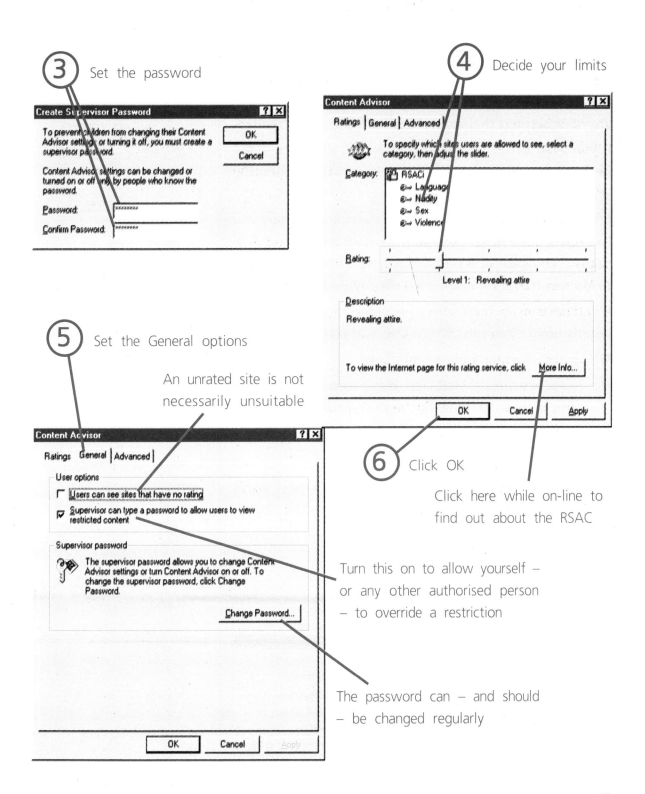

(3) Set the password

Create Supervisor Password   ❓✖

To prevent children from changing their Content
Advisor settings, or turning it off, you must create a
supervisor password.

Content Advisor settings can be changed or
turned on or off only by people who know the
password.

Password: ✱✱✱✱✱✱✱
Confirm Password: ✱✱✱✱✱✱✱

OK
Cancel

(4) Decide your limits

Content Advisor   ❓✖

Ratings | General | Advanced

To specify which sites users are allowed to see, select a
category, then adjust the slider.

Category: 🌐 RSACi
    ◉~ Language
    ◉~ Nudity
    ◉~ Sex
    ◉~ Violence

Rating: '   '   '   '

Level 1: Revealing attire

Description

Revealing attire.

To view the Internet page for this rating service, click   More Info...

OK   Cancel   Apply

(5) Set the General options

An unrated site is not
necessarily unsuitable

(6) Click OK

Click here while on-line to
find out about the RSAC

Content Advisor   ❓✖

Ratings | General | Advanced

User options
☐ Users can see sites that have no rating
☑ Supervisor can type a password to allow users to view
   restricted content

Supervisor password
🔑 The supervisor password allows you to change Content
Advisor settings or turn Content Advisor on or off. To
change the supervisor password, click Change
Password.

Change Password...

OK   Cancel   Apply

Turn this on to allow yourself –
or any other authorised person
– to override a restriction

The password can – and should
– be changed regularly

57

Making the connection

If you have an existing connection set up through Dial-Up Networking (see page 24), Explorer should have picked this up during installation. If you do not want to change any of its settings then no further work should be needed.

If you want to set up a new connection, or check – and perhaps adjust – an existing one, there is a Connection Wizard to simplify the process.

If you do not yet have an Internet service provider, you can select one from within the Wizard – have your modem ready if you want to do this, as the Wizard will go on-line to Microsoft to get the latest list of providers in your area.

If you have an account with a provider, then gather their details before you run the Wizard. You need to know:

● your provider's phone number;

● you provider's Mail and News servers' names – probably something like '*mail.myprovider.co.uk*';

● your user name, e-mail address and password.

You may also need:

● your provider's DNS Server Addresses – these are in the form of four sets of digits, like this: 190.99.134.29;

● your IP address – or not! Many systems allocate a new address when you log on;

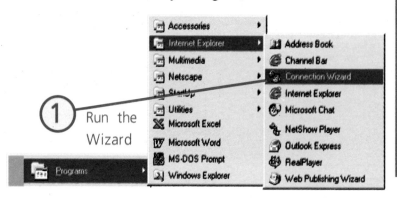

① Run the Wizard

1 Click on **Start**, point to **Programs**, then **Internet Explorer** and select **Connection Wizard**.

or

2 Click the Connect... button on the Internet Options Connection panel.

3 At the **Setup Options**, select *choose a new provider, set up a new connection to your provider* or *use your existing connection.*

4 Click **Next**.

5 If you are choosing a provider, the Wizard will download the list – select one and follow the prompts.

6 If you have an account with a provider, you can set up a new connection, or adjust the existing one. Follow the prompts, supplying information when requested.

③ Which setup?

Use the Wizard to find
a service provider

Use if you have a provider,
but have not yet connected

If you select this, the
Wizard will end after Next

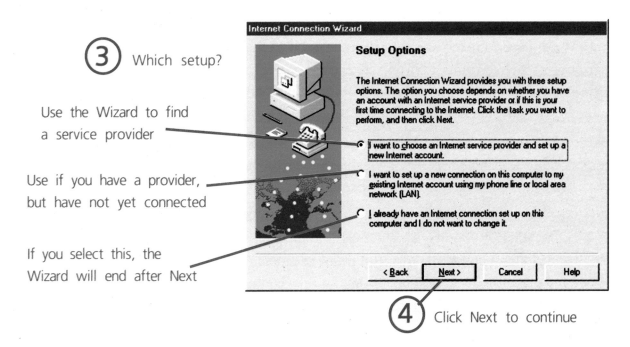

Internet Connection Wizard

Setup Options

The Internet Connection Wizard provides you with three setup options. The option you choose depends on whether you have an account with an Internet service provider or if this is your first time connecting to the Internet. Click the task you want to perform, and then click Next.

○ I want to choose an Internet service provider and set up a new Internet account.

○ I want to set up a new connection on this computer to my existing Internet account using my phone line or local area network (LAN).

○ I already have an Internet connection set up on this computer and I do not want to change it.

< Back   Next >   Cancel   Help

④ Click Next to continue

After the connection has been set up, you will see this panel when you start Explorer – tick the **Save password** box only if your computer cannot be accessed by unauthorised users.

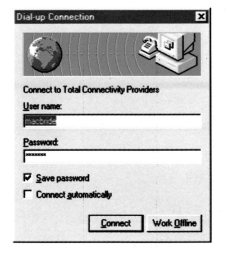

Dial-up Connection

Connect to Total Connectivity Providers

User name:
macbride

Password:
******

☑ Save password
☐ Connect automatically

Connect   Work Offline

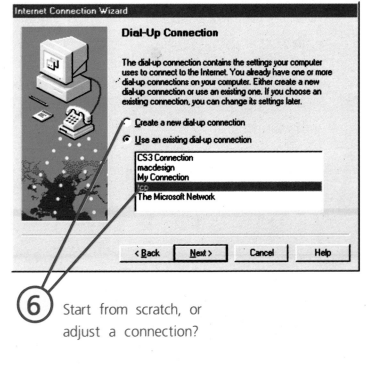

Internet Connection Wizard

Dial-Up Connection

The dial-up connection contains the settings your computer uses to connect to the Internet. You already have one or more dial-up connections on your computer. Either create a new dial-up connection or use an existing one. If you choose an existing connection, you can change its settings later.

○ Create a new dial-up connection

◉ Use an existing dial-up connection

CS3 Connection
macdesign
My Connection
tcp
The Microsoft Network

< Back   Next >   Cancel   Help

⑥ Start from scratch, or
adjust a connection?

59

Connection options

Running the Connection Wizard will have filled in the essential information on this panel, but there are a couple of options that need your attention. These are on the Dial-Up Settings panel, which is reached from the Connection panel of the Internet Options.

- Set the number of times to try to connect, and how long to wait before retrying – experience will show what is best with your service provider.

- Turn on the automatic disconnect if there is any possibility of you leaving the machine unattended and running up phone bills. But don't set too short a time or it will cut you off while you are reading a long page!

- Some Web sites run subscription services – you can arrange for them to send you news, sports results, weather and stock market reports (all mainly US), and other information. If you have subscribed to any of these, Explorer will by default go on-line and get the updates automatically. You may prefer to switch this off, and pick up your subscribed pages when you want them.

- Turn on the system security check if you want to ensure that the password is given before the system attempts to go on-line.

1 Open the **View** menu and select **Internet Options...**

2 Switch to the **Connection** panel.

3 Click Settings... .

4 Set the number of **redial attempts**, and the **delay** between trying.

5 Turn on **Disconnect if idle** and set the time limit.

6 Turn the **automatic update of subscriptions** on or off as needed.

7 Turn on the **security check** if needed.

8 Click **OK**.

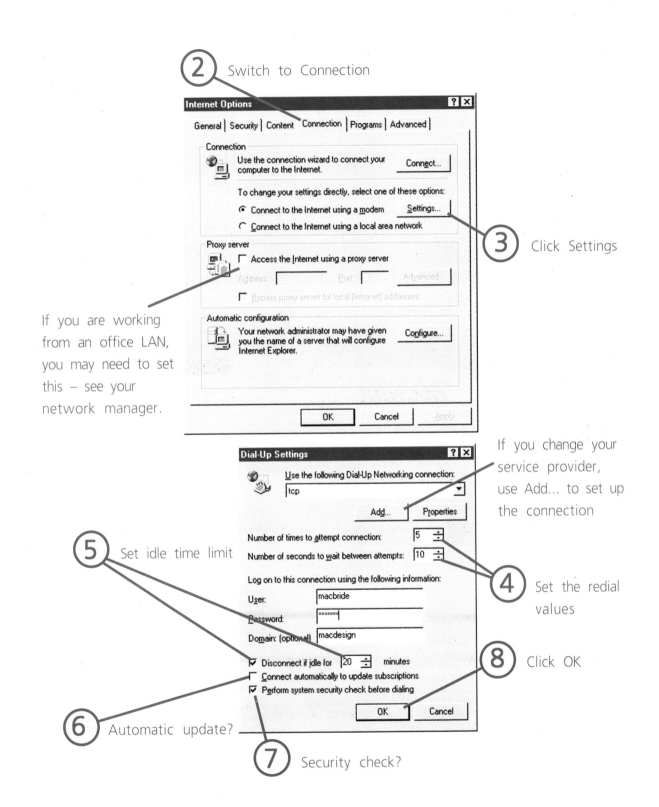

② Switch to Connection

③ Click Settings

If you are working from an office LAN, you may need to set this – see your network manager.

If you change your service provider, use Add... to set up the connection

⑤ Set idle time limit

④ Set the redial values

⑧ Click OK

⑥ Automatic update?

⑦ Security check?

61

Microsoft Home Page

Microsoft offers some useful and interesting services at their home page. Investigate them and see what you think.

You can reach the site from the Links or the Help menu.

Basic steps

1 Go on-line.

2 From the **Help** menu select **Microsoft on the Web**, then **Microsoft Home Page** or click the **Microsoft** Link

3 Read the news or pick from the **contents** list.

③ Start browsing

② Select Help – Microsoft on the Web – Home Page

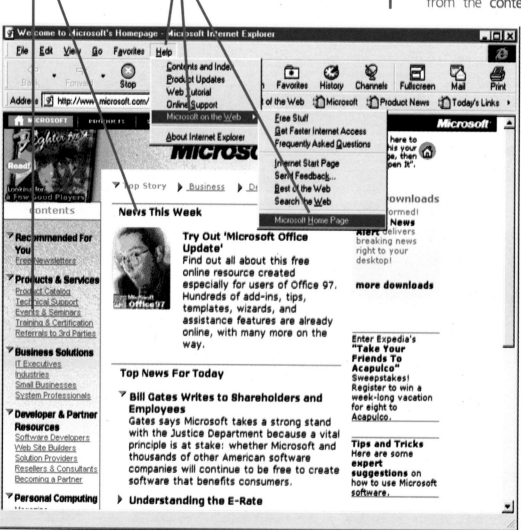

Best of the Web

If you are looking for a good place to start your browsing, why not try Microsoft's **Best of the Web**. This is a catalogue of selected links, grouped under topic headings. Just click on the **Links** button to connect.

Search takes you to Microsoft's search facility (page 132)

① Click Best of the Web

② Select an area

③ Pick a category

④ Start browsing

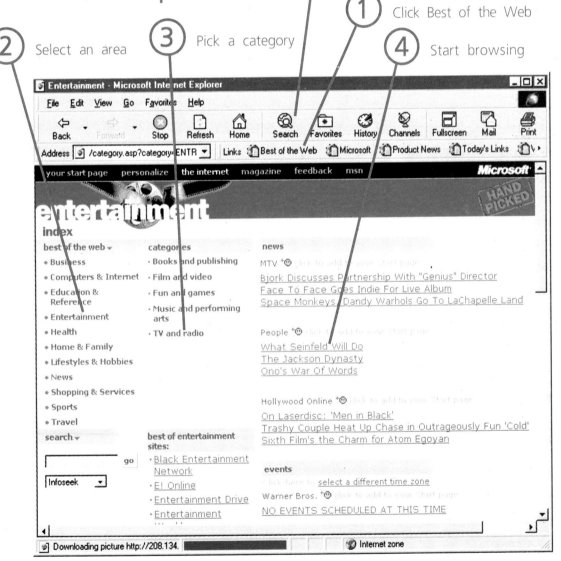

Summary

- **Internet Explorer 4.0** is the latest, and best version of Microsoft's Web browser.

- The software can be **downloaded** from Microsoft's home page, but is so large, that you are best getting it off a front-cover CD-ROM.

- Explorer 4.0 is very simple to install – you just let it get on with the job by itself!

- The **Explorer bar** can be opened as needed to display the Search, Favorites, History or Channels lists.

- To get Explorer working the way you want it, spend some time on the **Options panels**.

- Turning off some or all of the **Multimedia options** will speed up your travels round the Web.

- **Security** should initially be set to High, and only changed – if at all – when you have more experience of work on the Internet.

- If you have an established connection to an access provider when you install Internet Explorer 4.0, it will pick up those settings. If not, you will have to run the Connection Wizard.

- The Microsoft on the Web menu gives you easy access to several pages at Microsoft, any of which can be good places to start your browsing.

Which browser?

Netscape and Internet Explorer both do the same job in very similar ways. In the current versions, Netscape runs slightly faster, but Explorer offers child-protection features missing from Netscape. If you fill in a form on a Web page, Netscape can handle it properly, but Explorer can't.

Try them both out and see which you prefer.

5 Browsing the Web

Navigating the Web

The World Wide Web is held together by millions of hypertext links. These may take you from one page to another within a site or off to far-distant site – though some pages are dead-ends, which is when the Back button comes in handy!

The links may be underlined words embedded in the text or presented as a list, or may be built into pictures. They are usually easy to spot. When you point at a link, the cursor changes to 🖑 and the Status line shows the address of the linked page.

❑ When you find a page of interest, you can generally follow links from there to related pages, and explore the topic further. The trick is to find a suitable place to start your browsing. There are some starting points later in this chapter.

Click anywhere on the graphic

Hypertext links are usually underlined and coloured blue

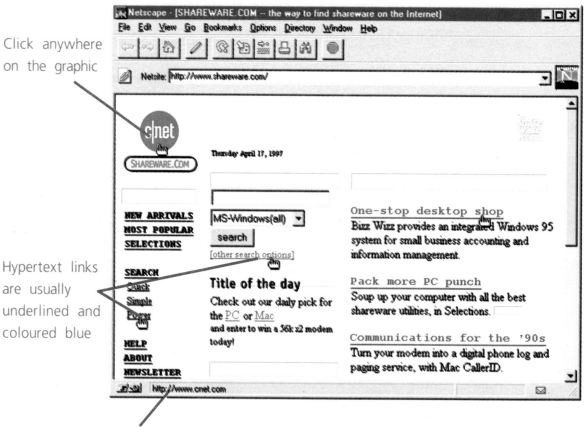

The address of the linked page

Image maps

Tip

If you want to include an image map in your own home page, you can easily create one using MapEdit — find it at:

http://www.boutell.com

Image maps are a special type of hypertext linked graphic. These can have any number of links embedded into them, each in its own area of the image.

In some image maps, like the Internet Resources Metamap it is quite clear what each part links to. In other more graphic ones, look for the hand icon. When you see it, you are pointing to a link.

Look for the hand

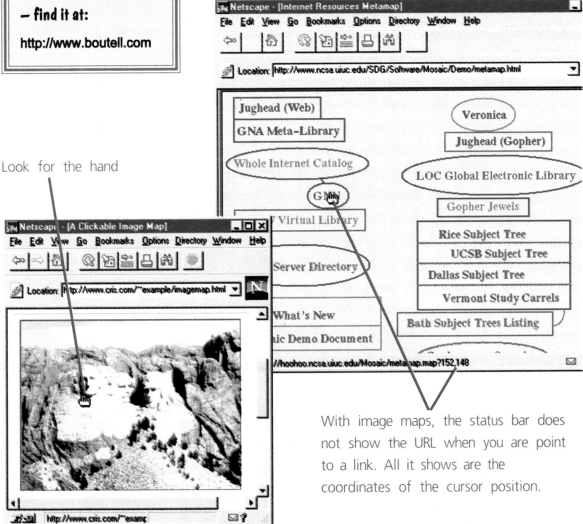

With image maps, the status bar does not show the URL when you are point to a link. All it shows are the coordinates of the cursor position.

67

VRML and Live 3D

VRML (Virtual Reality Modelling Language) can be used to create 3D objects or 'rooms'. Visitors can move around within the scene using the tools at the bottom of the screen. Some scenes are purely for fun; others are for navigating and have hypertext links embedded into them.

Though VRML has been around for several years, there are relatively few VRML navigation pages, perhaps because it takes a lot of hard work to build a good VRML image.

The VRML Weather Center (below) is one of examples from Netscape's Live 3D Cool Worlds list. Find it at:

http://search.netscape.com/uk/eng/live3d/worlds/weather/weather.html

Take note

To view VRML, you need Live3D. If you have Netscape, use Help — About Plug-ins to see if you have it. If not, you can download it from Netscape.

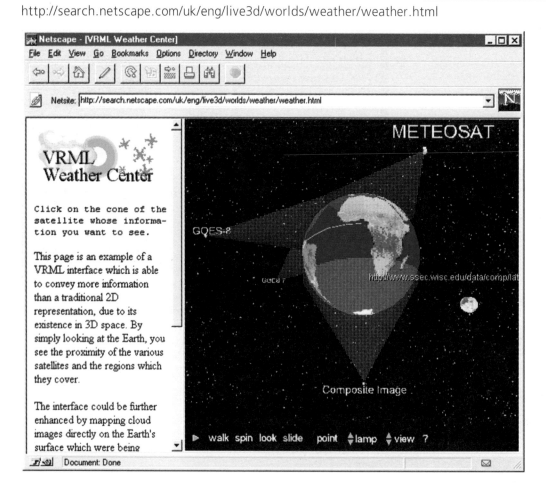

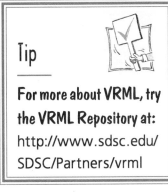

Tip
────
For more about VRML, try the VRML Repository at:
http://www.sdsc.edu/
SDSC/Partners/vrml

3D rooms are supposed to be more intuitive to explore than 2D maps. Perhaps. They are certainly more fun, but you need to practise before you can move around them smoothly. This screenshot is from Intel's demo site at:

http://pentium.intel.com/procs/intro/vrml

Look for the hand and a caption to find a link

Navigation controls

WWW URLs

Don't you just love the TLAs (Three Letter Acronyms)? The Internet is full of them. A **WWW URL** is a World Wide Web Uniform Resource Locator and it gives the location of a page.

The URL may be a simple name:

> http://www.cnet.com

This is the top page of the cInet site. **http://** identifies it as a WWW URL. **www** is how WWW addresses usually (but not always) start.

Some URLs are more complex:

> http://www.shareware.com/SW/Search/Popular

This takes us to the **Popular** page in the **/SW/Search** sub-directory at **shareware.com**. URLs are case-sensitive – you must use capitals and lower case as they are given in the URL. You must also get the punctuation right!

Using URLs

All Web browsers have routines for entering URLs. In Netscape and Internet Explorer they can be typed into the Location (or Address) slot, or into the Open dialog box that is reached from the File menu.

Finding URLs

Of course, before you can use a URL, you must know what it is. So where do you find them? There are several dozen scattered through this book; they are given in magazines and newspaper articles; they are even turning up in TV ads – and elsewhere. The URL for the BBC's news site (used opposite) came from the closing screen of the 9 O'Clock News.

Basic steps

1 Type the URL into the Location slot.

or

2 In Netscape 3.0, open the File menu and select Open Location.

In Navigator 4.0, use File – Open Page.

In Internet Explorer, use File – Open.

3 Type in the URL.

4 If your Netscape has an editor, select Open in Browser window.

5 Click [Open]

Tip

Once you start exploring the Web, you will find URLs all over the place. Make a careful note of any interesting ones, or add them to your Bookmarks or Favorites (pages 72 and 74).

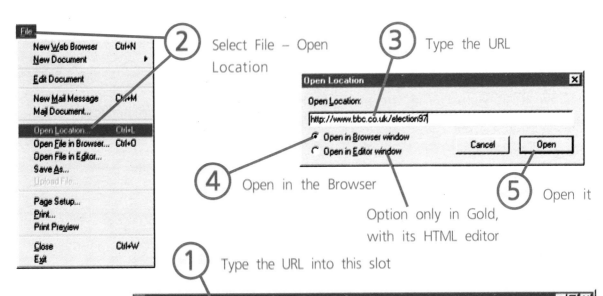

② Select File – Open Location

③ Type the URL

Open Location

Open Location:
`http://www.bbc.co.uk/election97`

⊙ Open in Browser window
○ Open in Editor window

Cancel   Open

④ Open in the Browser

Option only in Gold, with its HTML editor

⑤ Open it

① Type the URL into this slot

The / at the end marks this as the top page of the site. You don't need to type it.

Netscape Bookmarks

Some good places are easy to find; others you discover over a long and painful search or by sheer chance. If you want to return to those pages in future, add them to your bookmarks. This stores the title and URL of the page in a file, and puts the title onto the Bookmarks menu.

The more Bookmarks you have on the menu, the harder it is to spot one. Once you have more than a dozen or so Bookmarks, organise them into folders. These act as sub-menus on the Bookmark menu.

Before you start, work out which ones have something in common, and what to call their folders. Odds and ends can be left on the main menu and grouped later.

❑ Adding Bookmarks

1 When you find a page that you like, just click **Add Bookmark** on the **Bookmarks** menu.

❑ Using Bookmarks

2 Open **Bookmarks** and click on a page title.

❑ Organising Bookmarks

3 Open the **Bookmarks** menu and select **Go to Bookmarks**.

4 The new folder will be inserted below the selected item. For this first folder, select the Header – the top line.

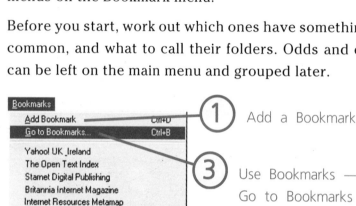

Add a Bookmark

Use Bookmarks —
Go to Bookmarks

Click to go to a page

Select where the
folder is to go

Use Item –
Insert Folder

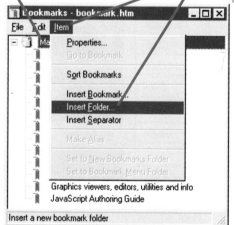

Tip

If you want to edit a Bookmark's title, select it, then use Item – Properties to open its Properties panel.

72

5 Open the **Item** menu and select **Insert Folder**.

6 Replace *New Folder* with a name to use on the Bookmarks menu.

7 Select an item and drag it onto the folder.

8 Repeat step 7 for all items for that folder.

9 Repeat steps 4 to 8 to create more folders.

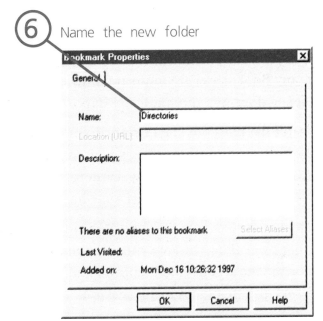

⑥ Name the new folder

⑦ Select an item and drag into place

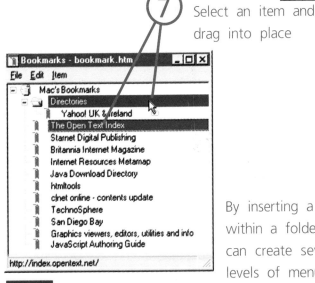

http://index.opentext.net/

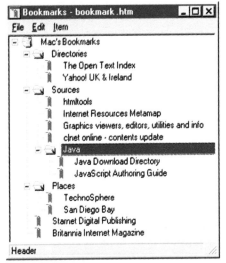

By inserting a folder within a folder you can create several levels of menus.

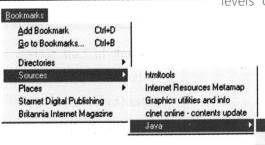

Take note

Bookmarks are handled in the same way in Navigator 4.0.

Explorer Favorites

Explorer Favorites are the same as Netscape Bookmarks. Indeed, if you have been using Netscape, then switch to Explorer, any Bookmarks are imported into its Favorites (but Netscape does not automatically import Favorites).

The Favorites list does not start empty. Explorer adds its own Links buttons and Channels, as well as Microsoft's on-line Clip Gallery and your My Directory folder (if present) – that's right, you can surf your hard disk!

The list can be opened from the Favorites menu, or in the Explorer bar by clicking the Favorites icon in the toolbar. This can be the most convenient approach if you want to visit several Favorite places in succession.

Basic steps

❑ Using the Explorer bar

1 Click the **Favorites** icon.

2 Click on a folder to open it.

3 Click on a link to visit its page.

4 When you have done, click the **Favorites** icon again to close the bar.

❑ Adding Favorites

1 Find a good page!

2 Open the **Favorites** menu and select **Add to Favorites**.

3 Edit the name if necessary.

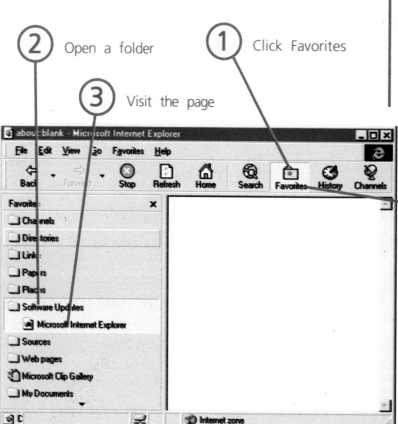

② Open a folder

③ Visit the page

① Click Favorites

④ Click to close

Tip

Switch to Full screen when the Explorer bar is open to give lots of room for the page display.

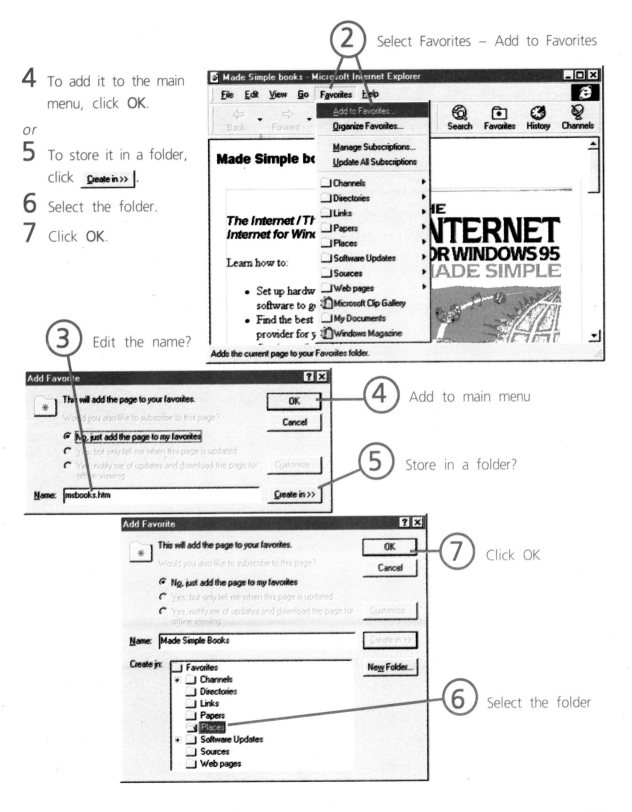

2 Select Favorites – Add to Favorites

4 To add it to the main menu, click **OK**.

or

5 To store it in a folder, click `Create in >>`.

6 Select the folder.

7 Click OK.

3 Edit the name?

4 Add to main menu

5 Store in a folder?

7 Click OK

6 Select the folder

Made Simple books - Microsoft Internet Explorer

File   Edit   View   Go   Favorites   Help

Add to Favorites...
Organize Favorites...

Manage Subscriptions...
Update All Subscriptions

Search   Favorites   History   Channels

Made Simple b

Channels
Directories
Links
Papers
Places
Software Updates
Sources
Web pages
Microsoft Clip Gallery
My Documents
Windows Magazine

The Internet / Tl Internet for Wine

Learn how to:

• Set up hardw software to g
• Find the best provider for y

Adds the current page to your Favorites folder.

NTERNET R WINDOWS 95 IADE SIMPLE

Add Favorite   ? X

This will add the page to your favorites.

Would you also like to subscribe to this page?

⦿ No, just add the page to my favorites
○ Yes, but only tell me when this page is updated
○ Yes, notify me of updates and download the page for offline viewing

OK
Cancel
Customize...

Name: msbooks.htm   Create in >>

Add Favorite   ? X

This will add the page to your favorites.

Would you also like to subscribe to this page?

⦿ No, just add the page to my favorites
○ Yes, but only tell me when this page is updated
○ Yes, notify me of updates and download the page for offline viewing

OK
Cancel
Customize...

Name: Made Simple Books   Create in >>

Create in: Favorites
  Channels
  Directories
  Links
  Papers
  Places
  Software Updates
  Sources
  Web pages

New Folder...

The History list

You will often find, when browsing, that you want to return to a page that you left not long before. Clicking the Back button will step you back through the links, but this is not always the best way to revisit. If the target page is more than a few jumps away, working backwards can be slow. If there is a framed page between you and the target, you may not be able to get out of the frames with the Back button. This is where the History lists come in handy.

Netscape 3.0

In Netscape 3.0, the History system only keeps track of the pages visited during the current session. If you want to retain a link for longer, then you should create a bookmark to it before you shut down for the day.

● The History window stays open – and on top – until you close it.

Navigator 4.0

Communicator's Navigator handles the History better. The most obvious improvements are:

● You can choose how long to retain the links (on the Navigator Preferences panel).

● The History window drops behind the Navigator window when you go to a link.

❑ Netscape 3.0

1 Open the **Window** menu and select **History**.

2 Select a link and click Go to.

or

3 Click Create Bookmark to add the link to your Bookmarks.

4 Push the History window out of the way or click Close.

❑ Navigator 4.0

5 Open the **Communicator** menu and select **History**.

6 To go to a page, double-click on its link.

or

7 Select the link, and use **File – Go to Page**.

8 Close the History window when you have done.

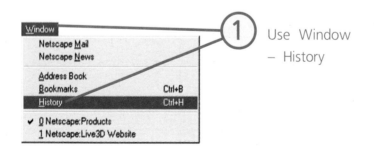

Use Window – History

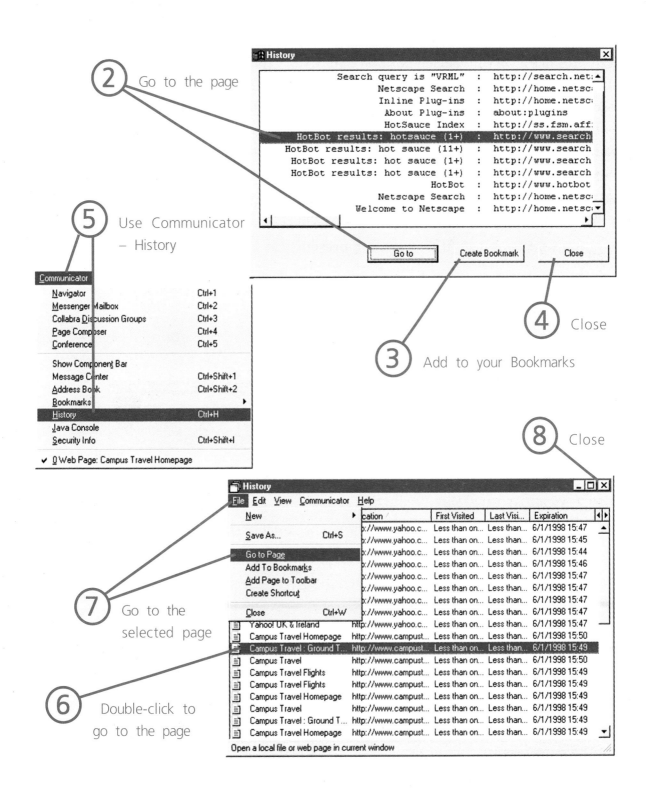

② Go to the page

⑤ Use Communicator
– History

④ Close

③ Add to your Bookmarks

⑧ Close

⑦ Go to the
selected page

⑥ Double-click to
go to the page

History

Search query is "VRML" : http://search.net:
Netscape Search : http://home.netsc:
Inline Plug-ins : http://home.netsc:
About Plug-ins : about:plugins
HotSauce Index : http://ss.fsm.aff:
HotBot results: hotsauce (1+) : http://www.search
HotBot results: hot sauce (11+) : http://www.search
HotBot results: hot sauce (1+) : http://www.search
HotBot results: hot sauce (1+) : http://www.search
HotBot : http://www.hotbot
Netscape Search : http://home.netsc:
Welcome to Netscape : http://home.netsc:

Go to   Create Bookmark   Close

Communicator

Navigator   Ctrl+1
Messenger Mailbox   Ctrl+2
Collabra Discussion Groups   Ctrl+3
Page Composer   Ctrl+4
Conference   Ctrl+5

Show Component Bar
Message Center   Ctrl+Shift+1
Address Book   Ctrl+Shift+2
Bookmarks   ▶
History   Ctrl+H
Java Console
Security Info   Ctrl+Shift+I

✔ 0 Web Page: Campus Travel Homepage

History

File Edit View Communicator Help

New   ▶   cation   First Visited   Last Visi...   Expiration
Save As...   Ctrl+S   p://www.yahoo.c... Less than on... Less than... 6/1/1998 15:47
                                      p://www.yahoo.c... Less than on... Less than... 6/1/1998 15:45
Go to Page   p://www.yahoo.c... Less than on... Less than... 6/1/1998 15:44
Add To Bookmarks   p://www.yahoo.c... Less than on... Less than... 6/1/1998 15:46
Add Page to Toolbar   p://www.yahoo.c... Less than on... Less than... 6/1/1998 15:47
Create Shortcut   p://www.yahoo.c... Less than on... Less than... 6/1/1998 15:47
                                      p://www.yahoo.c... Less than on... Less than... 6/1/1998 15:47
Close   Ctrl+W   p://www.yahoo.c... Less than on... Less than... 6/1/1998 15:47
Yahoo! UK & Ireland   http://www.yahoo.c... Less than on... Less than... 6/1/1998 15:47
Campus Travel Homepage   http://www.campust... Less than on... Less than... 6/1/1998 15:50
Campus Travel : Ground T... http://www.campust... Less than on... Less than... 6/1/1998 15:49
Campus Travel   http://www.campust... Less than on... Less than... 6/1/1998 15:50
Campus Travel Flights   http://www.campust... Less than on... Less than... 6/1/1998 15:49
Campus Travel Flights   http://www.campust... Less than on... Less than... 6/1/1998 15:49
Campus Travel Homepage   http://www.campust... Less than on... Less than... 6/1/1998 15:49
Campus Travel   http://www.campust... Less than on... Less than... 6/1/1998 15:49
Campus Travel : Ground T... http://www.campust... Less than on... Less than... 6/1/1998 15:49
Campus Travel Homepage   http://www.campust... Less than on... Less than... 6/1/1998 15:49

Open a local file or web page in current window

Explorer's History

Explorer has a very organised approach to History links. It sets up a folder for each day's surfing, and a folder for each visited site, and stores in it the links to the pages that you visited there. The resulting History list is compact, and it is easier to find links here than in either of the Netscape lists.

● If you use the History links after you have gone off-line, the page will be re-opened using the files stored on your hard disk (if they are still present).

Basic steps

1 Click the **History** icon on the toolbar.

2 Open the day's folder.

3 Open the folder for the site you want.

4 Click on the page link to open it.

5 Click the **History** icon again to close the Explorer bar.

(2) Open the day folder

(3) Open the site folder

(4) Go to the page

(1) Click History

(5) Close the list

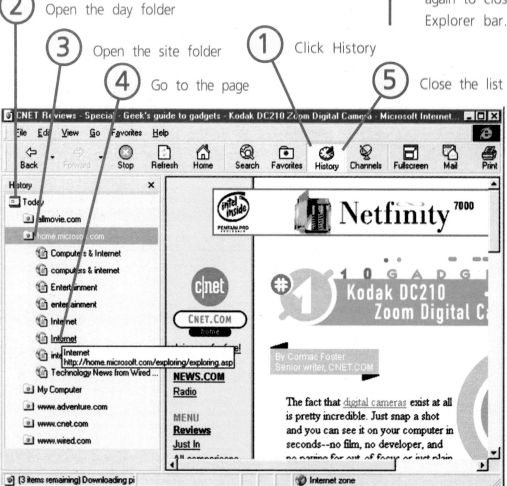

Basic steps

1 In Netscape, open the **History** list.

or

2 In Explorer, display the **History** list in the Explorer bar.

3 Locate the link.

4 Click on the link and drag it to the desktop.

5 Edit the shortcut's name if necessary.

Whether you use either Netscape or Internet Explorer, you can take links from the History list and turn them into shortcuts on your desktop. You may find it worth doing this for those sites that you make most use of.

The technique is the same for all browsers. Before starting, you must reduce the size of the browser window – and minimise any other applications – so that you can see some of the desktop beneath.

① Display the History list

③ Locate the link

⑤ Edit the name?

Shortcut to
Yahoo!

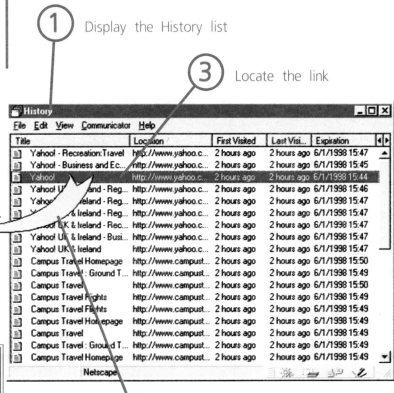

④ Drag onto the desktop

Tip

Don't overdo the shortcuts or you will have a very cluttered desktop!

Safe surfing

If you intend to let your children explore the Internet on their own, you would be advised to install some child-protection software. There are a number of programs available for this, mainly shareware and typically costing between £15 and £30. They tackle the job is several ways – some using a combination of approaches for more comprehensive control.

Acceptable and unacceptable sites

Some keep lists of acceptable sites, and ban access to all others. This is the basis of Surf Watch and Internet Explorer's Content Advisor, amongst others. It is effective, but can be over-restrictive. There may be many acceptable sites which have not yet asked for inclusion or been discovered by the keepers of the lists.

The alternative is to keep lists of unacceptable sites, and here the main problem is to keep the lists up to date as new sites are appearing all the time. Net Nanny (see next page) and others that take this approach issue regular updates to their registered users.

Text monitoring

Incoming and outgoing text can be checked for the presence of key words. This has the advantage of keeping on eye on e-mail and newsgroup use, as well as Web sites, but can let unacceptable pictures slip through.

Logging

This does not bar access, but it does keep track of where the browser has been, leaving it to parents to agree acceptable use with their children.

Take note

Some newsgroups carry pornography, sexist, racist, bigoted or other material which may offend. Software which simply controls access to Web sites may leave the door open to all news-groups. Some access providers, e.g. MSN and CompuServe, offer child-safe newsgroup access. Talk to your provider if this is a concern for you.

Net Nanny

□ Installation

1 Download the software and run it – it is a self-installing file.

2 Set the name and password for the administrator.

□ Net Nanny can be added to the StartUp folder so that it runs automatically when the PC is turned on.

Net Nanny is one of the best protection programs. It doesn't just control what Web sites can be accessed or what material can be read from the Internet, it also provides comprehensive supervision of all Windows-based activity. Net Nanny stores lists of unacceptable words and unsuitable Web sites and newsgroups. When an attempt is made to access a site or group on the list, Net Nanny can respond in one or more ways. It can:

- log the attempt, and leave you to take the appropriate action yourself after you have checked the logs to see what the kids have been doing.

- issue a warning.

- block the move.

- shut down the program – that'll teach 'em!

Net Nanny puts you in control. Amongst other things, it lets you:

- set up your own additional lists of unacceptable words and places;

- allocate override permission to authorised users;

- set it to monitor other Windows applications.

Try it free!

To get an evaluation copy of or more information about Net Nanny, go to the developer's site at:

http://www.netnanny.com

Take note

It's ironic, but Net Nanny is a great resource for people looking for 'adult' sites (see the screenshot on the next page). There doesn't seem to be any way to prevent people from reading these sites lists.

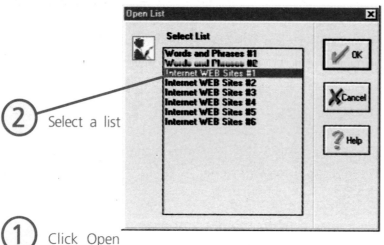

② Select a list

- ❑ Net Nanny options
- 1 Click the Open icon.
- 2 Select a word or site list.
- 3 Set the response options for that list.
- 4 Repeat for all lists.

① Click Open

③ Set the responses

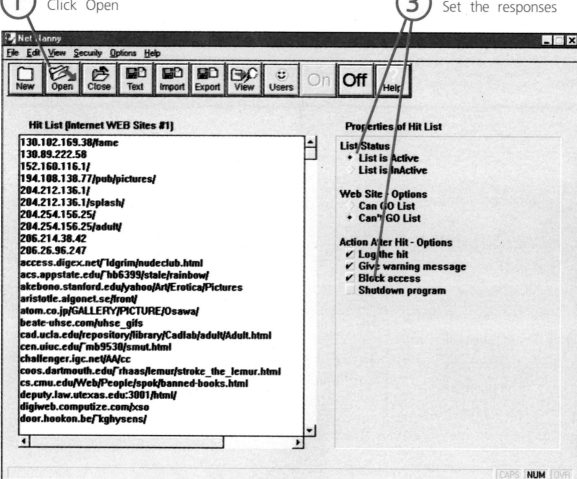

Hit List (Internet WEB Sites #1)

```
130.102.169.38/fame
130.89.222.58
152.160.116.1/
194.108.138.77/pub/pictures/
204.212.136.1/
204.212.136.1/splash/
204.254.156.25/
204.254.156.25/adult/
206.214.38.42
206.26.96.247
access.digex.net/~ldgrim/nudeclub.html
acs.appstate.edu/~hb6399/stale/rainbow/
akebono.stanford.edu/yahoo/Art/Erotica/Pictures
aristotle.algonet.se/front/
atom.co.jp/GALLERY/PICTURE/Osawa/
beate-uhse.com/uhse_gifs
cad.ucla.edu/repository/library/Cadlab/adult/Adult.html
cen.uiuc.edu/~mb9530/smut.html
challenger.igc.net/AA/cc
coos.dartmouth.edu/~rhaas/lemur/stroke_the_lemur.html
cs.cmu.edu/Web/People/spok/banned-books.html
deputy.law.utexas.edu:3001/html/
digiweb.computize.com/xso
door.hookon.be/~kghysens/
```

Properties of Hit List

List Status
- ◆ List is Active
- ◇ List is InActive

Web Site - Options
- ◇ Can GO List
- ◆ Can't GO List

Action After Hit - Options
- ✔ Log the hit
- ✔ Give warning message
- ✔ Block access
- ☐ Shutdown program

The Log file:

This records every significant action that occurs while Net Nanny is running. You will notice here that someone has been trying to get to the more exotic parts of the Internet!

The Log can be cleared – and should be cleared regularly to keep it to a manageable size. Anyone using the machine can do this, but the clear operation is also recorded.

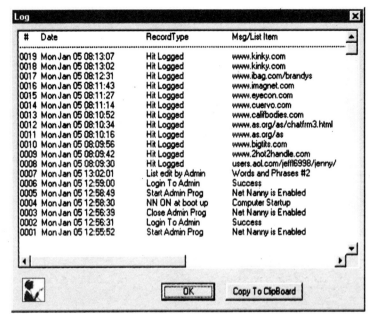

Authorised users

If you want to allow older members of the family to browse where they like, you can set them up as authorised users with the ability to override a shutdown or restart the program when Net Nanny swings into action.

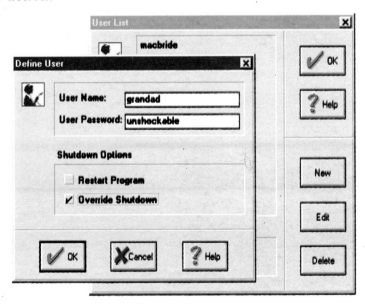

Take note

There is nothing to stop an unauthorised user from turning Net Nanny off – except that it will be noted in the log file.

To create a user, enter the Name and Password and set the options.

Summary

- Most **hypertext links** are built into text or attached to individual images, but you will also find them in **image maps** and **Live 3D** displays.

- Every **Web page has a unique URL** which gives the address of the site and the location of the page file.

- You can **go directly to a page** by typing its URL into the Location slot of your browser.

- When you find a page that you want to revisit, you can add it to your **Bookmarks** in Netscape, or your **Favorite Places** in Internet Explorer.

- Both browsers maintain a **History** list, keeping track of where you have been during a session. Use the links in the list if you want to return to a page.

- If you want quick and easy access to a Web page, you can set up a link as a **desktop shortcut**.

- There are places on the Internet which are not suitable for **family viewing**. If children are browsing from your computer, you should think about installing some safer surfing software. **Net Nanny** is one of the most comprehensive applications of this type.

6 Web directories

Yahoo

Yahoo is one of the best places to start. It has over one million links, and is well-organised and cross-referenced. Start at:

http://www.yahoo.com   or   http://www.yahoo.co.uk

Expect to go through at least two, and probably four or more levels of menus to get to any real meat. The top level lists broad areas of interest with sub-categories. You can start from the main headings or go straight to the next level of menus.

Yahoo categories

Arts and Humanities
Business and Economy
Computers and Internet
Education
Entertainment
Government
Health
News and Media
Recreation and Sport
Reference
Regional
Science
Social Science
Society and Culture

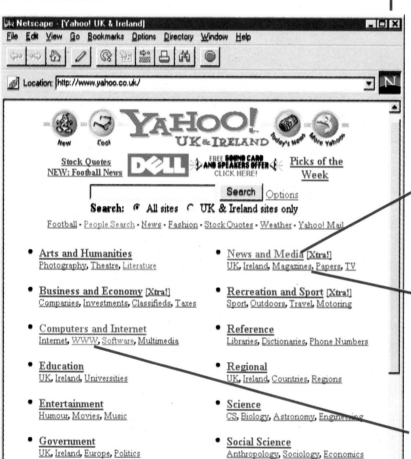

Click on a main heading to see the full list of categories in that area

An underline shows that text is a hypertext link – click on it to jump to the linked page

If the category you want is listed as a sub-heading, you can go straight to it

Menu pages

Tip

If you find a useful menu page, add it to your Bookmarks or Favorites – but go through them regularly to trim out those no longer needed, or you will get swamped!

The contents of menu pages vary, but you will always find a Search box at the top (see the next page).

The central area lists related categories and those of the next level down. These may be followed by:

@ showing a cross-link to another menu structure.

A number showing how many links it has.

Beneath these are links to pages, with a brief description of each.

This is a fourth level menu – there are more cross-references than sub-categories at this level

If a page (outside Yahoo) consists purely of links to material relevant to the menu topic, rather than information, Yahoo stores it in <u>Indices</u>

Message Boards are areas where visitors can discuss topics – much the same as newsgroups, but inside Yahoo.

This menu page had over 100 links – many of them worth a visit.

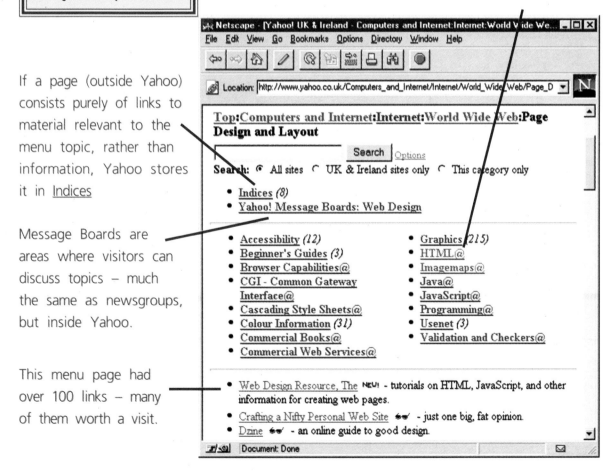

Searching Yahoo

If you are looking for information on a specific topic, organisation, artist, piece of software, or whatever, it is often quicker to search for it, than to work your way through menus or the descriptions of linked pages.

A successful search will give you a list of categories, if any, and a list of links that contain the given word(s).

Simple search

A simple search looks for pages that contain matches for all the words you enter (the *keys*), but treats the words as *substrings*. For instance, if you entered 'graphic software' it would look for pages with 'graphic', 'graphics' and 'graphical' and with 'software'.

- If you are in the UK, restrict the search to **UK & Ireland** only if you are looking for suppliers or societies, where being local is important.

- Restrict the search to **This category only** to reduce search times and cut out irrelevant material from other categories.

1 Enter one or more words to describe what you are looking for try to be specific.

2 Restrict the search, if appropriate.

3 Click **Search** .

4 When the results appear, go to a Category to browse through a menu page of related links.

or

5 Work through the Sites and select from there.

6 If the search does not deliver the goods, click **Options** (see page 90).

Tip

The Yahoo menu structure is very good, but it isn't always obvious where you should start looking for a topic. Rather than hunt up and down the menus, run a search to find the category headings.

Tip

If you are looking for a company on the Web, start in the Business section and just type the main part of its name.

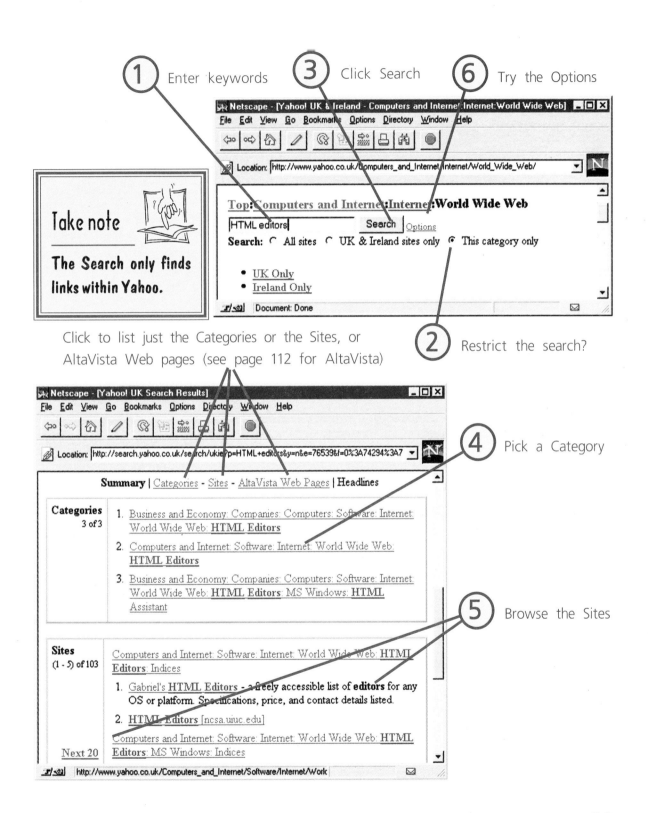

① Enter keywords

③ Click Search

⑥ Try the Options

Take note

The Search only finds links within Yahoo.

Top:Computers and Internet:Internet:World Wide Web

HTML editors   Search Options

Search: ○ All sites ○ UK & Ireland sites only ◉ This category only

- UK Only
- Ireland Only

Click to list just the Categories or the Sites, or AltaVista Web pages (see page 112 for AltaVista)

② Restrict the search?

④ Pick a Category

⑤ Browse the Sites

Summary | Categories - Sites - AltaVista Web Pages | Headlines

Categories
3 of 3

1. Business and Economy: Companies: Computers: Software: Internet: World Wide Web: **HTML Editors**

2. Computers and Internet: Software: Internet: World Wide Web: **HTML Editors**

3. Business and Economy: Companies: Computers: Software: Internet: World Wide Web: **HTML Editors**: MS Windows: **HTML** Assistant

Sites
(1 - 5) of 103

Computers and Internet: Software: Internet: World Wide Web: **HTML Editors**: Indices

1. Gabriel's HTML Editors - a freely accessible list of **editors** for any OS or platform. Specifications, price, and contact details listed.

2. HTML Editors [ncsa.uiuc.edu]

Computers and Internet: Software: Internet: World Wide Web: **HTML Editors**: MS Windows: Indices

Next 20

Search Options

With the Options, you can refine a search to focus on the most relevant material, or widen the search to bring more results into the net.

Match styles

- If your keywords are alternatives (e.g. Peking Beijing) then set it to **Matches on any word (OR)**.

- If you only want results that include all your key words, set it to **Matches on all words (AND)**.

- If the keyword could also be part of a larger, irrelevant word (e.g. 'lute' will also find 'flute', 'Klute', 'pollute') then set it to **An exact phrase match**.

Other options

You can search in **Yahoo**, in **Usenet** (for newsgroup articles) or for **e-mail addresses**. Within Yahoo, you can further restrict the search to **Categories**, **Sites** or **Today's News**.

If you are only interested in newer material, you can set a time limit, ranging from **1 day** to **6 months** – the default is during the past **3 years**.

The first page will always show a maximum of 5 results in each heading. You can specify the number to show on subsequent pages. Set this to 10 or less for a quicker response; or to a high number if you want to save the page as a file and examine the results at leisure, off-line.

Basic steps

1 Enter the keyword(s).

2 Select the area to search – **Yahoo**, **Usenet** or **e-mail addresses**.

3 Set the **match style**.

4 If you are searching Yahoo, restrict the search if appropriate.

5 Set a **time limit**.

6 Set the number of **results per page**.

7 Click Search .

8 When the **Summary** results appear, switch to **Categories**, **Sites** or **AltaVista Web** pages if you want to focus on one of these.

Tip

Cut down your phone bills by reading long page off-line. Use File – Save As, keeping the .htm ending then use Open – File to reload it into the browser.

90

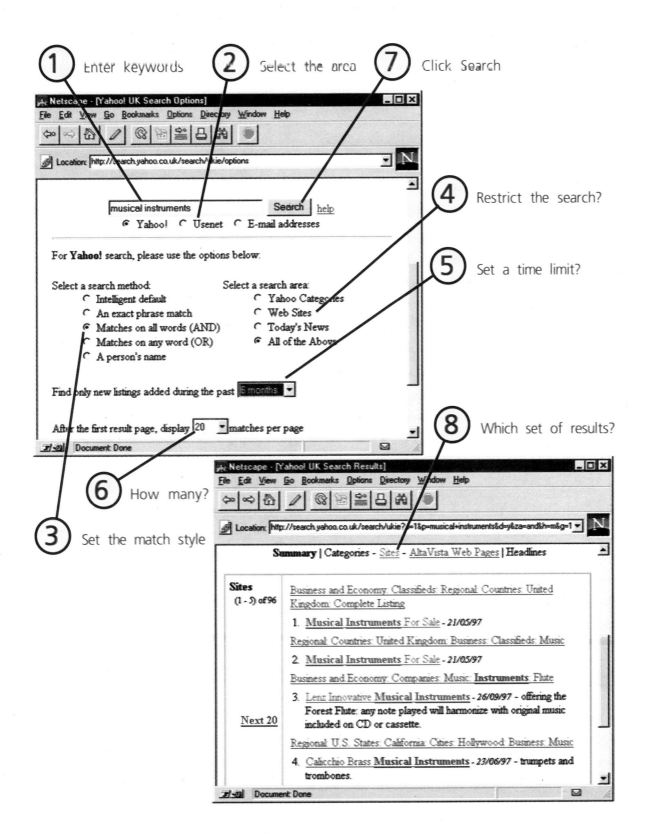

1. Enter keywords

2. Select the area

7. Click Search

4. Restrict the search?

5. Set a time limit?

8. Which set of results?

6. How many?

3. Set the match style

91

Excite

Excite is both a search engine and a directory. It lists 140,000 selected sites, of which 25,000 are reviewed – with the top 1% being checked and reviewed regularly. So, while you won't find as many links here as at Yahoo, they are likely to be more useful.

The content is geared to the home user, with good sources of information, but also plenty of links to commercial suppliers of goods and services. Layout is very clear, with an attractive magazine-style format on some pages.

Basic steps

1 Go to Excite at http://www.excite.com

2 Select a **Channel**.

3 Read the **News**.

Or

4 Go to the **Web sites**.

5 Go to a reviewed **Top Site** or pick a **Subtopic**.

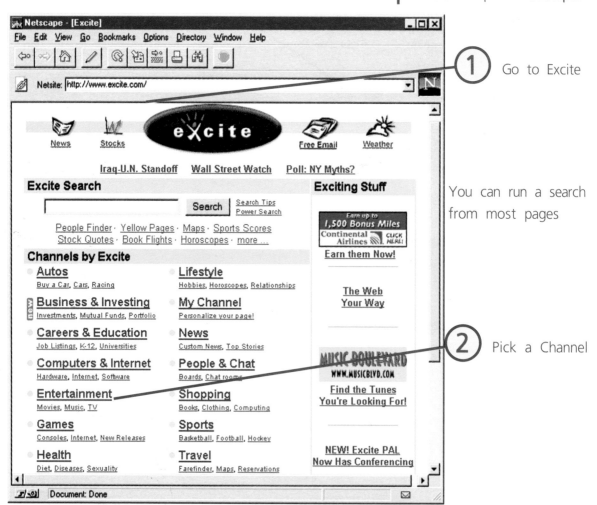

Go to Excite

You can run a search from most pages

Pick a Channel

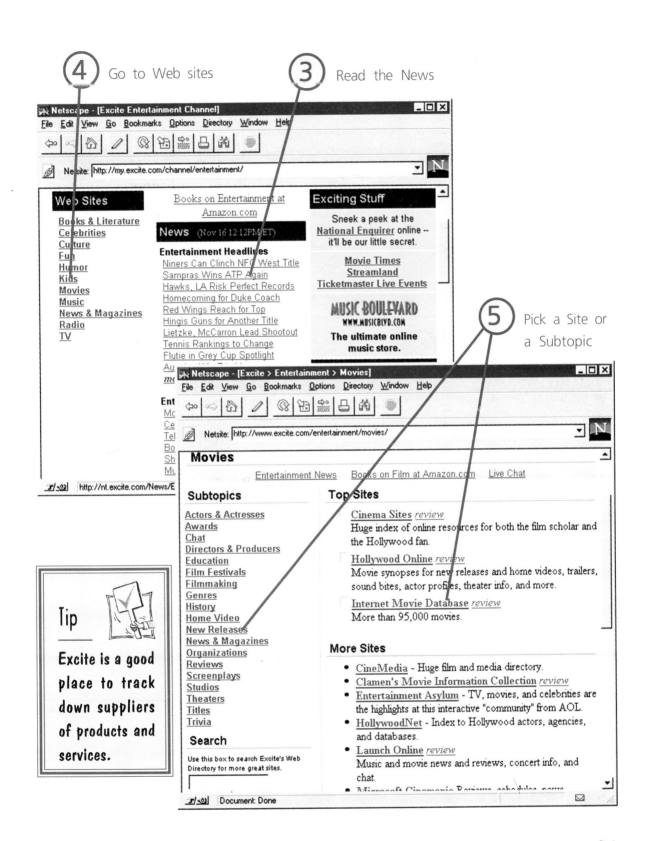

4 Go to Web sites

3 Read the News

5 Pick a Site or a Subtopic

Tip

Excite is a good place to track down suppliers of products and services.

My Channel

Excite, like most other directories and search sites, relies on advertising for its income – and rates depend upon readership. The personalised My Channel facility is one of the things that they hope will encourage you to keep coming back, and to spend more time there.

You can choose what topics to include on these pages, and set up your own selections of favourite links. The choices are stored on your computer, as a 'cookie' – coded data in Netscape's *cookie.txt* file, or Internet Explorer's *cookie* folder – so that they are in place when you revisit.

Basic steps

1 Go to Excite at http://www.excite.com

2 Select **My Excite Channel**.

3 Fill in the form and click **Submit** to go to your personal Channel.

4 Click the section's **Change** button.

5 Edit your choices and links then click **Submit**.

① Go to Excite

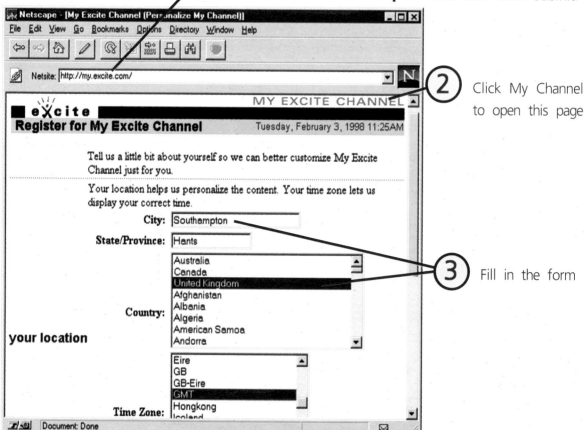

② Click My Channel to open this page

③ Fill in the form

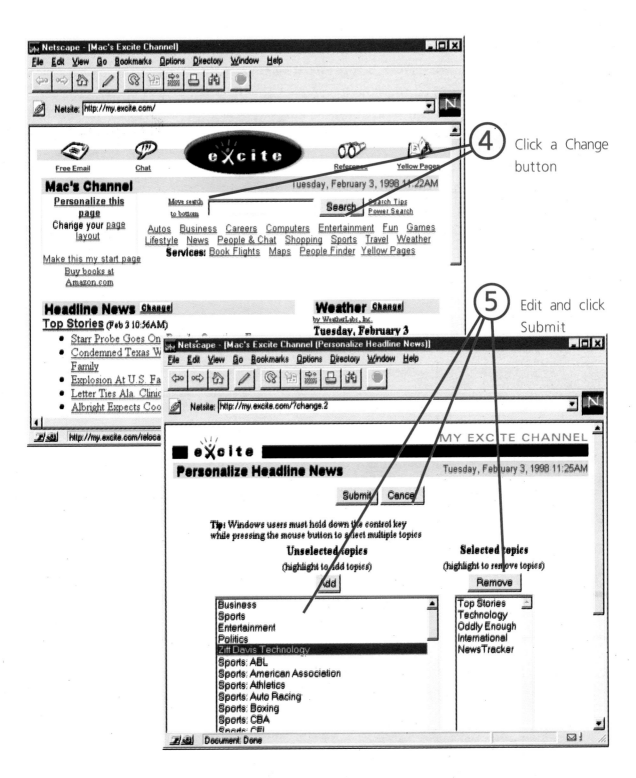

④ Click a Change button

⑤ Edit and click Submit

Lycos Top 5%

Lycos is one of the most popular sites on the Web, with a claimed 13+ million visitors a day! It is primarily a search engine – and we will return to this aspect on page 121 – but it also runs a directory of the Top 5% Sites, and offers a *Personal Guide* and other services.

Its Top 5% Sites are rated on content and/or design, and each link is accompanied by a brief review. So, although these cover only a small fraction of the Web, you can be reasonably sure that a site will be worth visiting and have what you want, before you link to it.

Basic steps

1 Go to Lycos Top 5% at
http://point.lycos.com

or

http://point-uk.lycos.com

2 Select a Topic.

3 Read through the list to find suitable sites.

or

4 Click on a heading for a more specialised list.

or

5 Sort the Content, Date, Design or Alphabet.

Go to Lycos Top 5% Sites

Click on a Topic

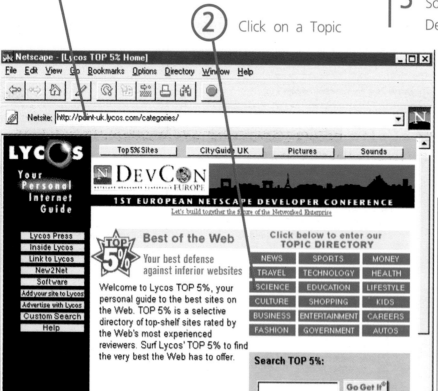

Tip

You can search the Top 5% from here – just type a keyword and click Go Get It!

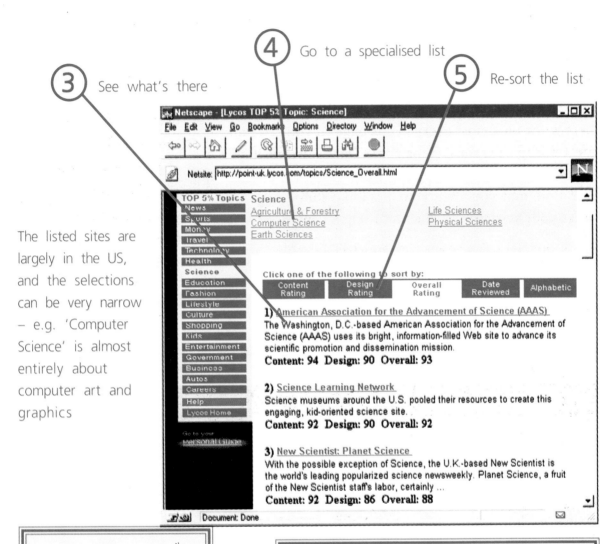

④ Go to a specialised list

③ See what's there

⑤ Re-sort the list

The listed sites are largely in the US, and the selections can be very narrow – e.g. 'Computer Science' is almost entirely about computer art and graphics

Take note

If you live in the UK you are automatically redirected to the UK version of the site.

Tip

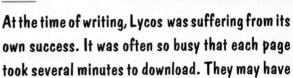

At the time of writing, Lycos was suffering from its own success. It was often so busy that each page took several minutes to download. They may have improved access by the time you read this.

Lycos Personal Guide

This is Lycos's equivalent to My Channel at Excite. There is more emphasis here on news than on links – though that does rather depend on how you set it up.

To start, click on a **Go to your Personal Guide** button – there's one on almost every Lycos page (if you can't find one, try http://personal.lycos.com). On the first visit, you are asked for details about yourself and your interests. Next time that you visit, your Personal Guide page will havve your selection of News and Top 5% links.

● Bookmark the page, and you will be able to leap straight to it.

Take note

Lycos offers other services including stores of pictures and sounds, and Chat rooms, where you can meet and 'talk' (type) with other surfers.

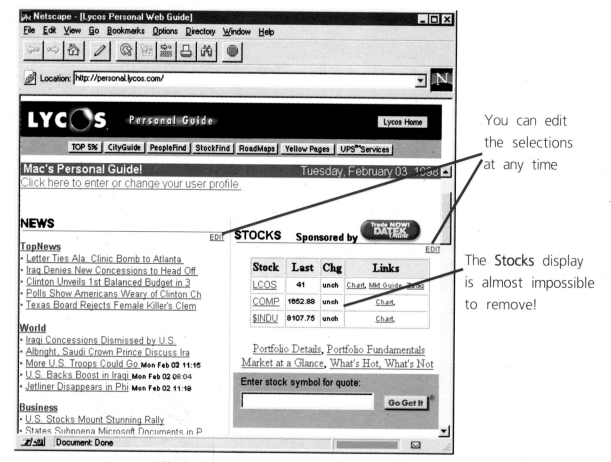

You can edit the selections at any time

The **Stocks** display is almost impossible to remove!

Infoseek Channels

Infoseek, like Excite and Lycos, offers a search facility – and a very good one, as you will see on page 118. For the moment, let's have a look at its Channels.

The Channels form a hierarchical directory, like Yahoo, but with only two or three levels. Each Channel carries a set of 'Web sites' which hold sets of links and which are further sub-divided into Topics. The major Web sites are listed, along with the Channels, on the Infoseek home page. The rest are easily accessed at the next level.

Infoseek is at **http://www.infoseek.com**

Tip

If you like using Infoseek, download its 'Desktop' software. This puts a slim Taskbar on your screen, giving you fast access to Infoseek's facilities.

Remember that you do not need to type the end / slash

You can also search for Companies here

You can download Infoseek Desktop from the top page

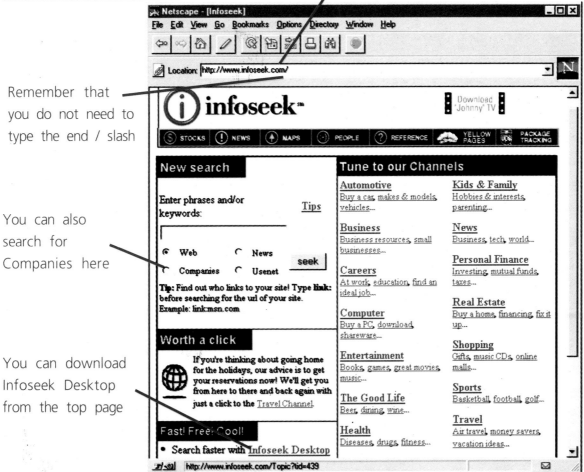

The contents of the Channels vary. There are normally some lead articles and News links, and there is always a set of links to their 'Web sites'. Some of those sites carry very many links – for instance, there were nearly 400 in Electronic Publishing topics when I visited.

Tip

Infoseek is one of the more commercial sites. It's a great place to go shopping if you live in the US – and not too bad if you don't, as there are plenty of links to international and non-US companies.

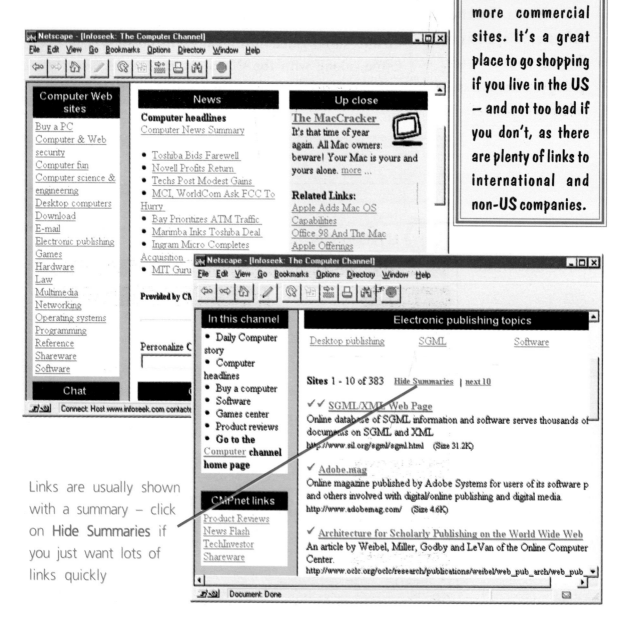

Links are usually shown with a summary – click on **Hide Summaries** if you just want lots of links quickly

Basic steps

1 Go to Starting Point at:
   http://www.stpt.com

2 Select a **Category** from
   the sidebar.

3 At the next level, pick a
   sub-category.

4 Browse through the
   links.

5 Click on a link.

Starting Point

Starting Point is a well-organised and easy-to-use directory. Particularly attractive features here are the brief but clear comments that accompany each link, and the presence of the main category list down the left of each page, so that you can switch to a new category without having to work your way back up the menu structure.

If you are looking for specific information, you can use Starting Point's Power Search. This links to major search engines to hunt down resources on the Web.

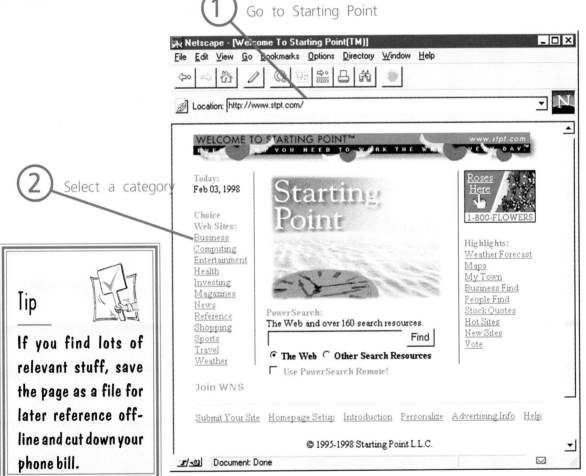

① Go to Starting Point

② Select a category

Tip

If you find lots of relevant stuff, save the page as a file for later reference off-line and cut down your phone bill.

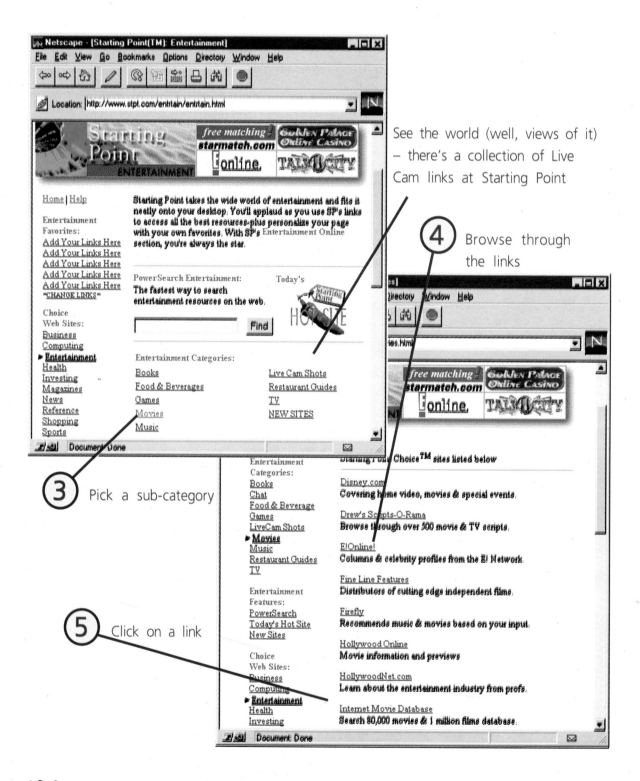

See the world (well, views of it) – there's a collection of Live Cam links at Starting Point

④ Browse through the links

③ Pick a sub-category

⑤ Click on a link

The IMDb

The Internet Movie Database (IMDb to its fans), is a great resource for movie buffs. It has the cast and credits of over 100,000 films – many with plot summaries, pictures and trivia.

It's fully searchable and cross-referenced, so that you can find out who played a part in one film, then get a list of all the others they've been in – you can follow the careers of directors, cameramen, even make-up artists!

When you enter a site URL, you may be taken directly to a special page. At the IMDb you go to the Welcome page.

Click here to search for your favourite actor/actress/director, or to find out who played a certain part in a film – and what else you can see them in.

WWW Virtual Library

The World Wide Web Virtual Library is a unique resource. Its catalogue is organised by subject, much as any ordinary (book) library. The main structure is defined and the links in the Overview kept up to date by Stanford University, but its component parts are maintained by specialists scattered throughout the world. The result is an extremely useful resource, particularly for academic research – at any level.

1 Go to the Virtual Library start page at http://vlib.stanford.edu/Overview2.html

2 Scroll through the Overview and select a subject.

3 Read through the page to find the section on the topic you want.

4 Follow the links.

5 Use the Back button to return to the Library for more links.

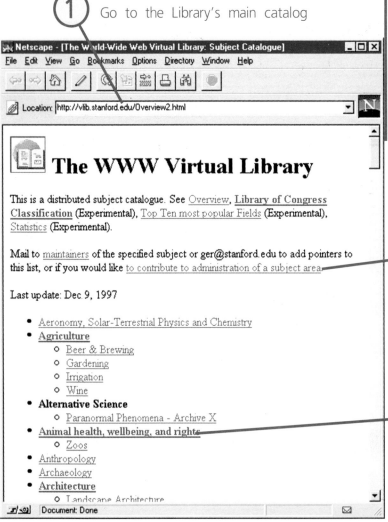

① Go to the Library's main catalog

If you are a specialist in a field that is not covered by the Library, why not volunteer to maintain a subject?

② Pick a subject

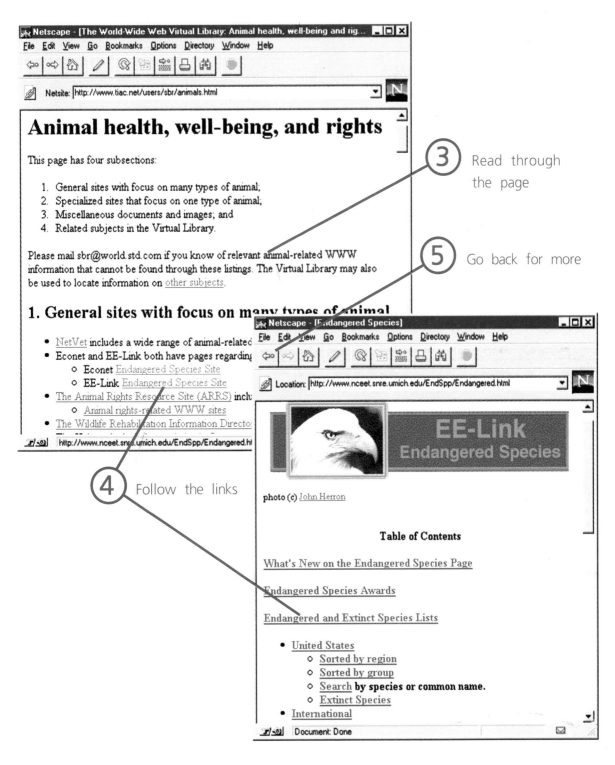

3 Read through the page

5 Go back for more

4 Follow the links

UK directory

If you want to find local suppliers, clubs, courses, the main Internet directories and search engines may not be the best place to look – simply because you will get too many irrelevant links. If you want local stuff, look in a local directory. In the UK, the first place to try is UK directory. It has links to UK businesses, shops, schools, colleges and government organisations, news, travel, entertainment and other services.

Unless you are looking for something very specific it is probably simplest to work your way through the well-organised catalog. If you do need to search, use the Full Search routine for better control.

Basic steps

1 Go to UK directory at:
http://ww.ukdirectory.co.uk

2 Browse through the catalog.

or

3 Click on **Full Search**.

4 Enter the search words.

5 Set the match to **ANY** or **ALL** words.

6 Enter any words to **Exclude**, if appropriate.

7 Click ➡**GO!**

if you get too many hits...

8 Click on a keyword to narrow the search.

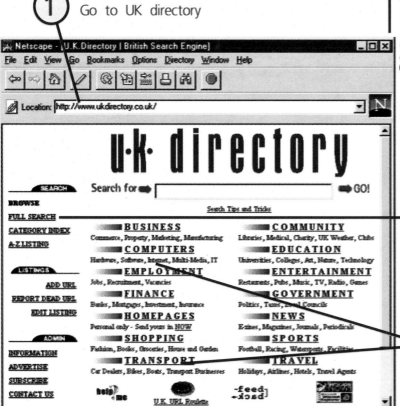

① Go to UK directory

③ Click Full Search

② Browse the catalog

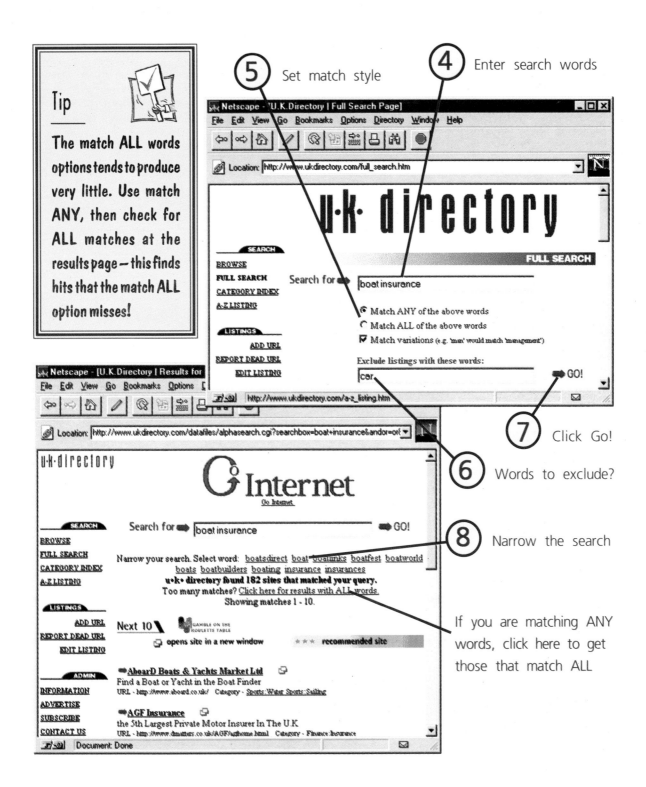

⑤ Set match style

④ Enter search words

⑦ Click Go!

⑥ Words to exclude?

⑧ Narrow the search

If you are matching ANY words, click here to get those that match ALL

Summary

- **Yahoo** is probably the best directory on the Web, and is always a good place to start browsing.

- Searches at Yahoo will find any matching links within the site.

- **Excite** holds many links to reviewed sites, with the best being revisited and checked regularly.

- You can set up a **My Channel** page at Excite, to give simple access to your favourite links, selected news and other information.

- **Lycos** has selections of the **Top 5%** of sites, as well as a very large database. You can customise your own sets of links in the **Personal Guide** at Lycos.

- At **Infoseek**, links to sites and to related news stories are organised into topic-based **Channels**.

- The **Starting Point** directory is well-organised and presented, making it simple to use – and it has some well-chosen sets of links.

- The **WWW Virtual Library** has its sets of links organised into subject areas, as in an ordinary library. It is a good place to start any academic research.

- If you want to find companies, organisations or people in the UK, the **UK directory** is the best place to start looking.

7 Search engines

Search techniques

Search engines vary, but the techniques that you must use to search their databases are broadly similar.

Simple searches

If you enter a single word, then – as you would expect – the engines will search for that word. If you enter two or more words, there are several possible responses:

- Most engines will search for pages that contain any of the words, but display first those those contain all of the words. e.g. a search for 'Beijing Peking' would find pages with references to the capital of China, however it was spelt. A search for 'graphics conversion software' would find all those pages containing the word 'graphics', plus those containing 'conversion' and those containing 'software' – and the total could run to millions. However, pages containing all three words – though not necessarily in that order, or related to each other – would be among the first results displayed.

- Some engines will only return those pages that contain all of the given words.

- If the given words are enclosed in "double quotes", most engines will search only for that phrase. Look for "greenhouse effect" and you should find stuff on global warming, and not get pages on gardening!

Plurals and other endings

Some engines automatically truncate and extend words to cater for different possible endings. With these, a search for '**music**als' would also find 'music' and 'musicians'.

Take note

Some search engines just search the title and keywords – if the page's author has defined any. Others also search through the top 10 or 20 lines of text. A few do full text searches, so that the whole page is indexed.

Advanced searches

These are much more varied than simple searches. Most support the use of logical operators.

Logical operators

Also known as Boolean operators, these can be used to link keywords. They are normally written in capitals.

AND every word must match to produce a hit

OR any matching word will produce a hit.

NOT ignore pages containing this word

If you use a mixture of operators, they will normally be evaluated in the order NOT, AND then OR, e.g.

boat AND sail OR yacht

will find pages with references to boats where sails are also mentioned, or to yachts.

boat AND sail OR paddle

will again find references to sailing boats, but will also pick up all 'paddle' pages – whether they relate to boats or not. This can be changed by putting round brackets () around the part you want to evaluate first. So, to find paddle boats or sail boats, you would need:

boat AND (sail OR paddle)

Include/exclude

Some engines will allow the use of the modifiers + (include) and –(exclude). Keywords marked + must be present for a page to match; pages containing keywords marked with – are to be ignored, e.g.

+"Tom Jones" Fielding –song

Should find pages about the book by Henry Fielding, but ignore the singer's fan clubs.

Tip

If you enter words only in lower case, most engines will ignore case when matching – so 'windows' also finds 'Windows'.

If you use capital initials, most engines will return only those pages with matching capitals, so that 'Gates' will find the boss of Microsoft, but ignore garden portals.

Words written entirely in capitals will rarely find anything!

AltaVista

AltaVista is regarded by many people as the king of the search engines. It's certainly very fast and has a huge database! Unless you are looking for something rare, a simple search can produce thousands of hits. There are three ways to focus a search – use the Advanced Search, the *Way-Cool topics map*, or Refine the results. We'll try refining first.

In this example, the search is sites that bring together potential pen friends – and we're looking for contacts for the kids! We'll start with 'pen friends' as the keywords.

Basic steps

1 Go to AltaVista at: http://altavista.digital.com

2 Set the **Search** area – the Web or Usenet newsgroups

3 Select the **language**.

4 Enter the keywords.

5 Click **Search**.

6 If you get a reasonable number of hits, follow the most likely links.

Otherwise...

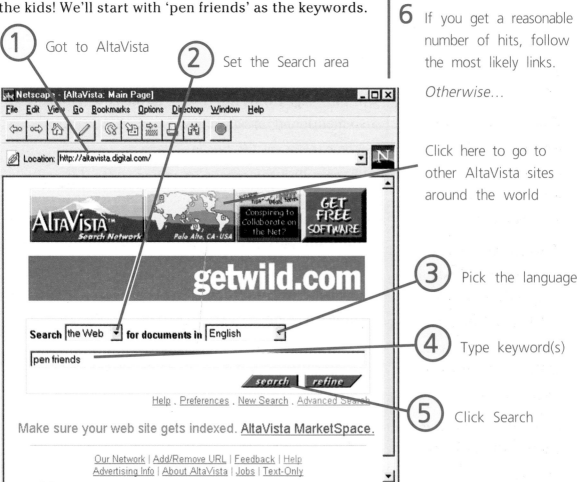

① Got to AltaVista

② Set the Search area

Click here to go to other AltaVista sites around the world

③ Pick the language

④ Type keyword(s)

⑤ Click Search

112

7 Click **Refine**.

8 Go through the list of topics, setting each one to **Require** or **Exclude** or ... if it doesn't matter.

9 Click **Search** again.

❑ You can Refine the search again to trim the list further.

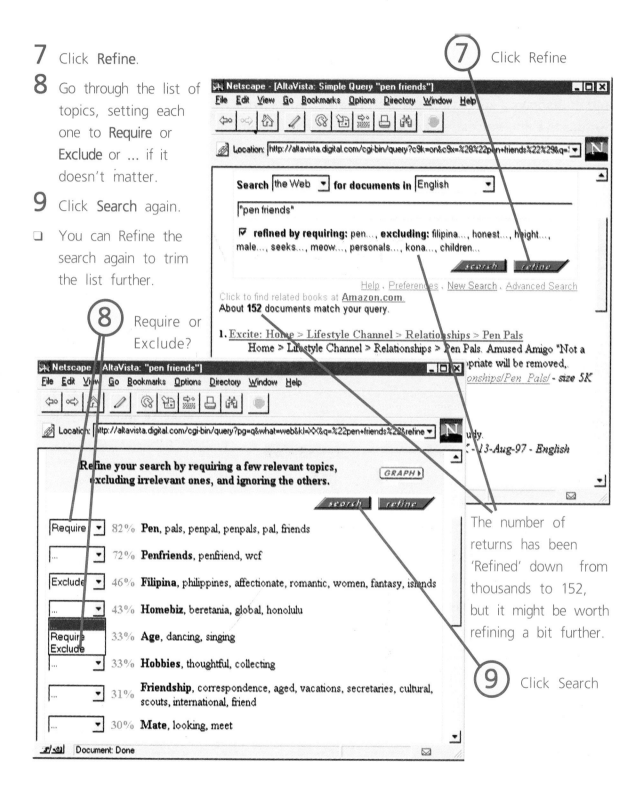

⑦ Click Refine

⑧ Require or Exclude?

The number of returns has been 'Refined' down from thousands to 152, but it might be worth refining a bit further.

⑨ Click Search

AltaVista's Way-Cool topics map

Now here's a different approach. This can be great if you are not entirely sure how to describe what you want to find. It displays a set of (not always!) related topics, with options in each. You can select words from the topic lists to add to your keywords, then rerun the search.

❑ Way-Cool topics map

1 Point to each heading.

2 If you find a useful word in the list, click on it to add it to your keywords.

3 Click **Submit**.

③ Click Submit

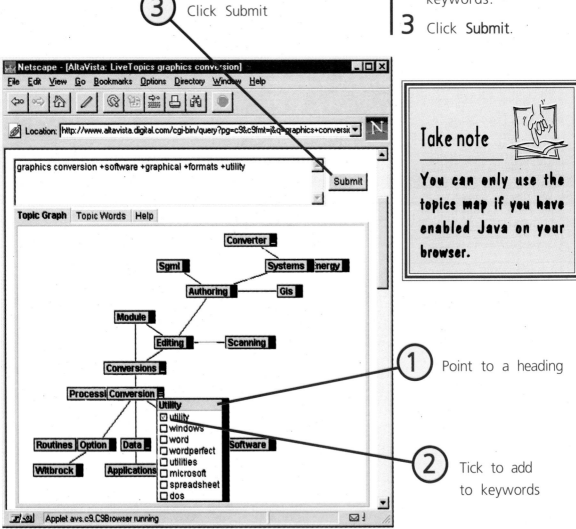

graphics conversion +software +graphical +formats +utility

Topic Graph | Topic Words | Help

Converter
Sgml   Systems Energy
Authoring   Gis
Module
Editing   Scanning
Conversions
Processi Conversion
Utility
☑ utility
☐ windows
☐ word
Routines Option Data   ☐ wordperfect   Software
☐ utilities
Witbrock   Applications ☐ microsoft
☐ spreadsheet
☐ dos

Applet avs.c9.C9Browser running

① Point to a heading

② Tick to add to keywords

Take note

You can only use the topics map if you have enabled Java on your browser.

114

Basic steps

Advanced Search

❑ Advanced Search

1 Type your keywords using AND, OR, NOT and NEAR to link them, as appropriate.

2 Enter the most crucial keywords in the **Ranking** textbox.

3 Set the dates if you want to restrict the search to certain limits.

4 Click **Search**.

AltaVista supports the usual logical operators **AND**, **OR**, and **NOT**, and the +/– modifiers.Note these special points about AltaVista advanced searches:

● You can link two words with **NEAR** to insists that they should be within the same block of text.

● If you want to accept plurals or other endings to words, add an asterisk (*****) after the core word.

● You can set date limits so that it only returns pages created between certain dates, or from a set date until now.

● If you enter words in the **Ranking** textbox, pages containing them will be listed first. This is of limited value, as it tends to override the main search expression.

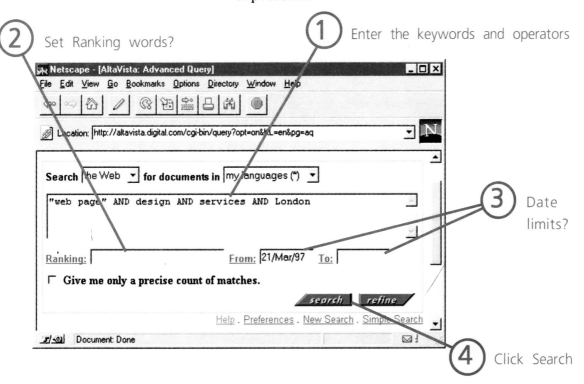

② Set Ranking words?

① Enter the keywords and operators

③ Date limits?

④ Click Search

HotBot

By the end of 1997, HotBot had indexed nearly 60 million sites. Searching this vast database can produce enormous sets of hits, but the drop-down menus on the interface page make it easy to set up a clearly focused search.

Type of search

all the words – the same as linking with AND.

any of the words – use when you are giving alternative spellings.

exact phrase – quotes are not needed.

Boolean phrase – select this if you want to write a complex search, using the AND, OR and NOT operators.

The search can also be for a person or page title.

Date

For newer pages only, turn this on and set the limit – from one week to two years.

Where to search

Another optional setting. Use it if you only want pages from a certain country or type of organisation in the US; e.g. if you are hunting for US government information, you would restrict the search to **North America (.gov)**.

Results display

How much detail do you want? When in doubt, select **brief descriptions** – **URLs only** is rarely much use.

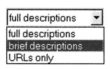

Basic steps

1 Go to HotBot at:
   http://www.hotbot.com

2 Set the **look for** type.

3 Enter the keywords.

4 If you want only newer pages, tick the **Date** checkbox and set the limit.

5 If you want to restrict the search to a Continent (or to types of organisations in the US), tick the checkbox and select the area.

6 Set the number of results per page, and the amount of information to be displayed.

7 Click **Search**.

Take note

You can also search for images, sounds and video clips – just set the Media options.

116

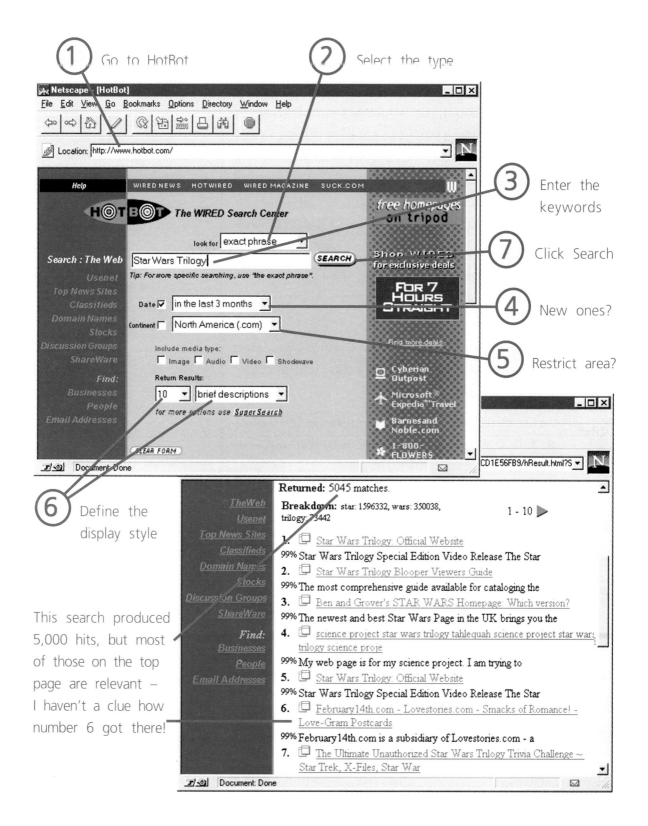

① Go to HotBot

② Select the type

③ Enter the keywords

⑦ Click Search

④ New ones?

⑤ Restrict area?

⑥ Define the display style

This search produced 5,000 hits, but most of those on the top page are relevant – I haven't a clue how number 6 got there!

117

Infoseek

Infoseek does full-text searching on over 30 million sites, and it offers an unusual, but brilliantly simple, way to search the Internet. When you get a set of results, you can search through those results – and do so to as many levels you like – so that you focus in on what you want. Instead of struggling to write one complex search expression, you simply give another defining word or set of words at each stage.

In the example, I'm looking for photographs of volcanoes in Hawaii, using the search words 'volcano', then 'Hawaii' and finally 'photo'.

● If you give several words, Infoseek will try to match any of them – e.g. 'mule donkey ass' will find any long-eared beast of burden.

● If you are searching for people, capitalise the names – e.g. 'Bill Gates' will find references to the man; 'bill gates' will find pages on birds, invoicing systems, logic chips and garden entrances.

● For phrase searching, enclose the words in "quotes" or link-them-with-hyphens. "Quoted phrases" also match any capitals.

● You can also search through the latest News stories, or through the Usenet newsgroups, or for company information on nearly 50,000 firms in the US.

1 Go to Infoseek at: http://www.infoseek.com

2 Enter the search word(s).

3 Select the **Web**, **News**, **Companies** or **Usenet**.

4 Click $\boxed{\text{seek}}$.

5 If there are too many results, enter the word(s) to narrow the search.

6 Click $\boxed{\text{Search These Results}}$.

or

7 If you are not finding what you want, go back and try another search word.

8 Repeat steps 5 to 7 until you have a small, but relevant, set of results.

Take note

If you really want to, you can write search expressions containing logical operators – read the Tips at Infoseek to find out how.

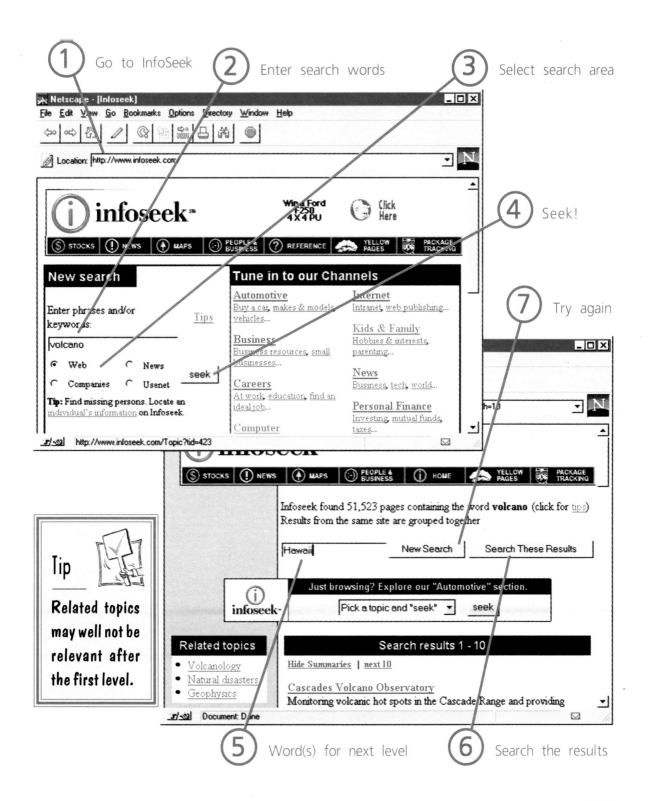

① Go to InfoSeek

② Enter search words

③ Select search area

④ Seek!

⑦ Try again

Tip

Related topics may well not be relevant after the first level.

⑤ Word(s) for next level

⑥ Search the results

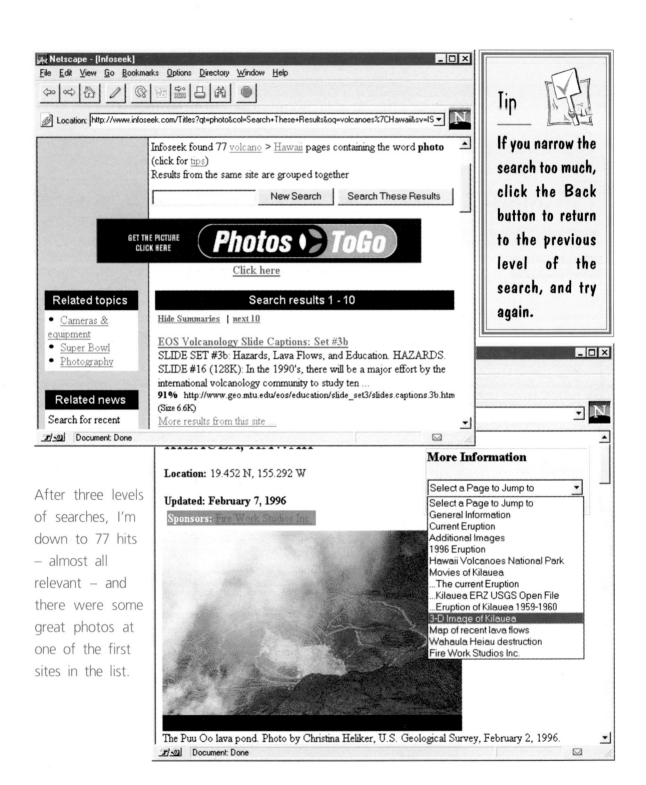

After three levels of searches, I'm down to 77 hits – almost all relevant – and there were some great photos at one of the first sites in the list.

Tip

If you narrow the search too much, click the Back button to return to the previous level of the search, and try again.

Netscape - [Infoseek]

File Edit View Go Bookmarks Options Directory Window Help

Location: http://www.infoseek.com/Titles?qt=photo&col=Search+These+Results&oq=volcanoes%7CHawaii&sv=IS

Infoseek found 77 volcano > Hawaii pages containing the word **photo** (click for tips)
Results from the same site are grouped together

New Search   Search These Results

GET THE PICTURE
CLICK HERE   **Photos ToGo**

Click here

Related topics

- Cameras & equipment
- Super Bowl
- Photography

Related news

Search for recent

Search results 1 - 10

Hide Summaries | next 10

EOS Volcanology Slide Captions: Set #3b
SLIDE SET #3b: Hazards, Lava Flows, and Education. HAZARDS. SLIDE #16 (128K): In the 1990's, there will be a major effort by the international volcanology community to study ten ...
91% http://www.geo.mtu.edu/eos/education/slide_set3/slides.captions.3b.htm (Size 6.6K)
More results from this site ...

Document: Done

Location: 19.452 N, 155.292 W

Updated: February 7, 1996

Sponsors: Fire Work Studios Inc

More Information

Select a Page to Jump to

Select a Page to Jump to
General Information
Current Eruption
Additional Images
1996 Eruption
Hawaii Volcanoes National Park
Movies of Kilauea
...The current Eruption
...Kilauea ERZ USGS Open File
...Eruption of Kilauea 1959-1960
3-D Image of Kilauea
Map of recent lava flows
Wahaula Heiau destruction
Fire Work Studios Inc.

The Puu Oo lava pond. Photo by Christina Heliker, U.S. Geological Survey, February 2, 1996.

Document: Done

Basic steps

1 Go to Lycos at:
http://www-uk.lycos.com

2 Select the **Search** area.

3 Enter the word(s) in the **for** slot.

4 Set the **Find** option –
all, any or the exact
phrase.

5 Click Go Get It.

The Lycos catalog holds the URLs of over 55 million pages – more than 90% of the Web. Around 20 million pages have been indexed on their headings, keywords and first twenty lines of text. Over 5 million graphics, sounds and programs files are also indexed.

Lycos normally truncates search words, so that alternative endings are matched, e.g. 'graphics' will also find 'graphic' and 'graphical'. You can prevent this by putting a dot after the word. Thus, 'graphics.' will only match 'graphics'.

The simple search has two main options. You can select:

● where to search – including **The Web** (the main index), the **UK and Ireland only**, **Pictures** and **Sounds**.

● how your search text should be treated – matching **all words** (AND), **any words** (OR) or **the exact phrase**.

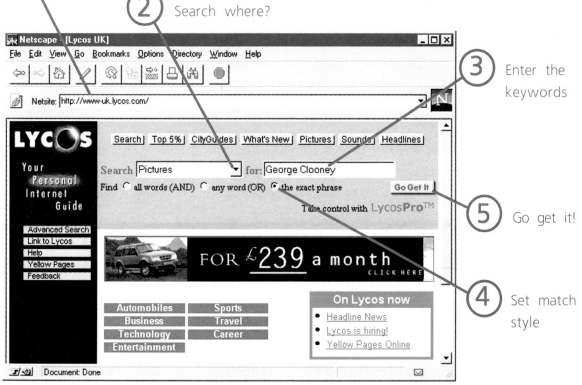

① Go to Lycos

② Search where?

③ Enter the keywords

④ Set match style

⑤ Go get it!

Magellan

Magellan has two unique features. First, it has a database of **Green Light** sites – sites that have been reviewed and found suitable for children. (It also has a database of 60,00 reviewed and 50 million unreviewed sites.)

The second feature is **concept-based searching**. As the search engine travels the Web building its index, it reads documents and learns which words and ideas are associated with one another. So, if you search for 'movies', it will also look for 'video', 'films', 'cinema' and similar.

Search expressions

With a simple list of words, Magellan will look for pages containing any of them, but put those that contain all – or most – at the top of the results list.

- You can use the operators AND, OR and AND NOT to link words. These must be written in CAPITALS.

- The + and – modifiers can be used to insist that words are present or absent from a page.

Find similar

If your keywords have several meanings, the initial results display may cover a range of topics. To focus on the ones you want, read through to find the most suitable result and click on its **find similar**. This is the concept-based searching in action! In the example, the search on 'amazon' found material on the river in Brazil, as well as stuff on parrots, the bookshop, sushi (!) and other irrelevancies. (And if it hadn't been restricted to Green Light sites, it would also have found feminist and girlie pages.) The **find similar** link by the Amazon home page turned up a wealth of material on the river basin – the object of the search.

Basic steps

1 Go to Magellan at: http://www.mckinley.com

2 Enter your search word(s) or expression.

3 Select the area to search – Reviewed sites, Green Light sites or the entire Web.

4 Click **search** .

5 Scroll through and view the results or click **find similar** to get more pages on the same topic.

Take note

Magellan also has organised its reviewed and Green Light sites into a subject-based catalog.

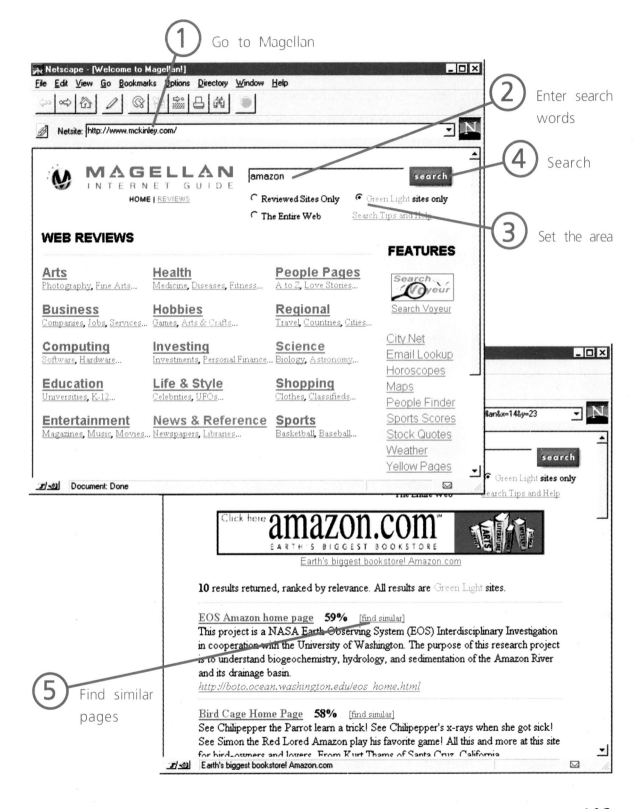

1 Go to Magellan

2 Enter search words

4 Search

3 Set the area

5 Find similar pages

Open Text

Open Text also has a full text index, but this is to over 5 million sites – and many millions of documents. Its database has FTP files (page 214), as well as the Web pages, and it is multilingual – including non-European character sets.

With a simple search, your only option is the match style – all the words, any of the words or the exact phrase.

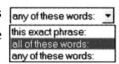

The Power Search has two sets of options, which can be applied to up to 5 words or phrases.

You can select where to look in a file – in its **Title**, **Summary**, **First Heading**, **URL** or **Anywhere**. The **Hyperlink** option is used to find pages that link to a given URL.

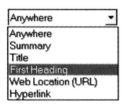

The words can be linked with the operators **And**, **Or**, **But not**, **Near** (within 80 characters) or **Followed by** (within 80 characters).

❏ Simple Search

1 Go to Open Text at: http://www.opentext.com

2 Select the match style.

3 Enter the keywords.

4 Click Search.

5 If you do not find what you want, click improve your search.

6 Set where to look for each word.

7 Set the operator to link each word to the next.

8 Click Search.

① Go to Open Text ② Set the match style ③ Enter the search words

④ Click Search

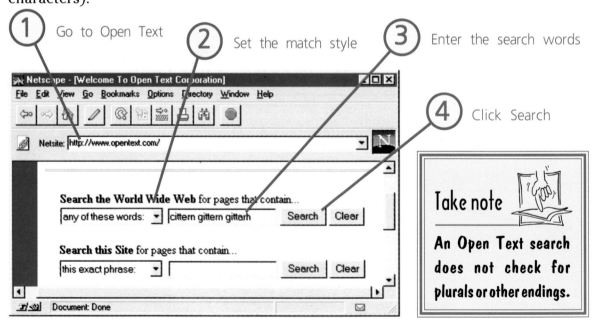

Take note

An Open Text search does not check for plurals or other endings.

124

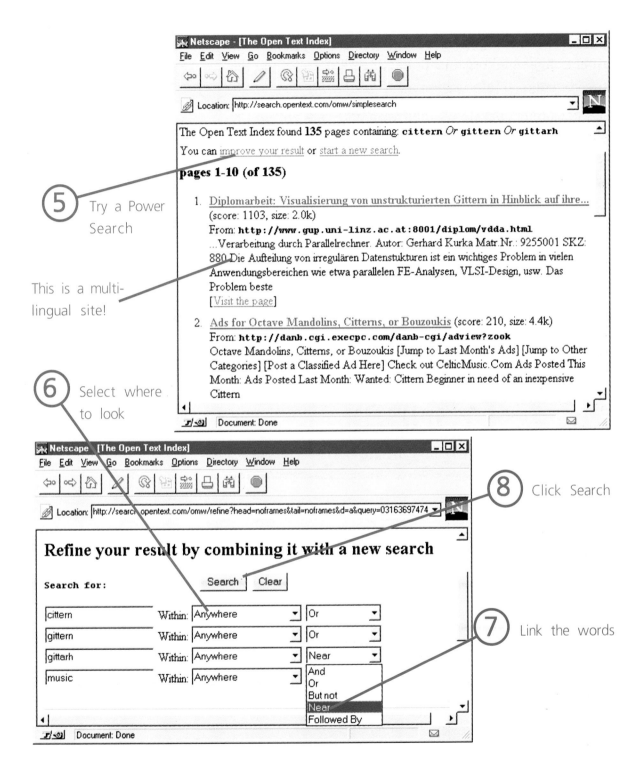

⑤ Try a Power Search

This is a multi-lingual site!

⑥ Select where to look

⑧ Click Search

⑦ Link the words

125

UK Index

The UK Index is a good source of links to suppliers and other commercial organisations, though not so good for non-commercial information.

Searches only operate on their own entries – not on UK Web sites and pages in general – but are simple to set up. The organisation of their entries by category makes it very easy to focus a search.

1 Go to UK Index at:
http://www.ukindex.co.uk

2 Enter one or two words or a phrase.

3 Select **And, Or** or **Phrase**.

4 Select the categories to be searched.

5 Click Submit.

① Go to UK Index – the simple URL takes you to this search page

② Enter search words

Netscape - [UK Index Search Form]

File Edit View Go Bookmarks Options Directory Window Help

Location: http://www.ukindex.co.uk/uksearch.html

③ Set the match style

UK INDEX™ SEARCH

Get much more with the

Enter a word in one or both boxes, and/or select your categories, then click the **submit** button.

web   AND ▾ design   Submit Clear

⑤ Submit it

☐ Arts   ☐ Business   ☑ Computing
☐ Culture   ☐ Education   ☐ England
☐ Environment   ☐ Health   ☐ History, Genealogy
☐ Index   ☑ Internet   ☐ Ireland
☐ Jobs   ☐ Language   ☐ Law
☐ TV, Radio, Video, Films ☐ Magazines, Newspapers etc ☐ Music
☐ Nature   ☐ News   ☐ Politics, Government
☐ Professional   ☐ Recreation   ☐ Reference
☐ Regional   ☐ Religion   ☐ Science
☐ Scotland   ☐ Sports   ☐ Travel
☐ Wales   ☐ Weird

④ Select categories

http://www.ukindex.co.uk/cathlp.html#2

Basic steps

1 Go to UK Search at: http://www.uksearch.com

2 Enter your keywords.

3 Select where to look.

4 Define the results display.

5 Click Search .

The UK Search database holds links to something over 250,000 UK sites, which must represent a high proportion of the total number.

The search options are limited. You can choose whether to look in the title, heading, text or all of each document. You can also set the style and number of the results displayed. When searching, it will try to match any of the words, but list first those that contain all of them. Logical operators and other search modifiers do not work here.

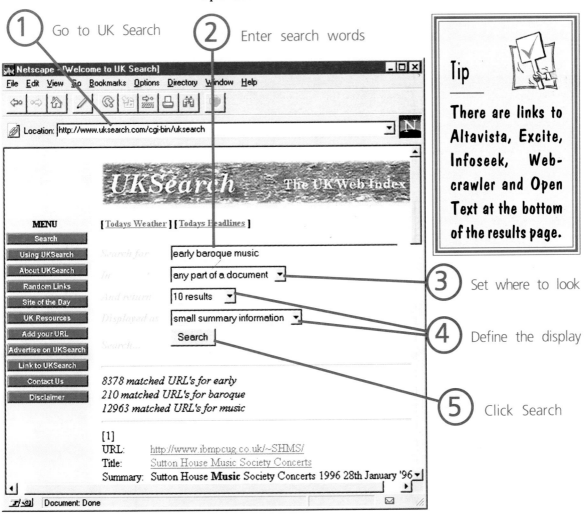

① Go to UK Search

② Enter search words

③ Set where to look

④ Define the display

⑤ Click Search

Tip

There are links to Altavista, Excite, Infoseek, Webcrawler and Open Text at the bottom of the results page.

Yell

Yell is more than just a directory. It is also the home of Electronic Yellow Pages – with links to Scoot – and hosts a comprehensive Film Finder, and a good London Guide.

It's a bright, jolly site, heavy on graphics, though it has such good telephone/modem links (well, it is run by BT!) that it pages download very quickly.

The directory to UK sites, and its search facilities, are in the Yellow Web.

1 Go to Yell at:
http://www.yell.co.uk

☐ Searching

2 Click on Yellow Web.

3 Select a heading and browse the catalog.

or

4 Enter the search words.

5 Select the match style.

6 Click Search.

① Go to Yell ② Click on Yellow Web

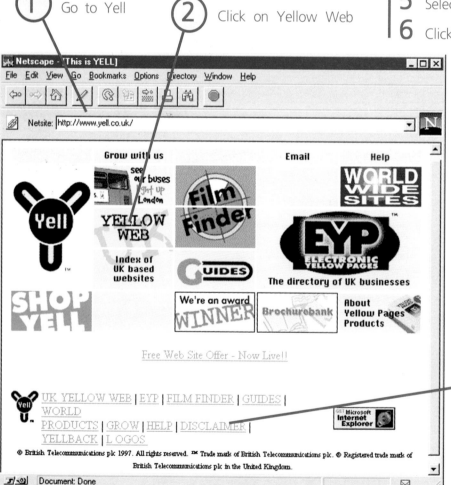

You can also navigate around the site using the main page titles – these are on the bottom of every page.

Searching at Yellow Web

Take note

These searches have been for early music links – which are fairly rare. Search for computer stuff, and you'll get lots from any **UK** search site.

This is another bare-bones search routine. You can only enter plain words – no operators or +/– symbols. The only real control is over the match style, and the options here are unusual.You can match all the words in the given order, or in any order, or match one or more words, or the words within other words (i.e. 'foot' also finds 'bigfoot' and 'football').

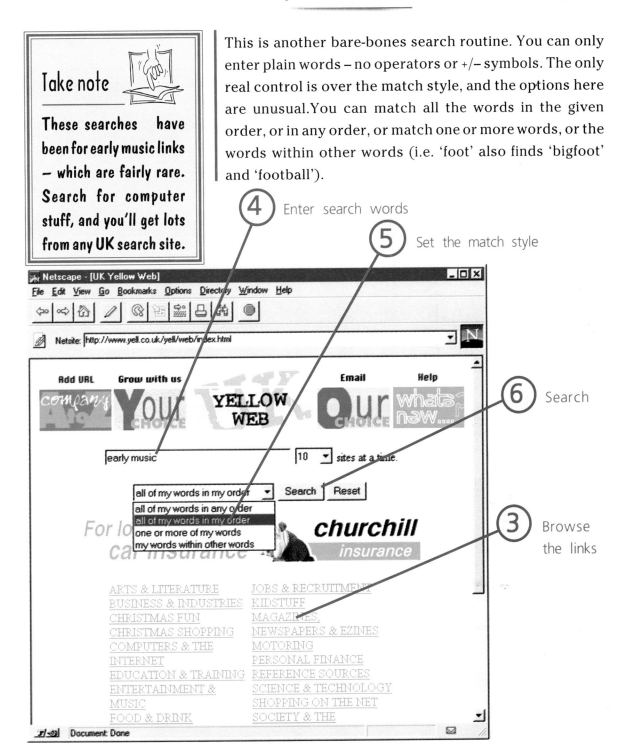

④ Enter search words

⑤ Set the match style

⑥ Search

③ Browse the links

Netscape Search

Netscape users have easy access to five of the best search sites, with links to a couple of dozen more through the Internet Search option on the Directory menu (on the Edit menu in Communicator). This links to the search page at Netscape's home site. You can set up simple searches, or select a catalog heading from here, and are then transferred to the search site for the results.

1 Open the **Directory** (or **Edit**) menu.

2 Select **Internet Search**.

3 When the page comes in, choose a search site.

4 Type the search words.

5 Click **Search**.

❏ If that site doesn't give you what you want, go back to Netscape Search and try another.

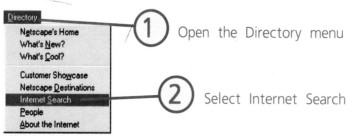

① Open the Directory menu

② Select Internet Search

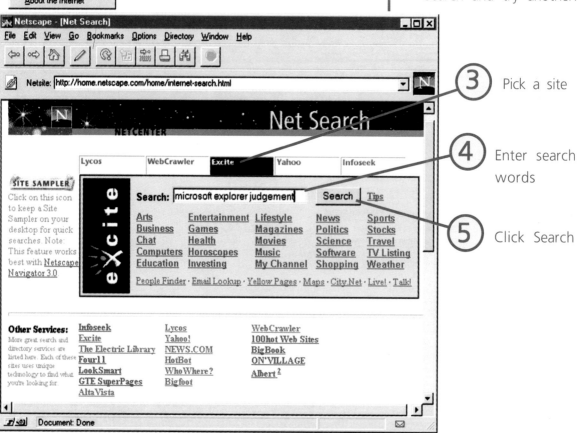

③ Pick a site

④ Enter search words

⑤ Click Search

The Site Sampler

1 Go to the Internet
Search page.

2 Select your search site.

3 Click **SITE SAMPLER**.

4 The new window will
be larger than the
sample panel – adjust it
down to size.

5 Run your searches as
normal.

6 When you are finished,
click the Close button
to exit the window.

If you want to search for a number of different items or
browse the catalog at a search site, you can open the Site
Sampler search panel in a separate window. It will then
stay open while the main window displays the data from
the search site.

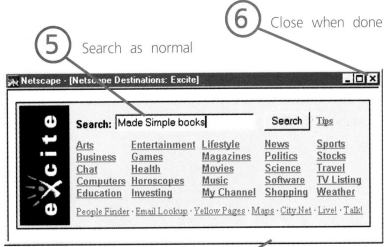

⑤ Search as normal

⑥ Close when done

④ Adjust the window size

Tip

**Even if you do not have Netscape, you can still use their
search page. Just point your (other) browser at:**

http://home.netscape.com/home/internet-search.html

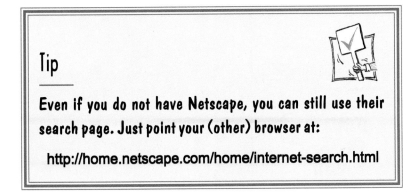

IE Exploring

With Internet Explorer 4.0, Microsoft has introduced a screen layout that is very convenient for searching. Searches are run in the left-hand panel, and the results are displayed and found pages are viewed in the main panel. If you want to see more of a page, the search panel can be closed with a click of a button, then re-opened later with its contents still in place.

Basic steps

1 Open the **Help** menu, point to **Microsoft on the Web**, and choose **Search the Web**.

or

2 Click Search.

3 Type the search words.

4 Select a search engine.

5 Click Search.

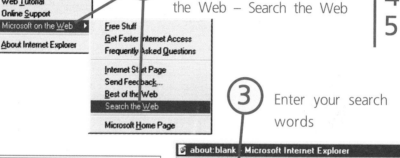

Select Help – Microsoft on the Web – Search the Web

③ Enter your search words

② Click Search

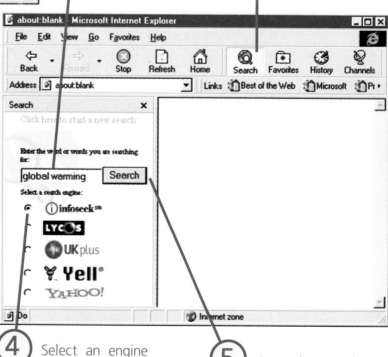

④ Select an engine

⑤ Start the search

Take note

This search technique can only be used with Internet Explorer. Microsoft do offer an 'All-in-One' search page for use by other browsers, but it has a different style. To try it, go to:

www.microsoft.com/ access/allinone.asp

You can run more searches or refine your existing one, at the same engine

Click here to return to the initial search panel, with its set of search engines

Toggle the search panel display on and off by clicking the Search button

Only links are displayed, but if you want to know more about a hit, point to it and wait for the pop-up panel to give you any other available information

If you follow up links, the new pages will be displayed in this panel, without affecting the search panel

Summary

- **Simple searches** – just using keywords – are handled in almost the same way by all search engines. Most also accept the AND, OR and NOT **logical operators** and the +/– **modifiers**.

- At **AltaVista** you can keep the returns down to a reasonable level by refining the search, using the Way Cool topics map, or specifying an advanced search.

- **HotBot** has indexed almost all the Web, but its option-based search form makes it easy to focus a search.

- At **InfoSeek** you can narrow a search down in stages, searching within a set of results for a new keyword.

- **Lycos** offers a good full-Web search, and is an excellent place to look for pictures and sounds.

- **Magellan's Green Light** sites make this a prime site for children to use – but it also has reviewed sites across the full range of topics, and links to most of the Web.

- **Open Text** has a full text index of over 5 million sites, with FTP and gopher files as well as Web documents. It is probably the best site for multilingual use.

- The **UK Index** and **UK Search** are good sources of links within the UK, but if you want phone numbers or (snail mail) addresses of UK businesses, look in the **Electronic Yellow Pages** at Yell.

- Both **Netscape** and **Microsoft** offer access to several search engines from their search pages.

8 The Interactive Web

On-line services

It would be an impossible task to list all the services that are now available over the Internet – there are just too many, with new ones appearing all the time. There are thousands of firms large and small, government departments, voluntary organisations and individuals who are providing information, offering services or selling goods over the Internet.

What follows in the next few pages is just a taster of the possibilities. If you want to know more about what's available on-line – with the focus on the UK – head for the UK directory at:

http://ukdirectory.com

Take note

There's more about the UK directory on page 106. The other good place to start looking for UK sales and services is Yell – see page 128.

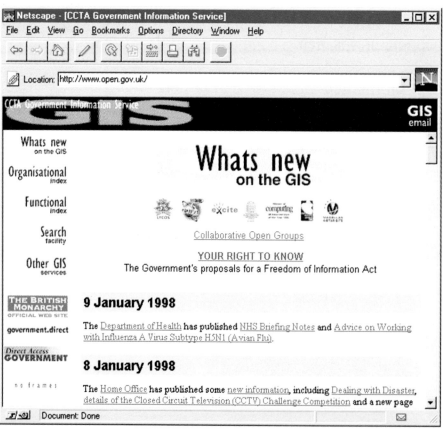

The UK government is still not as open as the US, but an increasing amount of information is available on-line through GIS, the Government Information Service. Go to: http://www.open.gov.uk

British Midlands is just one of the airlines offering on-line bookings – the graphics make this simple, but slow, to use.

And if you are travelling by road, the RAC's traffic reports will help you miss the jams – go first to: http:// www.rac.co.uk

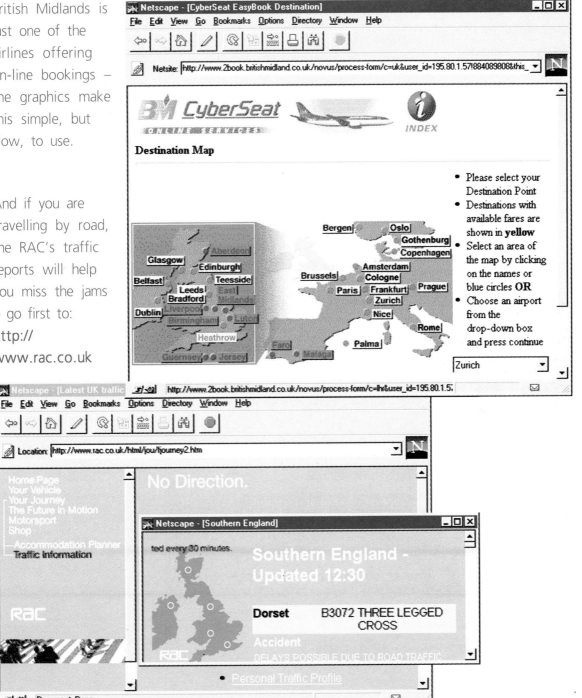

Looking for a new job? Try the Telegraph's Appointments Plus page – this search produced some interesting possibilities for me, though not quite tempting enough to give up writing!

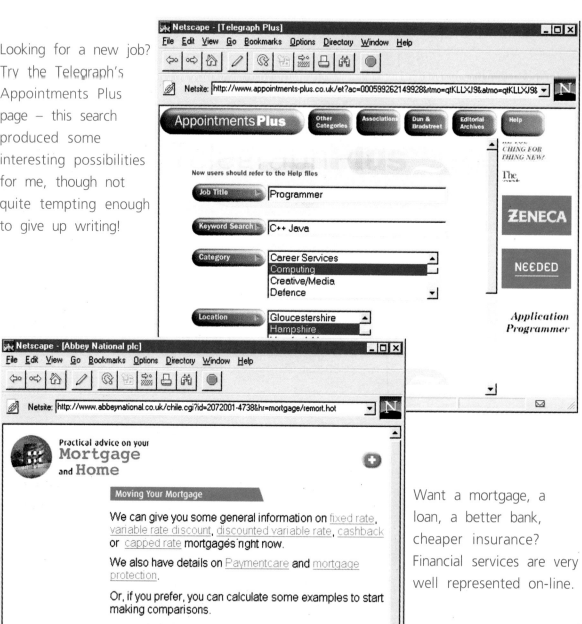

Want a mortgage, a loan, a better bank, cheaper insurance? Financial services are very well represented on-line.

Shop safely

The Internet has its fair share of crooks, but if you observe a few sensible precautions, you should be able to buy goods and services on-line as safely as you can by mail order or in the high street.

Too good to be true?

It is cheaper to trade on the Internet than it is in the high street, or even by by mail order or telephone, so you should expect to get a better deal, a faster service or a lower price. But if an offer sounds too good to be true, it probably is!

Who are these people?

Don't deal with people you don't know or with those that you can only contact over the Internet. If a firm is new to you, check that they really exist by looking up their address in the Electronic Yellow Pages (page 128) or the Companies lists at Yahoo.

It's not just credit card fraud

In fact credit card fraud made up less than 20% of Internet fraud in 1997. Most victims paid by cheque, cash, money orders or bank debits.

You are as safe paying by credit card over the Internet as you are over the phone – which is not completely safe. Make sure that the *SSL security checking* is enabled on your browser – on the **General Options** in Netscape, and the **Advanced Internet Options** of Explorer. This ensures that the transactions you have with the firm cannot be 'eavesdropped' over the Internet.

Take note

In 1997, on-line fraud cost Internet users an estimated £200 million.

Tip

If you want to know more about fraud, go to Yahoo and select **Computers and Internet: Internet: Business and Economics: Fraud**, or head for **Internet Fraud Watch** at: http://www.fraud.org

Shopping on the Web

So what do they sell on the World Wide Web? You will find the kinds of goods that, five years ago, would have been sold by mail order or over the phone – the Web is a natural extension of these approaches.

The Web is a good place to sell anything which people buy on specification rather than by sitting on or trying on, e.g. computer hardware and software, books and CDs. It is also a logical place to sell those specialist goods that you can be difficult to find in your local high street – organic foods, collectors' items, anything hand-made.

Tip

The most common type of fraud in 1997 was the sale of Internet services (Web design, domain registration, etc). The second most common was in the sale of goods.

We've been using the phone to order flower deliveries for years via Interflora. Now you can do it on the Web and see what you will get for your money! Chocolates, champagne, teddy bears – all sorts of gifts for delivery – can be ordered via the Web.

Blackwell's is one of many on-line bookstores serving the UK. If you have to order a book, it is often faster to do it through an on-line store than a high street shop.

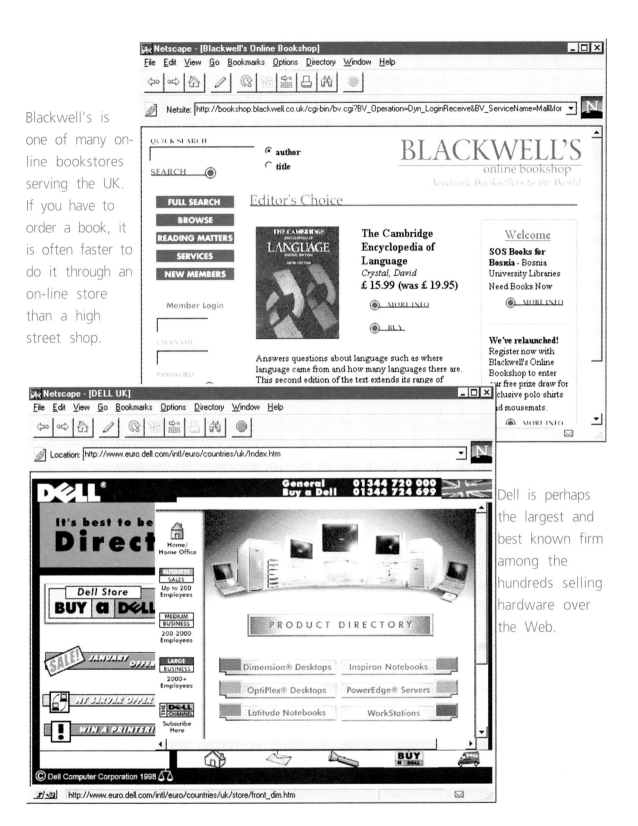

Dell is perhaps the largest and best known firm among the hundreds selling hardware over the Web.

Shops on the Web

High street shops are using the Web in three main ways:

- to advertise their goods;
- to take orders;
- as virtual shops.

The last is perhaps the most exciting aspect, though at present few of us can experience it. Tesco now has a number of stores across London that offer Home Shopping. You need the right software, on CD-ROM, and an account with them. Once equipped, you can take a virtual tour of their shelves and fill your trolley, which they then deliver to you – replacing the virtual goods with real ones!

Fortnum & Mason do not take orders or restaurant bookings over the Web – yet. At present their site is just a tastefully designed advert.

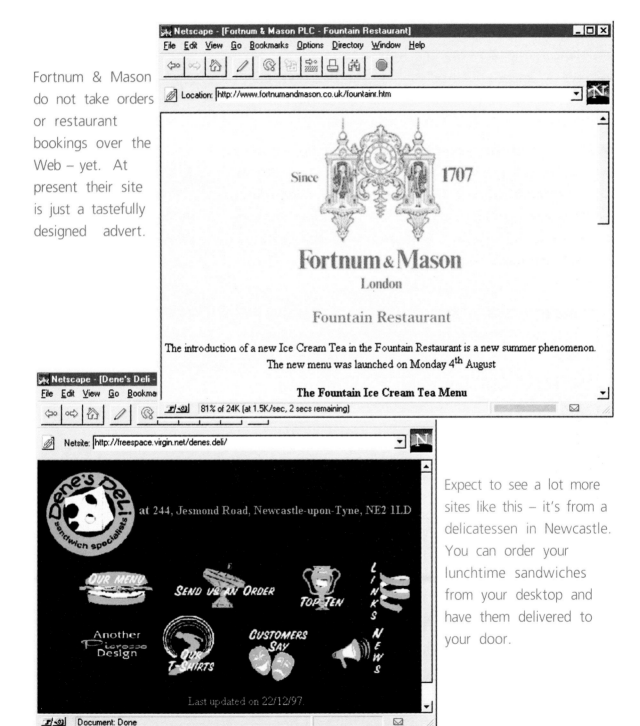

Expect to see a lot more sites like this – it's from a delicatessen in Newcastle. You can order your lunchtime sandwiches from your desktop and have them delivered to your door.

Chat rooms

Chat rooms are the CB radio of the Internet. Some people find them a good place to while away the hours – but I have to confess I am not one of them. It is very difficult to find a chat room where you can get an interesting conversation going. There are some practical problems:

- Most chat rooms will accommodate anything up to 20 or 30 people at a time. It is difficult to get this number of strangers chatting together, even where you are meeting face to face. If you are lucky and find a room with only a few guests, there's a better chance of starting a sensible conversation.

- The 'chat' is typed and takes a few seconds to reach the screen. In between you reading something that you want to respond to and your response appearing, several other messages could have hit the screen.

- Too many chat users seem to be there for getting off or showing off. This is true even for those rooms that are supposed to be centred on a specific topic.

But don't let me put you off trying. You may get more out of chat rooms that I do.

Places to go

The major directories all run chat rooms. Two of the busiest are at Yahoo (**http://chat.yahoo.com**) and Excite (**http://www.excite.com**).

Some individuals and organisations also run them – Spurs fans should try their room at **http://www.link-it.com/soccer/spurs**.

If you want to set up your own chat room, you can get what you need from Ultranet at **http://www.ultranet.org**.

Tip

A chat rooms can be a good place to meet up with existing friends and family from around the world. You can set up private rooms at most chat sites. Agree a time and a site (by e-mail or during the last meeting) and get together on-line.

Take note

Most chat rooms work through a Java applet — make sure Java is enabled before you start.

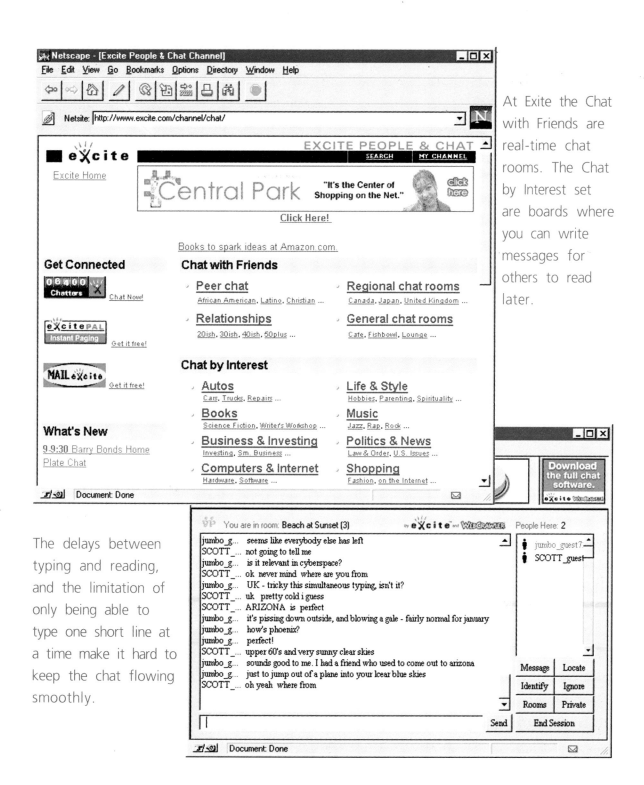

At Exite the Chat with Friends are real-time chat rooms. The Chat by Interest set are boards where you can write messages for others to read later.

The delays between typing and reading, and the limitation of only being able to type one short line at a time make it hard to keep the chat flowing smoothly.

Summary

- A great deal of information from governments, commercial and voluntary organisations is now available on-line.

- There are risks in purchasing goods and services over the Internet, but if you take sensible precautions, it should be no riskier than buying by mail or in the high street.

- Cheaper running costs should enable Internet-based traders to offer better deals than you could get elsewhere – but amazing bargains are often a sign of a con man at work.

- A wide range of goods can now be bought over the Internet and delivered to the door.

- High street shops are using the Web to advertise, and sometimes to sell their goods.

- Chat rooms are where people can get 'together' in real-time to exchange ideas and gossip – though in many rooms the level of conversation is not impressive.

Take note

With a microphone, sound card and speakers, you can turn your PC into an 'Internet telephone' – at least, that's the theory. At present, it does not work very well in practice – the connections are simply not fast enough for a proper conversation, but it is improving all the time. Watch out for developments, especially if you have friends and family overseas and would like to cut down your phone bill!

9 E-mail

Electronic mail

These are messages sent to other individuals on the Internet. Think of them more like memos than postal mail. A message can be easily copied to other users; and when you receive an incoming message, you can attach your reply to it, or forward it on to a third party. You can also attach documents and graphics files to messages. (See *Files by mail*, page 160.)

The mail will sometimes get through almost instantly, but at worst it will be there within a few hours. The delay is because not all of the computers that handle mail are constantly in touch with each other. Instead, they will **log on** at regular intervals to deal with the mail and other services.

Key points about e-mail:

● Even the simplest connection to the Internet can handle e-mail;

● Every service provider offers **e-mail** access;

● The cheapest and most convenient way of dealing with your mail is to read and compose it **off-line**;

● As with snail mail, to send someone e-mail you need their address. (See *Finding people*, Chapter 10.)

Definitions

Log on – connect to a multi-user computer, either directly or over a phone line.

E-mail – electronic mail.

Snail mail – the good old postal service.

Off-line – disconnected from the Internet. Netscape and Explorer can be run off-line. You can also get off-line readers – software that sends and collects mail from the provider, and lets you read it and compose messages after you have hung up the phone.

Take note

There are many organised **MAIL LISTS** on the Internet, each dealing with its own topic of interest. Subscribers can post messages to a central point, from which they are sent out in a block to all other subscribers. As a means of sharing ideas, they are very similar to Newsgroups – see Chapter 11.

E-mail addresses

Tip

There are utilities on the Internet that will help you to find people's e-mail addresses (page 166), but the simplest way to do it is to phone them and ask them to e-mail to you. Every message carries its sender's address.

The standard pattern for a person's e-mail address is:

> name@provider

However, there are quite a few variations to the basic pattern. Here, for example, are some of the names that I have had while researching this book.

> macbride@tcp.co.uk

We met this one earlier (page 11). Total Connectivity Providers follow the standard pattern.

> 100407.2521@compuserv.co.uk
>
> macbride@compuserv.co.uk

When I joined CompuServe it gave its users numbers. Now you can have a name as well, if you like.

> macbride@macdesign.win-uk.net

At **WinNet**, they allocate domain names (**macdesign**) to their users, as well as personal names (**macbride**). This is because they use the same format for companies and for home users. You will see the same pattern in commercial and other organisations. For example, to send e-mail to my publishers – perhaps to ask about some other Made Simple books – their address is:

> bhmarketing@repp.co.uk

Take note

It is easy to mistype an e-mail address, but you should only have to type it once for each person. Every mail system has an Address Book file where you can store addresses.

Netscape Mail

This is where you read, write and organise your e-mail messages. In Netscape 3.0 the window has three panes:

- The top left displays the mail folders
    - ◆ Inbox
    - ◆ Outbox, for message awaiting delivery
    - ◆ Sent, for copies of outgoing mail
    - ◆ Trash stores deleted messages. To remove them completely, you empty the Trash.

    New folders can be added if needed.

- The top right lists the message headers.

- The bottom pane is where messages are displayed – just click on one in the list to pull it into this pane.

Basic steps

1 Run Netscape. Open the **Window** menu and select **Netscape Mail**

2 To link to your on-line mailbox, to send or receive mail, type your user password and click **OK**.

3 If you just want to read or organise existing mail, no password is needed. Press **Cancel**.

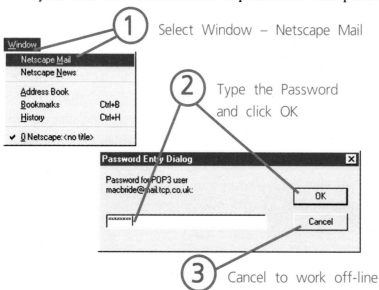

Select Window – Netscape Mail

Type the Password and click OK

Cancel to work off-line

Tip

If you are the only one who has access to Netscape Mail, you can skip the Password Entry Dialog. Go to the Options – Mail and News Preferences. On the Organisation panel, turn on Remember Mail Password.

Take note

Communicator's Messenger has separate windows for folders, headers and messages, but the commands are virtually the same.

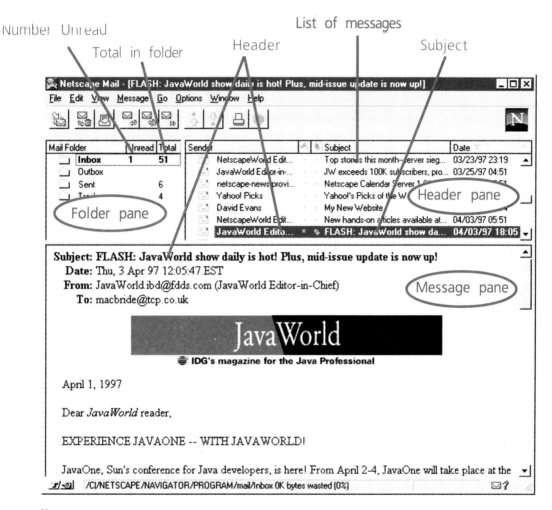

Number Unread

Total in folder

Header

List of messages

Subject

Folder pane

Header pane

Message pane

The Toolbar

You can handle all the routine Mail tasks with these. The Reply and Forward buttons copy the message into the Compose window ready for editing and sending on.

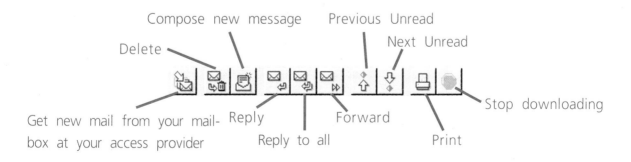

Compose new message

Previous Unread

Next Unread

Delete

Stop downloading

Get new mail from your mail-box at your access provider

Reply

Reply to all

Forward

Print

Explorer Mail

The first time that you try to use Explorer Mail, a Wizard will run to collect and install the details that are needed to create the mail connection. Have this information to hand:

- your user name and password;
- your e-mail name, e.g. JoSmith@mynet.co.uk;
- the names of your service provider's Incoming and Outgoing Mail Servers – these may well be the same.

The Mail window is similar to that of Netscape, though here the folders are in a drop-down list.

These three copy the message into the New Message window for editing and sending on

Send messages and get new mail

Create new message   Reply   Reply to all   Forward   Delete

Folder list

Header

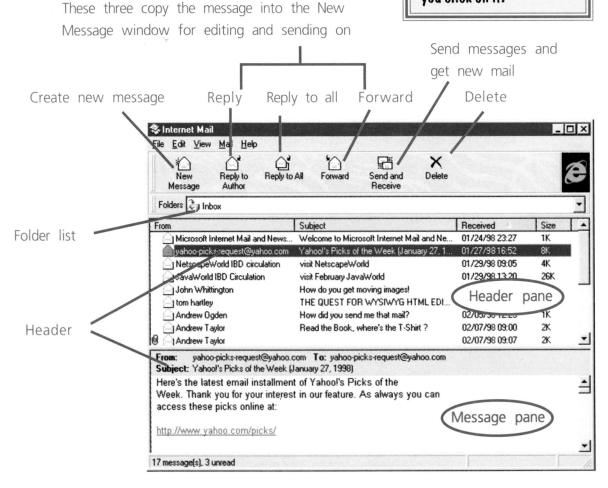

Basic steps

- ❏ Selecting header items
1 Open the **View** menu, and select **Columns**.
2 Select an item from the **Available** list and click `Add >>` to include.
3 Select an item from the **Displayed** list and click `<< Remove` to remove.
4 Adjust the positions with the **Move** buttons.
- ❏ The Preview Pane
5 Open the **View** menu, select **Options** then pick your **Split**.

Display options

You can choose which items from the headers to include in the message lists, and how to split the screen.

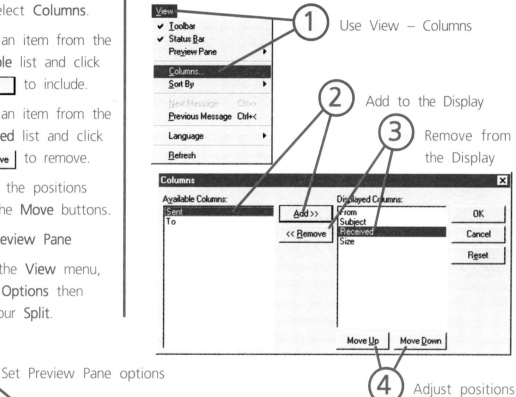

① Use View – Columns

② Add to the Display

③ Remove from the Display

④ Adjust positions

⑤ Set Preview Pane options

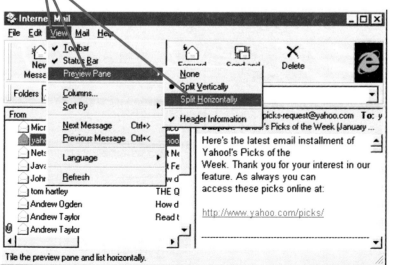

Take note

Netscape is used for the remaining examples in this chapter. Explorer's screen and the commands are almost identical.

Sending messages

To send e-mail, all you need is the address – and something to say! Messages can be composed and sent immediately if you are on line, or composed off-line and stored for sending later.

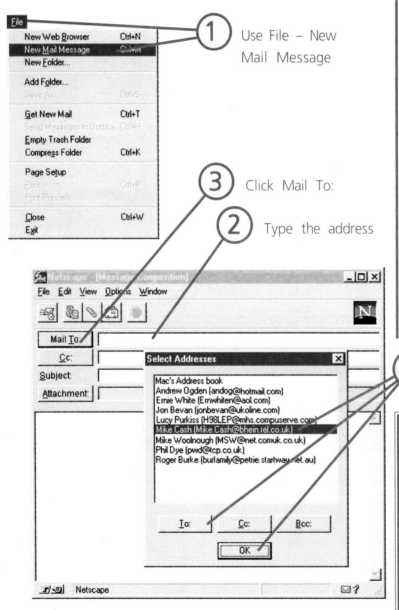

Use File – New Mail Message

Click Mail To:

Type the address

Copy the address

1 Open the File menu in the Browser or Mail window and select **New Mail Message**.

or

Mail – **New Message** in Explorer.

2 Type the address in the **Mail To:** slot.

or

3 Click **Mail To:** to open the Select Addresses panel.

4 Select a name and click the **To:** button, then **OK** to copy the address.

Take note

Cc (Carbon copy) recipients can see who else received the message. Bcc (blind carbon copy) recipients don't see the circulation list.

❏ If sending copies to others, repeat from step 2 for the **Cc:** slot.

5 Type a **Subject**.

6 Type your message.

7 Click 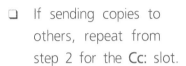 to send the message imediately.

or

8 If you are off-line, use **File – Send Later**.

9 When you are on-line, use **File – Send Messages in Outbox** to deliver the mail.

⑦ Send it now...   ⑤ Type the Subject

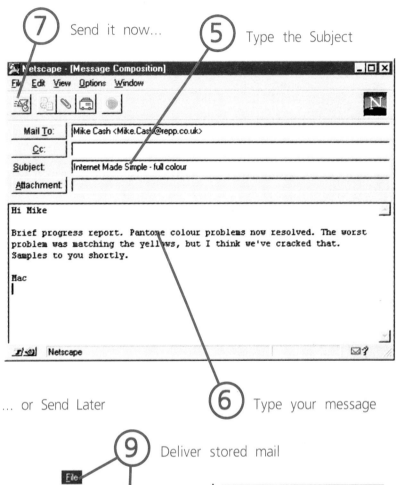

⑧ ... or Send Later   ⑥ Type your message

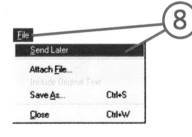

⑨ Deliver stored mail

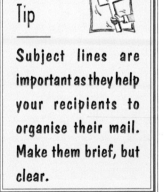

Tip

In Netscape 4.0, you can use HTML (Chapter 15) to format your text, and add links and images. Explorer also lets you format the text and add links.

Tip

Subject lines are important as they help your recipients to organise their mail. Make them brief, but clear.

Replying

When you reply to an incoming message, the system will open the Compose window and copy the sender's address into the To: slot

- If you want the sender's address, copy it now, and paste it into your Address Book. The e-mail address is in <angle brackets>.

- The original message is normally also copied into the main text area with > at the start of each line. This can be very handy if you want to respond to the mail point-by-point. You can insert your text between the lines, and any unwanted lines can be deleted.

Tip

Copying messages into a Reply is an option. If you don't want it, go to your system's Mail Options (or Preferences) and turn it off.

Copy the address from here if wanted

Insert your new text anywhere you like

Delete unwanted lines

E-tiquette rules

- ❏ **Small is beautiful**. Short messages are quick and cheap to download.

- ❏ **Test first**. When sending anything other than plain text, try a short test file first to make sure that the other person can receive it properly.

- ❏ **Zip it up!** If you are sending files, compress them with WinZIP (page 163).

- ❏ **Subject matters!** Always type a Subject line so that the other person can identify the message.

- ❏ **Short signatures**. If you have a signature (see page 159), keep it short – no more than half a dozen lines. Long files, no matter how clever, are an irritating waste of space.

When you send someone a paper letter, you know that what they receive will be the same as you send, and if you enclose lots of material, you will pay the extra postage.

E-mail is different. Your recipients actively download your messages, which takes time and can cost money. Further, if they are using different Mail software to yours, it can affect the appearance – and sometimes the *delivery* – of your messages.

Text and data files

A lot of business users, and some individuals, have e-mail systems that can only handle plain text. If you want to send files to these people, the files must first be converted to text. That is easy for you – just set the option when attaching the file (page 160). However, there are several formats for sending data files as text, and your recipient must have a suitable converter to extract the file at the other end (page 162).

Size

Some e-mail systems set a limit to the size of messages. 1,000 lines (roughly 70Kb) was the accepted maximum. You are hardly likely to write this much, but an attached file can easily push the message size over the limit.

Even where there is no limit, file size is still a factor. The larger the file, the longer it takes to download, and the higher your recipients' phone bills – especially if they are paying long-distance charges to their providers. With a good modem and a standard phone line, e-mail usually comes in at under 1Kb per second, or 1Mb in 20 minutes.

Use the standard WinZIP (or PKZip) software to compress data files before attaching them. Graphics and documents files can be reduced to 10% or less of their original size this way. Even executable files – the most difficult to compress – show some reduction.

Subject lines

A clear Subject line identifies a message. Your recipients need this when the mail arrives, to see which to deal with first – and which to ignore completely! They also need it when organising old mail, so that they know which to delete and which to place in what folder.

Emphasis

If your recipient's Mail system can handle formatted text, then you can use <u>underline</u> or **bold** for emphasis. If you are sending plain ASCII text, and want to make a word stand out, enclose it in *asterisks* or _underscores_, or write it in CAPITALS.

Smileys

E-mail messages tend to be brief, and as your receipients cannot see your expression or hear the tone of your voice, there is a possibility of being misunderstood – especially when joking. Smileys, also known as *emoticons,* are little pictures, composed of ASCII characters, that can help to convey your meaning.

The basic smiley of **:-)** is the one you will see most often, though there are many other weird and wonderful smileys around. A few of the more common ones are shown here.

Smileys

:-)	It's a joke
'-)	Wink
:-(	I'm feeling sad
:-o	Wow!
:-C	I don't believe it!
(-:	I'm left handed
%-)	I've been staring at a screen for hours!
8-)	I'm wearing sunglasses

Abbreviations

BTW	By The Way
BWQ	Buzz Word Quotient
FYI	For Your Information
IMHO	In My Humble Opinion (ironic)
MOTSS	Member Of The Same Sex
POV	Point Of View
TIA	Thanks In Advance
TTFN	Ta Ta For Now
WRT	With Reference To
<g>	Grin

Saving space and typing

If you are an indifferent typist, or like to keep your messages short, or are likely to be getting mail from old 'netties', then it's worth learning a few of the standard abbreviations. You will also find these used in real-time conferences and chat lines, and in newsgroup articles.

If you want to track down more abbreviations or the acronyms used elsewhere in the computing world, an excellent list called Babel is maintained by Irving Kind at Temple University in the States. Get a copy by FTP (page 214) at this URL:

> ftp.temple.edu/pub/info/help-net/babel97b.txt

Signatures

A signature file can be added to the end of every message. This is a plain text file, usually saved as *personal.sig* or something similar, containing your name, e-mail address and any other contact details you want to give. People's signatures often also contain a favourite quote, advert, or a picture or name created from ASCII characters, e.g.

Example 1

```
--------------
P.K. McBride    |macbride@tcp.co.uk
Computing's Made Simple at http://www.bh.com
--------------
```

Example 2

```
                        _\  |  /_
                         @  @    =
_____ooO_(_)_Ooo_____
Declan Quinn,
```

Files by mail

Files of any type – graphics, word-processor and spread-sheet documents, audio and video clips – and URL links, can be attached to messages and sent by e-mail. Compared to sending them printed or on disk in the post, e-mail is almost always quicker, often more reliable and – up to a point – cheaper. The larger the file, the longer it takes to get through, and the greater the chance of errors – increasing transmission time even more. Somewhere over 1Mb, depending upon the time and cost of postage, the time you and your recipient spend on-line will start to outweigh the postage costs.

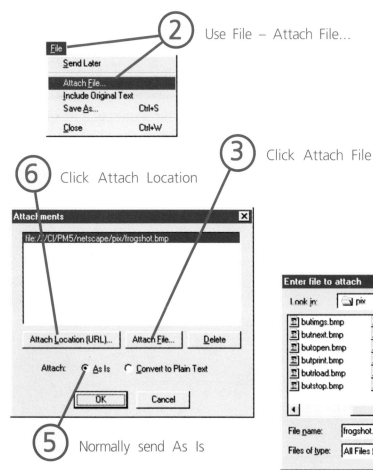

Use File – Attach File...

Click Attach Location

Click Attach File

Basic steps

1 Compose the message as normal.

2 Open the **File** menu and select **Attach File...**

or

In Explorer, use **Insert – File Attachment.**

❑ To attach a file

3 Click Attach File...

4 Browse for the file and click **Open**. The name will be shown in the Attachments list.

5 Use **Convert to Plain Text** only if you know your recipient cannot handle the file in its original **As Is** form.

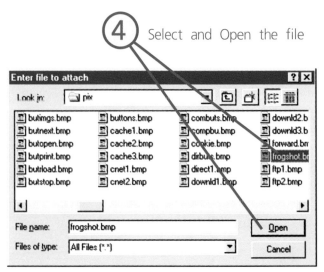

Select and Open the file

Normally send As Is

❑ **To attach a URL**

6 Click **Attach Location**

7 Enter the full URL, including *http://* for a Web page or *ftp://* for a file.

8 Click **OK**.

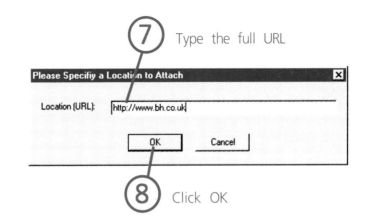

⑦ Type the full URL

Please Specifiy a Location to Attach ✕

Location (URL): http://www.bh.co.uk

OK   Cancel

⑧ Click OK

When you receive a message with an embedded file, Netscape will display it if it can. If it cannot, right click on the **Part...** icon and select **Browse** or **View** from the short menu.

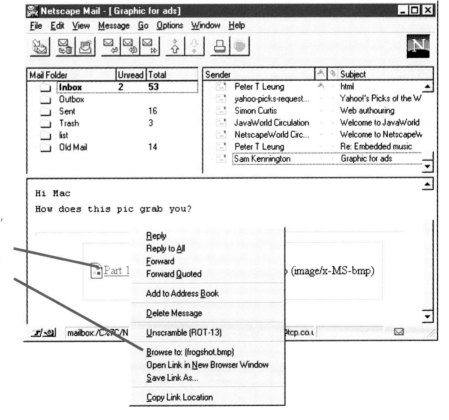

161

Detaching binary files

Detaching binary files from mail messages used to be hard work – they had to be cut out from the text of the message and processed through special decoding software.

Now, it's easy thanks to the Mail facilities in the new browsers. Both Netscape and Explorer will display graphics, if they can. Those that they cannot display, and other binary files will be clearly marked as an attached file. They can be opened or saved from the dialog box or icon.

Basic steps

☐ Viewable files

1 Scroll past the message to see the image.

2 Right click on the image to open the short menu.

3 Select **Save Image As...** and save as normal.

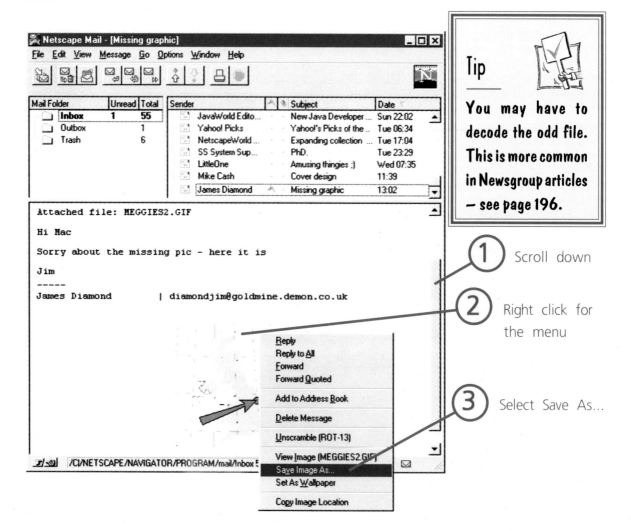

> ## Tip
>
> **You may have to decode the odd file. This is more common in Newsgroup articles – see page 196.**

1 Scroll down

2 Right click for the menu

3 Select Save As...

Basic steps

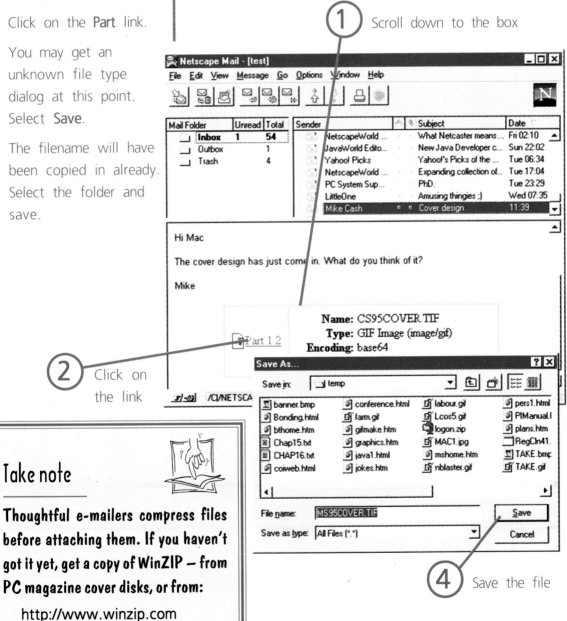

☐ **Other files**

1 Scroll down to the attached file box.

2 Click on the **Part** link.

3 You may get an unknown file type dialog at this point. Select **Save**.

4 The filename will have been copied in already. Select the folder and save.

Graphics for which you have not installed a viewer, and other types of binary files, can be detached and saved with a couple of mouse clicks.

① Scroll down to the box

② Click on the link

④ Save the file

Take note

Thoughtful e-mailers compress files before attaching them. If you haven't got it yet, get a copy of WinZIP – from PC magazine cover disks, or from:

http://www.winzip.com

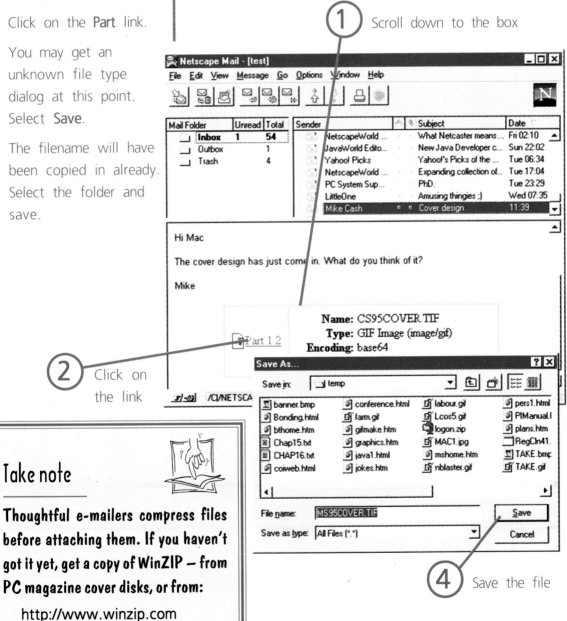

Summary

- **Electronic mail** is faster, cheaper and probably more reliable than the post.

- E mail addresses normally follow a pattern, but there's no way you can guess someone's address. Generally, the best way to get an address is to ask the person to send you an e-mail.

- In **Netscape**, the Mail window is divided into three panes, for the folders, headers and message text.

- **Explorer's mail window** has two panes, with the folder being selected from a drop-down list.

- When **sending messages**, start by selecting who they will go to. You should always write the nature of the message in the Subject line.

- When **replying**, the mail system can copy in the original message for you to add your comments to.

- **E-mail etiquette** is based on not wasting other people's time (and phone bills). Mail should be kept short, and should have a clear Subject line.

- Abbreviations and smileys can help to cut down on typing while getting your message across.

- **Signatures** can add something extra to your mail — and long ones can add far too much!

- **Files can be attached** to e-mail messages and detached at the other end. This is usually a simple process, but may sometimes require a bit of work on your part.

164

10 Finding people

Finding e-mail addresses

As the Internet has no central controlling organisation, it is not surprising that there is no single, central Internet address book. So, if you want to send e-mail to people, how do you find their e-mail address?

The simplest solution is to phone them and ask. If they do not know their own address – and occasional users may well not have the details at their fingertips – ask them to send you e-mail. All mail software has, somewhere within it, a means of seeing the address of the sender.

If the phone-up-and-ask approach is not feasible, there are several databases of e-mail addresses on the Internet which between them cover quite a large proportion of users. Service providers often have member directories that other members can access to find addresses. We will cover a selection of these in this chapter.

Take note

The phone books run by the people-finding sites are US-only. Their directories of e-mail addresses, though geared towards the US, are more international.

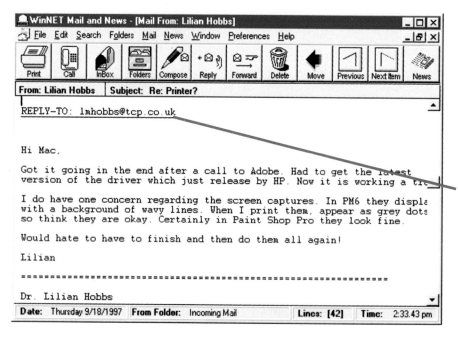

If you get e-mail from someone, you have their address

Basic steps

1 Go to WhoWhere? at:
http://www.whowhere.com

2 Enter the Last Name.

3 Enter the First Name, or at least an initial.

4 Select E-Mail.

5 Click Find.

cont...

The first place to look for e-mail addresses is at WhoWhere? It's quick, efficient and seems to have more addresses – especially outside the US – than its competitors. There are two main problems you may have to deal with:

● Common names will produce far too many hits – you must find some way of restricting the search;

● First names can be written in different ways – full names, initials, nicknames. Even last names do not follow strict rules – are you sure of the spelling?

If the simple search from the top page of WhoWhere? does not give you what you want, you can refine the search at the next stage.

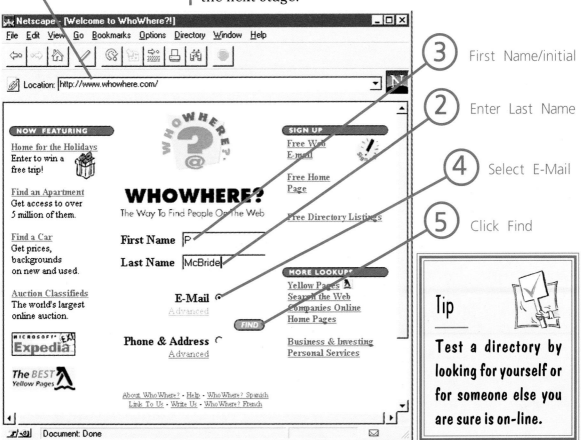

① Go to WhoWhere?

③ First Name/initial

② Enter Last Name

④ Select E-Mail

⑤ Click Find

Tip

Test a directory by looking for yourself or for someone else you are sure is on-line.

Refining the search

The standard search looks for an **exact match**, and will display those names which contain the given names exactly – so looking for 'P McBride', would find 'P K McBride' or 'Peter McBride' (if you are looking for me!) as well as any other person whose name started with 'P' or had 'P' as a middle initial.

If **all matches** is selected, 'P McBride' will also find any 'MacBride' and 'McBride' with different initials.

You can restrict a search to a **domain**. This could be the name of the service provider, if known, e.g. 'aol' or 'msn'. Outside of the US, you could useful give the country code as the domain.

❑ If you get too many...

6 Enter the **Domain** – the country code

7 Select **only exact matches**.

❑ If you don't find it...

8 Select **all matches**.

9 Click **Search**.

Tip

If you find several possible addresses, send e-mail to them all – few people mind a brief 'Is that you?' message.

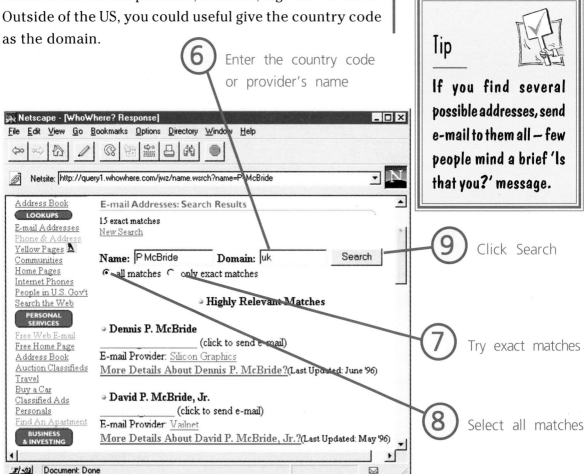

⑥ Enter the country code or provider's name

⑨ Click Search

⑦ Try exact matches

⑧ Select all matches

Detour — Web e-mail

While you are at WhoWhere? you may like to take up their offer of free Web e-mail – the service is supported by advertising (on the site, not junk e-mail).

MailCity accounts are particularly useful for:

● people who access their normal e-mail through their business, college or other organisation, especially those who are away from their desk a lot. Web mail can be read and sent from any computer with access to the Web – not just your own computer on your desk at work.

● families, as all members can have their own mailbox, instead of sharing the one at the service provider's.

Handling your mail at MailCity is almost identical to working in Netscape or Explorer mail – the only difference is that you have to go to the MailCity site (and read the adverts)

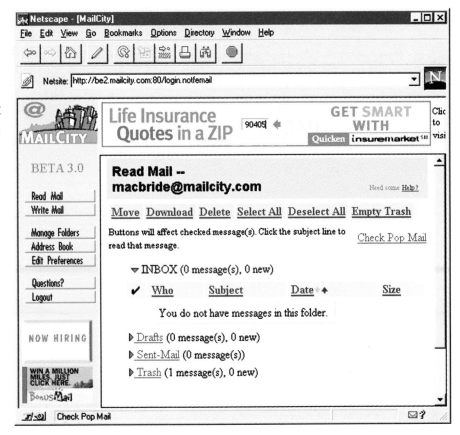

NetGuide

If you are a Netscape user, you have easy access to NetGuide, where you will find a choice of four people-finding directories. One of these is WhoWhere?, which we have already seen. The useful thing about working from NetGuide is that if WhoWhere? fails to deliver, you have three others to go at.

Let's start with BigFoot.

1 In Netscape, open the **Directory** menu.

2 Choose **People**.

3 Click on **Bigfoot**.

4 Select **E-Mail**.

5 Enter the **Name** – initial or first name and last name.

6 Click **Begin Search Now**.

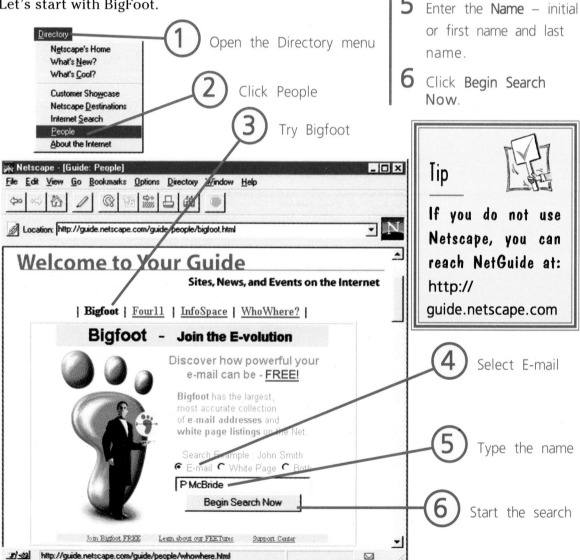

Tip

If you do not use Netscape, you can reach NetGuide at: http:// guide.netscape.com

170

InfoSpace

1 In Netscape, open the **Directory** menu.

2 Choose **People**.

3 Click on **InfoSpace**.

4 In the **Find E-mail** section, enter the **First** and **Last Name**.

5 Pick the **Country** from the drop-down list.

6 Click **Find It**.

The search form at InfoSpace asks for the first and last name, the City and State (in the US) or Country. As a result, if the person is in their database, you are more likely to find them first time here, than at either WhoWhere? or Bigfoot. Unfortunately, their database does not have particularly good coverage of countries outside the US.

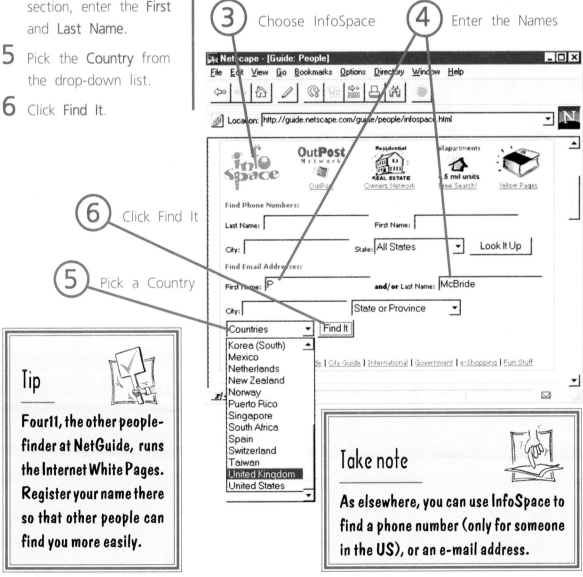

③ Choose InfoSpace

④ Enter the Names

⑥ Click Find It

⑤ Pick a Country

Tip

Four11, the other people-finder at NetGuide, runs the Internet White Pages. Register your name there so that other people can find you more easily.

Take note

As elsewhere, you can use InfoSpace to find a phone number (only for someone in the US), or an e-mail address.

Exploring for people

If you are an Internet Explorer user, Microsoft's Search the Web page would seem to be a good place to start looking for people. Use it with care! The search will return phone numbers and addresses – of all matching names in the US – as well as e-mail addresses of people on the Internet. So, give as much as you can of the name.

1 In Internet Explorer, open the **Help** menu and point to **Microsoft on the Web**.

2 Choose **Search the Web**.

3 Select a **White Pages** service in the bottom panel.

4 Enter the **First name** or initial – and **Last Name**.

5 Click **Search**.

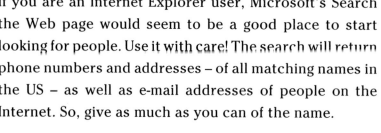

Select Help – Microsoft on the Web

Choose Search the Web

Enter the Names

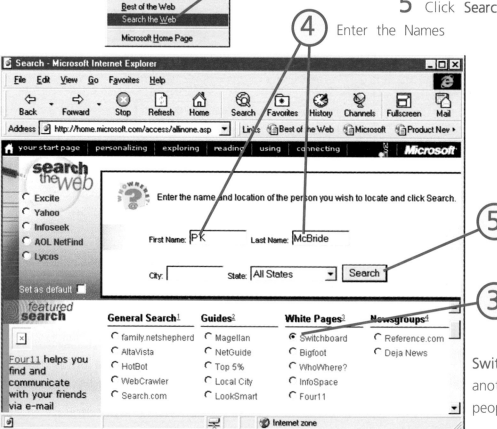

Click Search

Select a service

Switchboard is another good people finder

172

AOL's E-mail Finder

Basic steps

1 Go to AOL at:
http://www.aol.com
and select **NetFind**.

2 Switch to the **E-Mail Finder** page.

3 Enter the **First name** or initial — and **Last Name**.

4 Click **Find**.

Let's have a look at one last Web people-finder before we explore some alternative means of tracking down folk.

There is an E-mail Finder at AOL Netfind. It runs a simple name search, but at least you don't have to worry about geting swamped with phone numbers!

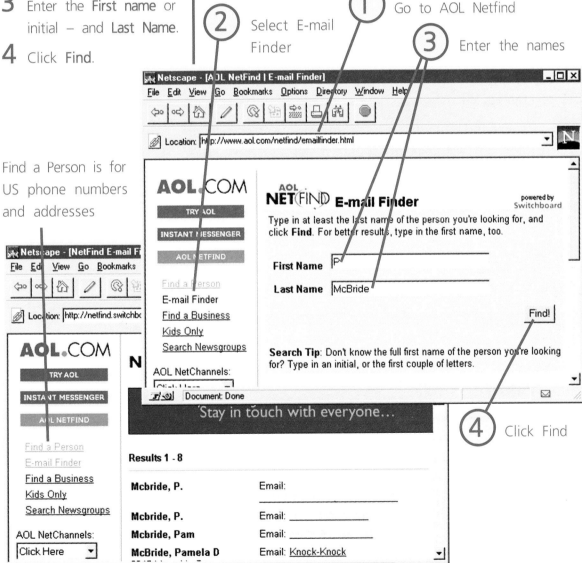

Whois

Whois is a standard tool on Unix systems with Internet connections. It can query databases held on Whois servers and – in theory – you can simply give a name and it will give you the e-mail address. In practice, Whois only works for those organisations that submit details of their users to the servers' databases.

WinWhois

This is another Winsock compliant program, like WS_FTP, so log on to the Internet through Dial-Up Networking before starting WinWhois.

This compact and efficient piece of software is on the Net as 'winwhois.zip'. Amongst other places, you can find it at:

ftp.sunet.se/pub/pc/windows/winsock-indstate/whois/

Basic steps

1 Log in through your **Winsock** software.

2 Run WinWhois.

3 Enter the **Name** – try the surname or surname, firstname.

4 Click **Make Query** and wait for the host to reply.

5 If the person you wanted is there, get the address.

6 Exit when done.

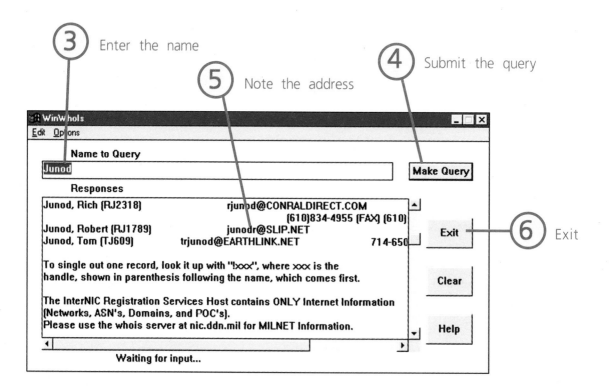

③ Enter the name

⑤ Note the address

④ Submit the query

⑥ Exit

Whois through the Web

1 Go to Internic at:
http://rs.internic.net/
cgi-bin/whois

2 Type in a name and
press [Enter].

3 Wait for the list of
names or a 'no
matches' message.

If you do not have WinWhoIs, or would like to try it out
before you get it, you can access Whois servers through
the Web.

There are links to half a dozen at *Yahoo.* Step through the
menus: *Computers and Internet – Internet – Directory
Services – Whois.* You can also go direct to the Internic
server through the Web.

Go to Internic

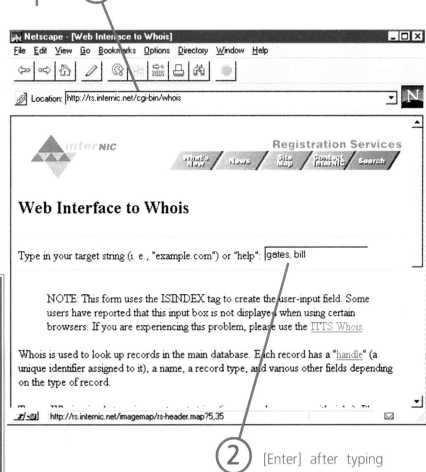

Take note

**Internic is one of the
central organisations
of the Internet.**

**Browse their site and
find out what they do.**

(2) [Enter] after typing
to start the search

Finger

Finger is a utility found on most Unix – and some other – systems. When prompted with part or all of a user's name, it will return more information on that person – including their e-mail address. Within a site it is often used to see whether or not someone is logged on.

Finger varies. On some systems a request to 'finger john' would tell you about all the people on that system with 'john' in their proper name or user ID. On other systems, you have to give the official user ID (which could be like this – 'cs1024jbs') to get any response.

When used over the Internet, rather than within a site, you also have to supply Finger with the name of the domain. You may have to know someone's e-mail address before you can finger them!

Your fingering may be in vain because:

- Some sites only give on-site users access to Finger;

- Some computers do not have a Finger utility;

- Finger is case-sensitive on some Unix computers, so that 'smith' will not find 'Smith'.

To run Finger over the Internet, you will need suitable software, like WsFinger (opposite), or work through a Web gateway. You will find one at Yahoo.

Take note

Most computers will show a list of who is logged on at the time if you just type:

    finger @host

For example:

    finger@doc.ic.ac.uk

Watch out! A busy site, during working hours, can produce screensful of information.

Basic steps

WsFinger

❑ Finger queries

1 Click ___Finger___ to open the window.

2 Enter the query as *name@domain*.

3 Click **OK** to start the search.

4 If you get more than one match, scroll through to the results.

❑ WhoIs queries

5 Click ___WhoIs___ to open the **WhoIs** window.

6 Enter the **name**.

7 Enter a Whois **Host** – e.g. rs.internic.net.

8 Click **OK**.

This Winsock software gives a neat way to run Finger queries, and also offers a Whois facility – though as you have to enter the server name by hand, it is not as reliable or as easy to use as WinWhoIs.

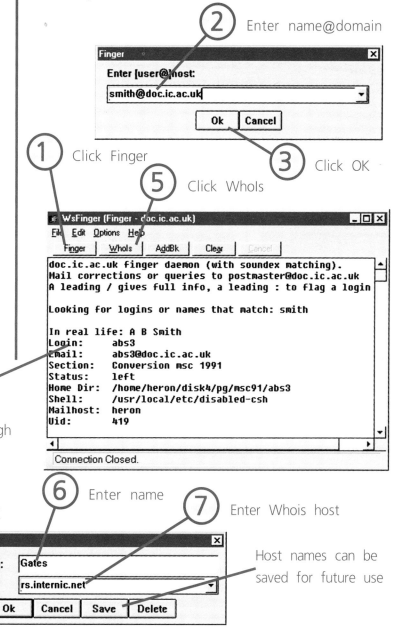

② Enter name@domain

Finger

Enter [user@]host:

smith@doc.ic.ac.uk

Ok   Cancel

① Click Finger

③ Click OK

⑤ Click WhoIs

WsFinger (Finger - doc.ic.ac.uk)

File Edit Options Help

Finger   WhoIs   AddBk   Clear   Cancel

doc.ic.ac.uk finger daemon (with soundex matching).
Mail corrections or queries to postmaster@doc.ic.ac.uk
A leading / gives full info, a leading : to flag a login

Looking for logins or names that match: smith

In real life: A B Smith
Login: abs3
Email: abs3@doc.ic.ac.uk
Section: Conversion msc 1991
Status: left
Home Dir: /home/heron/disk4/pg/msc91/abs3
Shell: /usr/local/etc/disabled-csh
Mailhost: heron
Uid: 419

Connection Closed.

④ Scroll through the results

⑥ Enter name

⑦ Enter Whois host

⑧ Click OK

WhoIs Query

Query String: Gates

Host: rs.internic.net

Ok   Cancel   Save   Delete

Host names can be saved for future use

Member directories

Bigger organisations keep directories of their members, which other members can search. If you connect through a national service, it may be worth trying their directory when looking for a lost friend or other contact.

Basic steps

❏ CompuServe

1 Log on to CompuServe.

2 Open the **Mail** menu and select **Member Directory**.

3 Type in enough details to identify the person – **Last Name** and **Country** may be enough.

4 Click **Search**.

5 If the search produces too many results, you will have to go back to step 3 and add **First Name** or **City** to narrow the search.

6 Double-click on a name in the results display to get fuller details of the person.

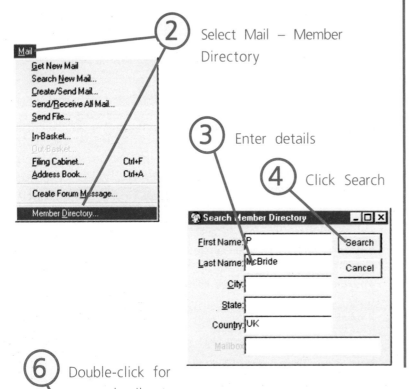

② Select Mail – Member Directory

③ Enter details

④ Click Search

⑥ Double-click for more details

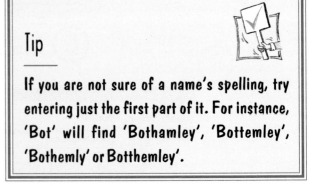

Tip

If you are not sure of a name's spelling, try entering just the first part of it. For instance, 'Bot' will find 'Bothamley', 'Bottemley', 'Bothemly' or Botthemley'.

Basic steps

❑ MicroSoft Network

1 Log on to **MSN** and open your **Inbox**.

2 From the **Tools** menu select **Address Book**.

3 For **Show Names from the:** select **Microsoft Network**.

4 Open the **Tools** menu and select **Find**.

5 Enter known details on the **General** tab.

6 Click **OK**.

7 Click on a name in the **Search Results** list for more on the person.

① Open the Inbox

② Select Tools – Address Book

③ Show Names from MSN

⑤ Enter details

⑥ Click OK

⑦ Click for more info

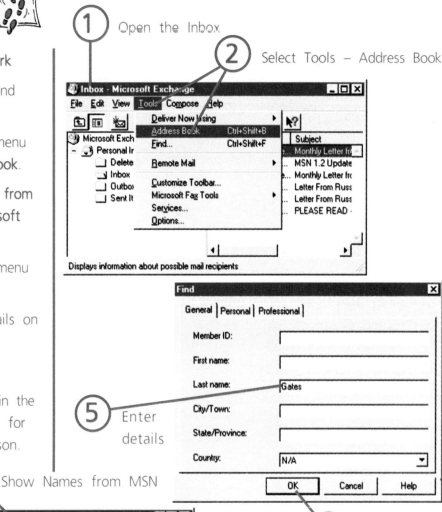

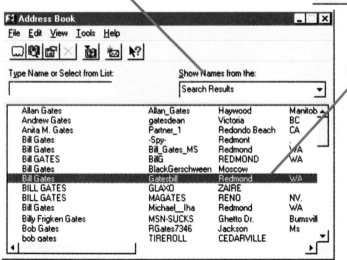

Tip

If you find too many names, you can search again through the 'Search Results' list.

Summary

- There is no simple, guaranteed way to find someone's e-mail address — the Internet just isn't that organised.

- **WhoWhere?** is the first place to look when you are searching for people. It holds the e-mail addresses of many people throughout the world, and also has access to the US phone books.

- Most of the people-finding sites — and some others — offer **free Web-based e-mail**. This can be useful for people who are often away from their desk, and for families who share one e-mail account.

- **BigFoot**, **Four11** and **InfoSpace** are good people-finding sites. These can be reached directly or through NetGuide at Netscape and the People search pages at Microsoft.

- There is a simple E-Mail Finding page at **AOL NetFind**.

- **Whois** can give you the addresses of people working for those organisations that submit their e-mail details to the Whois servers — not all do.

- **WinWhoIs** is a Windows program that will handle Whois queries for you.

- Whois can be run through the Web — you can find **gateways to Whois** at Yahoo.

- Where a person is in an organisation that uses **Unix machines**, you can usually **Finger** them to find their address.

- Large service providers often maintain **directories** of their **members**, which members can use to find each others' addresses.

11 Reading the News

News

Newsgroups have developed from e-mail, and consist of groups of users linked so that an **article** sent to the group is **posted** to all its members. There are thousands of groups, each dedicated to a different interest – professions and obsessions, programming languages and TV programs, software, hobbies, politics.

Key points about newsgroups

- **Subscribing** to a group is easy, free of charge and free of entry restrictions.

- The quality and quantity of the communications vary enormously. Some newsgroups circulate large volumes of interesting and relevant information; others carry few articles – or few of any interest.

- Some newsgroups are moderated, i.e. they have someone who checks all incoming articles before broadcasting them to the members. This reduces the quantity of irrelevant and/or boring post.

- The seedier and steamier side of the Internet is mainly in the newsgroups. If you do not want anyone to access this from your system, there are programs that will filter it out for you (see page 80).

- Some groups are mainly for discussions, others are more like open help-lines, where people can ask for – and get – solutions to technical problems.

- As newsgroups bring together people who share a common interest, they can be a good place to make new friends.

- If you decide that a newsgroup is not for you, you can leave at any time.

Definitions

Article – message sent to a newsgroup.

Post – submit an article for broadcasting.

Subscribing – this doesn't involve going onto any kind of membership list. In the Netscape and Explorer News systems, this simply places the newsgroup name in a folder for easy access.

Tip

If you are new to the Internet, there is a group specially for you. It's *news.announce.newusers.* (For subscribing see pages 184, 187 or 189.) And look out for Emily Postnews' Etiquette for USENET News Postings. It's posted fairly often.

Some major groups

alt – alternative set: a vast and varied collection, largely unmoderated

comp – computing: a great source of help and a good place to meet fellow enthusiasts

rec – recreation: for sports, arts, hobbies and pastimes

sci – science: for academic and amateur scientists

uk – groups mainly for UK residents. There are similar sets for most countries and many smaller regions

Newsgroup names

Newsgroups are organised into a branching structure, with major sections sub-divided by topic. Their names reflect this structure; e.g, *comp.lang.basic.visual.database* is in the *comp*uter section, which amongst other things covers programming *lang*uages, including *basic*, and this has a *visual* subsection containing four groups, one of which is concerned with *database* programming.

● The names and natures of some of the larger top-level groups are listed on the left.

● The hierarchy of groups can be seen in this screen from Netscape News. It is presented there in the familiar folder/sub-folder format.

When you are on-line, the number of current articles is shown here

Click on a folder to open it out

A tick shows you have subscribed to the group

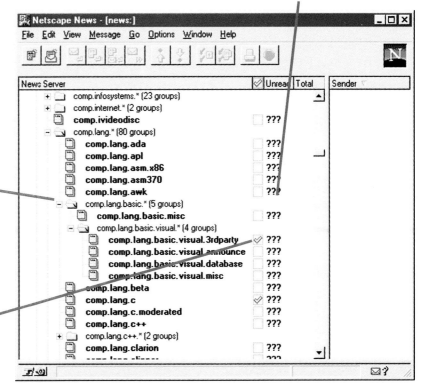

News from Netscape

In Netscape 3.0, access to newsgroups is handled through the News window. This looks very like the Mail window, and is used in much the same way.

The top left pane shows the newsgroups; the top right holds the headers of the current articles in the selected group; the large lower pane will display the text of an article when it is selected.

When the window opens, the top left pane shows only those groups to which you have subscribed. If you are on-line at the time, the system then downloads the headers for these groups.

● If you want to dip into other groups, or see what's available so that you can subscribe to some, you must display all the newsgroups.

1 From the **Options** menu, select **Show All Newsgroups**. The first time you do this, Netscape downloads the list from the server – it takes a while!

❏ **Sampling the news**

2 Open folders to see the groups they contain.

3 Click on a group to download its headers.

4 Click on a header to read the article.

❏ **Subscribing**

5 Just tick the box.

Subscribed groups are listed when you start

Use Options – Show All Newsgroups

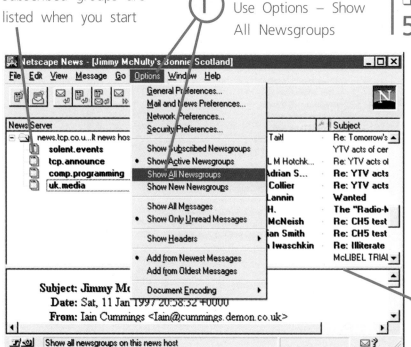

You can adjust the pane sizes by dragging the dividing lines

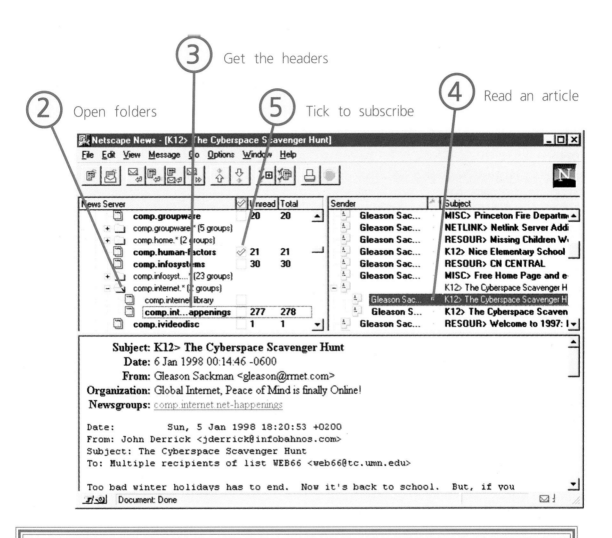

(2) Open folders

(3) Get the headers

(5) Tick to subscribe

(4) Read an article

Subject: K12> The Cyberspace Scavenger Hunt
Date: 6 Jan 1998 00:14:46 -0600
From: Gleason Sackman <gleason@rrnet.com>
Organization: Global Internet, Peace of Mind is finally Online!
Newsgroups: comp.internet.net-happenings

Date: Sun, 5 Jan 1998 18:20:53 +0200
From: John Derrick <jderrick@infobahnos.com>
Subject: The Cyberspace Scavenger Hunt
To: Multiple recipients of list WEB66 <web66@tc.umn.edu>

Too bad winter holidays has to end. Now it's back to school. But, if you

---

Take note

Your *news server* may well not carry all newsgroups. Some access providers refuse to carry those groups that circulate graphics and other binary files as the sheer volume of data adds heavily to the traffic on their lines; many also filter out those groups that may carry material that may result in prosecutions. Censorship and self-censorship are subject to lively debate on the Internet. If you want to follow this further, the main UK discussion site is at:

http://www.leeds.ac.uk/law/pgs/yaman/yaman.htm

Communicator's Collabra

Basic steps

In Collabra, you start in the Message Center. When you select a group from there, you are taken to the main mail and news window where you can read and reply to articles.

① Run Collabra

② Double-click to open

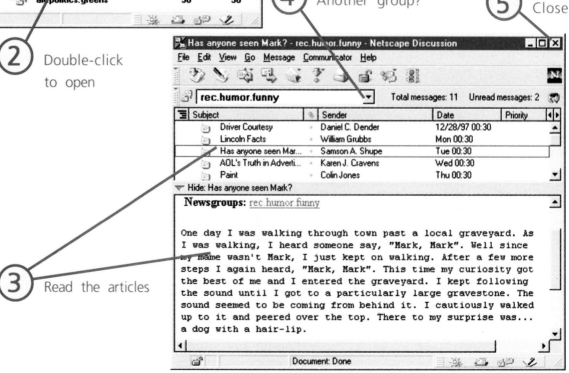

④ Another group?

⑤ Close

③ Read the articles

1 Run **Collabra** from the **Start** menu, or from the **Communicator** menu in **Navigator**.

2 Double-click on a newsgroup to open the main news window.

3 Read the news as in Netscape 3.0.

4 Select another group from the drop-down list, if wanted.

5 Close the windows.

Basic steps

1 In the **Message Center** click the **Subscribe** icon.

2 Switch to the **Search for a Group** panel.

3 Type a word to find in the newsgroup name and click **Search Now**.

4 Select a newsgroup and click **Subscribe**.

5 Click **OK**.

❏ The group will be added to the Message Center list.

Tip

To remove a group from your subscribed list, return to the Subscribe panel, select it and click Unsubscribe.

Sampling newsgroups in Collabra

There is no easy way to do this! You can only get to a newsgroup's articles from the Message Center or the mail and news window, and the only newsgroups that are listed are those to which you have subscribed. If you want to sample a newsgroup you must first add it to your list of subscribed groups – you can remove it later if you don't want to access it regularly.

② Open the Search panel

③ Search for a name

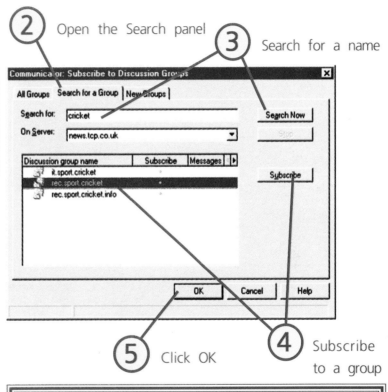

⑤ Click OK

④ Subscribe to a group

Take note

It doesn't matter how many groups you subscribe to. The articles are not downloaded automatically, so they will not choke your phone line or block up your system.

Explorer News

Basic steps

In Explorer 4.0, news and mail are handled by the same software – normally Outlook Express, unless you specified your own alternative during the initial setup.

The mail and newsgroups folders are listed on the left, with article headers for the selected folder in the top pane, and the text of a selected article in the lower pane.

Basic steps

1 In Explorer, click the **Mail** button and select **Read News**

2 Select a newsgroup.

3 Open the **Tools** menu and select **Download this Newsgroup...**

4 Tick **Get the following items** then select the items you want.

5 Click OK and wait.

6 Click on a header to read the article.

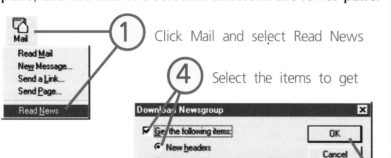

① Click Mail and select Read News

④ Select the items to get

⑤ Click OK

② Pick a group

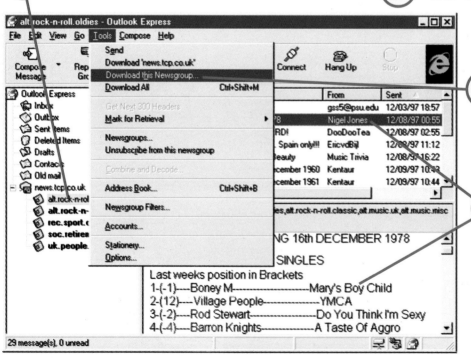

③ Download this group

⑥ Read an article

188

Sampling and subscribing

1 From the **Tools** menu, select **Newsgroups**...

2 Open the **All** groups panel.

3 Type a keyword (or several) to filter the list.

4 Select a group.

5 See what's there by clicking **Go to**.

or

6 Join the group by clicking **Subscribe**.

If you want to browse through the groups, or see what's available so that you can subscribe to some, open the newsgroups panel.

In Explorer news the groups are presented as a single continuous list. This is initially daunting, but in practice, it's often easier to find a group in Explorer than in Netscape News' folder display. Just type in one or more words that you might find in the name, and Explorer will search for matching groups. This is particularly useful where a group's place in the hierarchy is not obvious.

Tip

When reading news with Explorer, save download time. Get *New headers* first, mark the articles you want, then select *Get marked messages*.

③ Type keyword(s)

④ Select a group

⑥ Click Subscribe

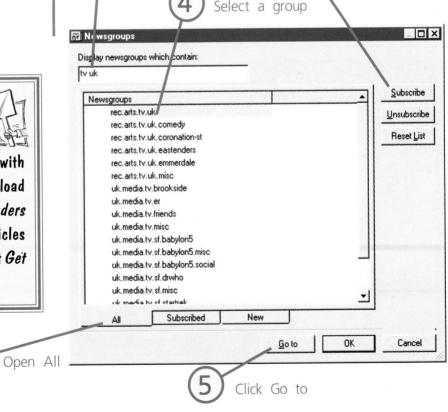

② Open All

⑤ Click Go to

189

Posting and replying

Posting articles to a newsgroup is very similar to sending mail, but with a couple of significant differences:

- when posting to a newsgroup, your message goes to thousands of people – observing the netiquette (page 192) is very important;

- when responding to an article, you have the choice of replying to the author, posting to the whole group or both.

❏ Responding to articles

1 Select the article.

2 Decide whether you want to reply to the author only, or post to the whole group.

3 Use the appropriate **Message** option or Toolbar button.

4 Edit out any unwanted lines from the quoted article.

5 Type your reply.

6 Click the **Send** button.

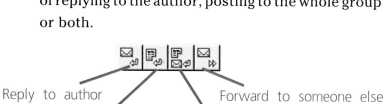

Reply to author

Post to group

Reply and post

Forward to someone else

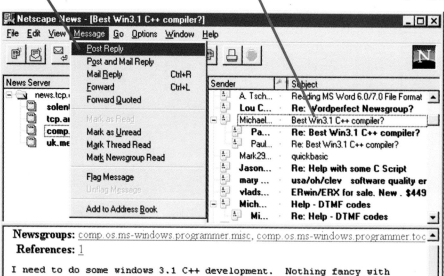

③ Post or mail your reply

① Select the article

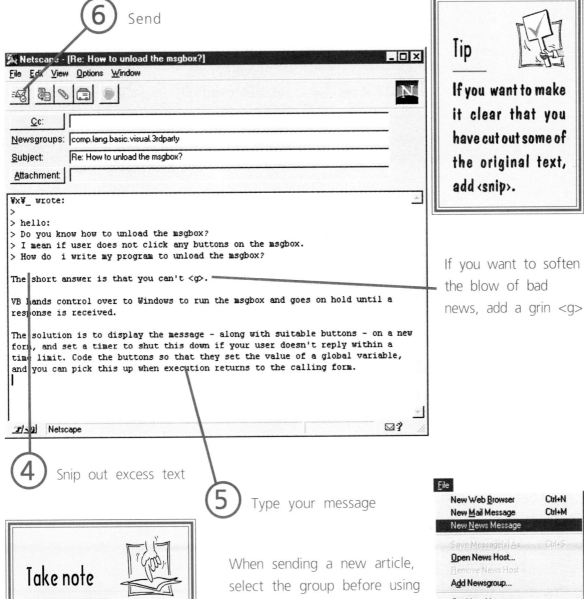

Tip

If you want to make it clear that you have cut out some of the original text, add ‹snip›.

If you want to soften the blow of bad news, add a grin ‹g›

④ Snip out excess text

⑤ Type your message

Take note

Netscape 3.0 is used for all the examples in the rest of this section.

When sending a new article, select the group before using File – New News Message. The group's name will then be copied into the Mail To: slot, ready for you.

Netiquette

Newsgroups have their own etiquette, and you would do well to observe it if you don't want to be shot down in **flames**. The key is to remember that any article that you post to the newsgroup will be received by all of its members – hundreds, or even thousands of people – and that it will cost each of these phone time to receive it and personal time to read it. As some service providers charge for mail and article storage, it can also cost money.

If a newsgroup has 1,000 members (many have more), a 1kb article takes up 1Mb of net traffic and disk space. Even if members only scan the Subject line, and do not read it, the total time spent will be a couple of hours.

Key points of netiquette:

● When you first join a newsgroup, **lurk** for a while. Read its articles to get a feel of its flavour and level.

● Before you post any questions of your own, read the **FAQs**. These are usually circulated regularly.

● If you post a reply to an article, trim out any unnecessary text, to save everyone's time and **bandwidth**.

● If your reply will only really be interesting to the original author, e-mail it, don't post it.

● Keep your own postings brief and to the point.

● Don't **spam**. Post your articles only to the newsgroups where they will be appreciated.

Definitions

Bandwidth – strictly the capacity of the comms lines, but taken to mean on-line time/ mailbox storage.

FAQ – Frequently Asked Questions, and their answers, lists compiled by groups' moderators (organisers) and great sources of information.

Flame – overreaction to a breach of netiquette or tactless remark. Can lead to **flame wars** if the victims believe they are right.

Lurk – read articles, without posting. It's OK to lurk.

Reply – send an e-mail in reply to an article, rather than posting the reply to the group.

Spam – send article to inappropriate groups. The worst spammers are those promoting 'Get rich quick' schemes.

Files from the News

A key feature of the news (and e-mail) system is that it is based on 7-bit transfers. That is, the bytes coming down the wires only use 7 bits for data, with the eighth bit being using for error-checking. This is fine for plain text, as this only uses the first half of the ASCII set (characters 0 to 127) and these can be represented with only 7 bits.

Graphics, zipped files, executable programs and similar files – known as binaries – present a problem, as you have to use all 8 bits to express the values in these. To transfer a binary file through the mail or news systems, it must be converted to 7-bit format for transfer and converted back to 8-bit before it can be used.

To make matters worse, some systems set a limit to the size of articles and messages (around 60Kb). Large binary files have to be split into smaller chunks before transfer.

Binary files can be sent, and received, through the news system either in binary form or encoded into ASCII text.

- In Netscape, the file will be displayed within the article if you have a suitable viewer. If not, you will see a box marked '**Attachment**'. Either way, these can be saved and are ready for use directly.

- In Explorer, an attached file is initially shown as an icon. Clicking on it will display the image, if appropriate, or take you to a Save routine,

- If the file has been split over several articles, only the first will be displayed – showing part of the image. To see it, save all the related articles, join them together and decode them (page 200).

- If the file was converted to text, it must be saved as a text file and decoded (page 194).

Take note

Netscape's Save As... options only have HTML and TXT, but don't let this fool you. Use TXT if the file is encoded, otherwise write the extension – GIF, JPG, or whatever – into the filename. The extension will be present in the default filename that Netscape will have given it at the start of the routine.

Multi-part files must be decoded

① Open the article

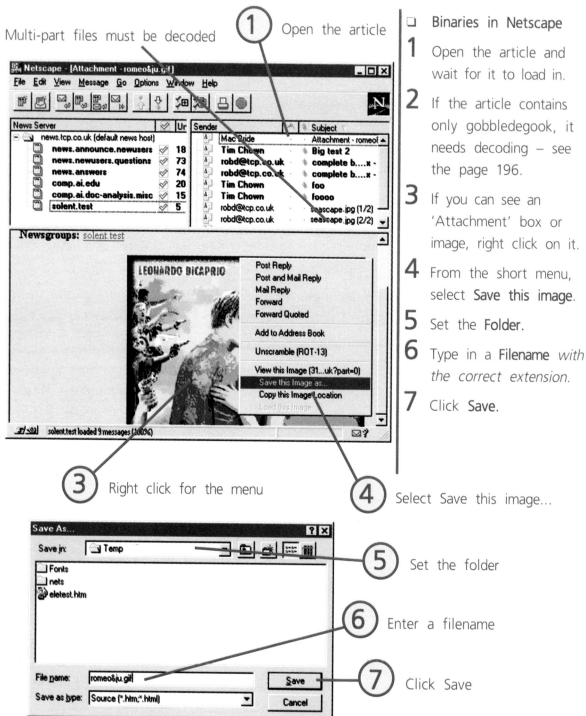

③ Right click for the menu

④ Select Save this image...

⑤ Set the folder

⑥ Enter a filename

⑦ Click Save

❑ **Binaries in Netscape**

1 Open the article and wait for it to load in.

2 If the article contains only gobbledegook, it needs decoding – see the page 196.

3 If you can see an 'Attachment' box or image, right click on it.

4 From the short menu, select **Save this image**.

5 Set the **Folder**.

6 Type in a **Filename** *with the correct extension.*

7 Click **Save**.

Basic steps

❑ **Binaries in Explorer**

1 Check the Subject line. If it says (1/1) at the end, it is a simple one-part file, and you can carry on.

2 Open the article.

3 Click the Paperclip icon to display the filename.

4 Click the filename to open the file.

5 Some files generate a warning message – only open the file if it is from a reliable source or not executable.

❑ If possible, the file will be opened in Explorer or in a viewer, and can be saved from there. If it is not viewable, you will be offered a Save As option.

Once you are sure that a file type is safe, tick this box and skip the warnings in future

The filename is usually in the Subject line

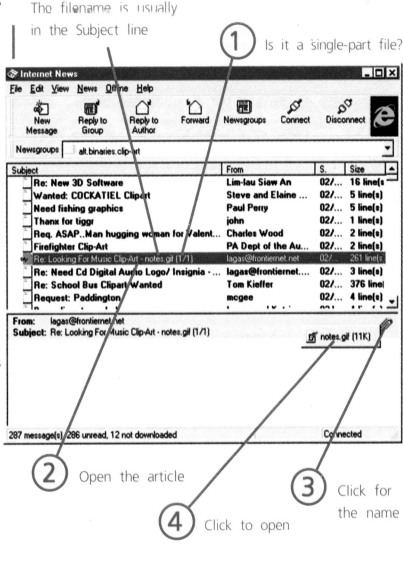

① Is it a single-part file?

② Open the article

③ Click for the name

④ Click to open

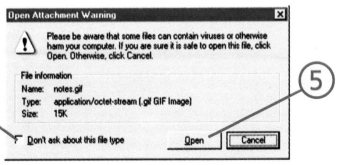

⑤ Open if safe to do so

Decoding binaries

Binary files can be represented as ASCII text in several different formats. The two most commonly used are **MIME** (see page 198) and **uuencoding**. To decode them you need special software, but it is readily available over the Net.

The decoding process is a bit long-winded, but normally straightforward. Briefly, you have to get the coded part(s) out of the article(s), joining them together if necessary, to create one text file. This is then passed through the appropriate decoder, which outputs the binary file.

Uuencoding

UU stands for Unix to Unix – a reminder that the Internet is based on Unix machines. Don't let this worry you – it works perfectly well on the PC. The decoding software is *uudecode.exe*, a DOS program. Your access provider should have a ready-to-run copy in their databanks. FTP a copy and store it in your DOS or Windows directory. Alternatively, there is a good Windows version that you can find at:

http://www.infocom.net/~elogan/wuudoall.html

Uuencoded files can be recognised by their first line, which always starts:

begin 644

This is followed by the name of the original binary file. The last line of the code is marked by:

end

Multi-part files will usually have breaks marked by:

- - - cut here - - -

❏ One-part files

1 Use the **File – Save** option to save the article as a text file.

2 Open the file in an editor and delete everything down to the 'begin' marker.

3 Delete any text after the 'end' marker.

4 Save the file – *as text*.

5 Run the **DOS** prompt.

6 Change to the directory containing the file.

7 Type:
uudecode *whatfile.txt*
(use its proper name!)

8 Check out the new file.

Tip

When cutting the coded part out of the article, make sure you include the 'begin' and 'end', but crop out any 'cut here' lines.

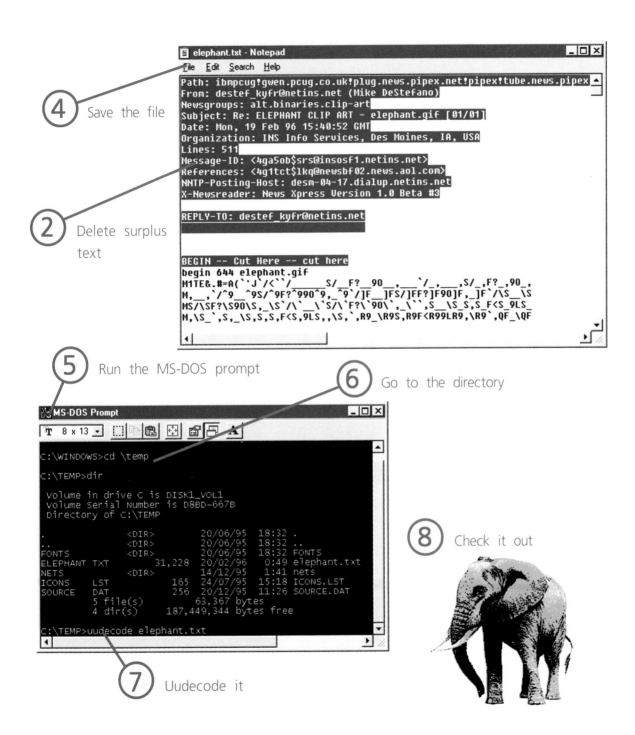

④ Save the file

② Delete surplus text

elephant.txt - Notepad

File Edit Search Help

```
Path: ibmpcug!gwen.pcug.co.uk!plug.news.pipex.net!pipex!tube.news.pipex
From: destef_kyfr@netins.net (Mike DeStefano)
Newsgroups: alt.binaries.clip-art
Subject: Re: ELEPHANT CLIP ART - elephant.gif [01/01]
Date: Mon, 19 Feb 96 15:40:52 GMT
Organization: INS Info Services, Des Moines, IA, USA
Lines: 511
Message-ID: <4ga5ob$srs@insosf1.netins.net>
References: <4g1tct$lkq@newsbf02.news.aol.com>
NNTP-Posting-Host: desm-04-17.dialup.netins.net
X-Newsreader: News Xpress Version 1.0 Beta #3

REPLY-TO: destef_kyfr@netins.net


BEGIN -- Cut Here -- cut here
begin 644 elephant.gif
M1TE&..#=A=A=A=+H.#`#&W_#B&''____//H$?J`#H`O_##9x9t,!
M,,...
MS/\SF?\S90\S,_\S`/\`__\`S/\`F``\90\`__\`_`__S__\S_S,S,_S_F<S_9LS_
M,,\S_`,S,_\S,S,S,F<S,9LS,,\S,`,R9_\R9S,R9F<R99LR9,\R9`,QF_\QF
```

⑤ Run the MS-DOS prompt

⑥ Go to the directory

MS-DOS Prompt

T 8 x 13

```
C:\WINDOWS>cd \temp

C:\TEMP>dir

 Volume in drive C is DISK1_VOL1
 Volume Serial Number is D8BD-667B
 Directory of C:\TEMP

.              <DIR>        20/06/95  18:32 .
..             <DIR>        20/06/95  18:32 ..
FONTS          <DIR>        20/06/95  18:32 FONTS
ELEPHANT TXT        31,228  20/02/96   0:49 elephant.txt
NETS           <DIR>        14/12/95   1:41 nets
ICONS    LST           165  24/07/95  15:18 ICONS.LST
SOURCE   DAT           256  20/12/95  11:26 SOURCE.DAT
         5 file(s)        63,367 bytes
         4 dir(s)    187,449,344 bytes free

C:\TEMP>uudecode elephant.txt
```

⑦ Uudecode it

⑧ Check it out

MIME

MIME stands for Multipurpose Internet Mail Extensions and is one of the standard techniques for transferring binary files through the mail or news systems. If you want to encode files into MIME format, you need **mpack** – perhaps more importantly, if you receive a MIME file, you need **munpack** to decode it.

mpack and **munpack** were written by John G. Myers (jgm+@cmu.edu). They are available for most types of machines, but note that the PC version is a DOS, rather than a Windows program. When hunting for it in FTP sites, look for ZIP files, with names starting 'mpack...'.

At the time of writing, the latest PC version was **mpack15d.zip**. This unzips into two programs, **mpack.exe** and **munpack.exe**. For ease of use they should be stored in your DOS or Windows directory, or any other directory that is in your standard path.

● You can use the same steps as for uudecode, simply substituting 'munpack' at the MS-DOS prompt. The steps shown here take a slightly different route to reach the same end.

Basic steps

❑ **Decoding one-part files**

1 Select the MIME message or news article, with its headers and use **Edit–Copy** to copy it to the Clipboard.

2 Open **Wordpad** or any other word-processor and **Edit–Paste** in the selected text.

3 Save it as a text file.

4 Open the MS-DOS prompt and switch to the text file's directory.

5 Give the command:
munpack *textfile*

❑ If the message contains a filename to use for the MIME part, that name is used for the output file. If not, the names 'part1', 'part2', etc will be used.

6 Check the directory for your new file.

Tip

You can get MPACK and MUNPACK from:

ftp://ftp.andrew.cmu.edu:pub/mpack/

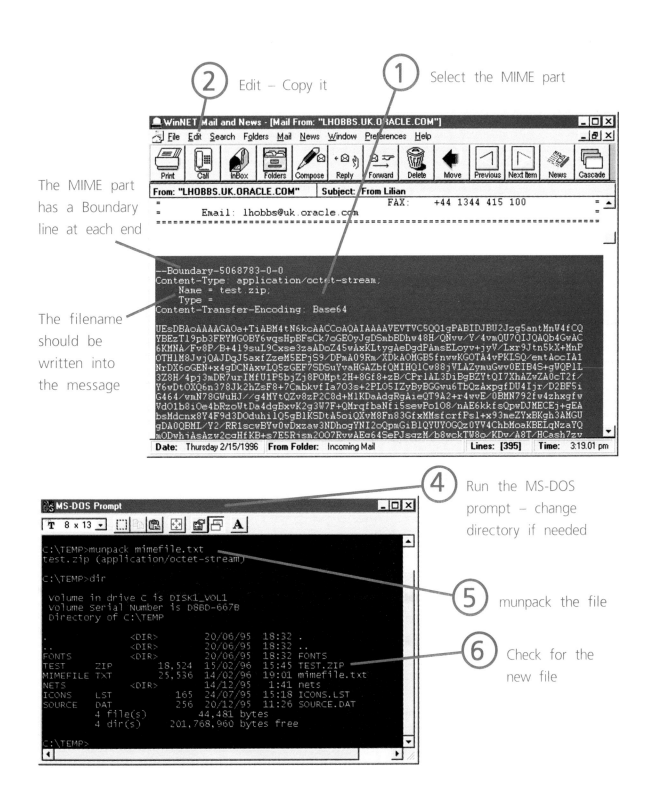

(2) Edit – Copy it

(1) Select the MIME part

The MIME part has a Boundary line at each end

The filename should be written into the message

Run the MS-DOS prompt – change directory if needed

(5) munpack the file

(6) Check for the new file

199

Multi-part binaries

Decoding a multi-part binary file is simple – once you have amalgamated the chunks from the incoming articles. All you have to do is run the MS-DOS prompt and *uudecode* or *munpack* it. The amalgamation is the tricky part!

There are three likely causes of error:

● The parts are out of order – saving methodically will prevent this. The headers have numbers at the end to show how many there are in the set, and where the article fits, e.g. 02/05 is the second in a five-file set. One labelled 00/05 would be the accompanying description – don't save this.

● You have left line breaks or surplus text between the parts – check the joins. (If your first few amalgamations show that you can cut and paste perfectly, you can omit this from your routine.)

● One or more parts of the file has been corrupted – you cannot do anything about this, but fortunately it does not happen very often.

Take note

The amalgamated file will be too large for Notepad to handle. Stick them together in WordPad, Write or a word-processor. This will also give you the Find facility that you need for checking the joins.

1 Save the articles, with numbers in the names – 'part1.txt', 'part2.txt', etc.

2 Edit each article down to its coded text and save it again.

3 Open the first part in **WordPad** and move to the very end.

4 Open the next part, in WordPad or NotePad and make a note of its first 6 or 7 characters.

5 Select the text, copy it and paste it at the end of the first file.

6 Run the **Find** routine in your main file, looking for the first characters of the new part, and check that they follow directly on from the previous text.

7 Repeat steps 4 to 6 for any other parts.

8 Save the complete file under a new name – *as a text file*.

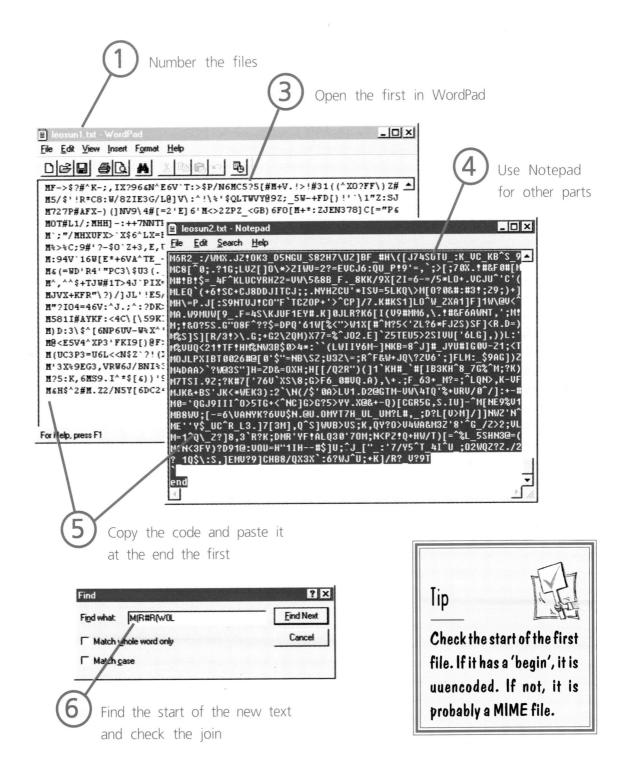

① Number the files

③ Open the first in WordPad

④ Use Notepad for other parts

⑤ Copy the code and paste it at the end the first

⑥ Find the start of the new text and check the join

Find

Find what: M[R#R(W0L

☐ Match whole word only

☐ Match case

[Find Next] [Cancel]

Tip

Check the start of the first file. If it has a 'begin', it is uuencoded. If not, it is probably a MIME file.

Summary

- There is a **newsgroup** for almost every conceivable interest, hobby, profession or obsession.

- Newsgroups are **organised into a hierarchy**, branching down from broad areas to highly specialised topics.

- The first stage in using any News system is to **download the list of newsgroups** from your server.

- **Netscape 3.0's News** window is divided into three panes, for the groups, headers and text of articles. Initially only subscribed groups are displayed.

- In **Communicator's Collabra**, you start in the Message Center to select your group, then read and reply in the main mail and news window.

- **Internet Explorer's News** window also follows the same style as its mail window, using a two-pane display and a drop-down list of subscribed groups.

- Newsgroups can be **sampled** to see what's there.

- **Subscribing** to a group adds it to your quick access set.

- When **responding to an article**, you can post a follow-up article to the group, reply to the author, or both.

- You can **post articles** to any subscribed group. Articles should only be posted to relevant newsgroups.

- Some **binary files** can be viewed and saved easily. Others will have been encoded into text and must be decoded before they can be viewed.

- **Multi-part binary files** must be saved as text, joined together in a word-processor and then decoded.

- **Uuencoding** and **MIME** are the two most common formats for transmitting binaries through newsgroups.

12 Files from the Net

Software at c|net

Amongst c|net's many activities, it runs **Software Central** – a great place to find freeware, shareware and commercial software for PCs or Macintosh computers.

The simplest way to find software is to work through the catalog. The categories are well organised, with the first jump taking you to the program listings. These show the dates and the number of times it has been downloaded – a reasonable indicator of its quality. Some listings are very lengthy, though sorting by downloads should bring the best to the top. When you select a program, you are taken to a page showing a longer description, its size, price, etc. You can download from there with a click.

Go to Software Central

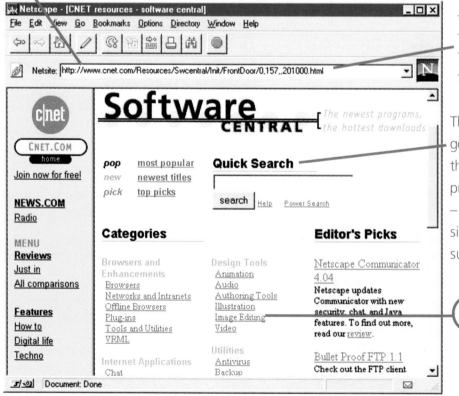

Just head for cnet – you will be taken to the current front page

The Quick Search is good if you know the name of the program you want – otherwise it is simpler to look in a suitable Category

Select a Category

204

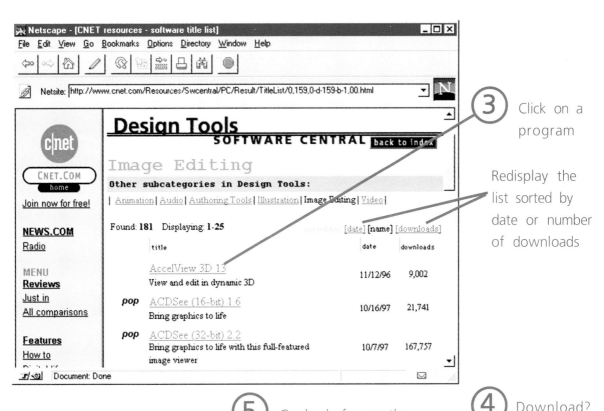

3 Click on a program

Redisplay the list sorted by date or number of downloads

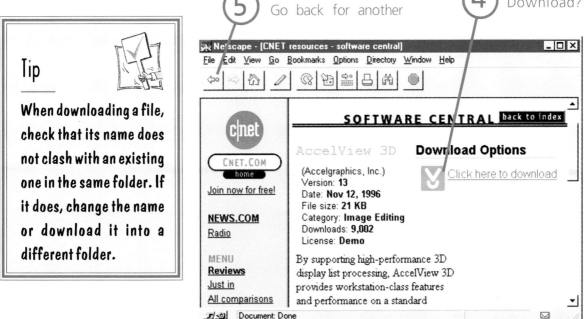

5 Go back for another

4 Download?

Tip

When downloading a file, check that its name does not clash with an existing one in the same folder. If it does, change the name or download it into a different folder.

shareware.com

Another valuable c|net service is **shareware.com.** It has literally megabytes of shareware (and freeware) programs. This is a place for searching, not browsing!

The Search routine looks for a match in the names and in the descriptions of the programs.

● If you are just starting to build your shareware collection, try the Most Popular selection.

1 Go to: http://www.shareware.com

2 In the **Quick Search** box type the name or a key descriptive word.

3 Set the computer type.

4 Click **Search** and wait.

5 Read the descriptions to find the right file.

(1) Go to shareware.com

(2) Type the name or a keyword

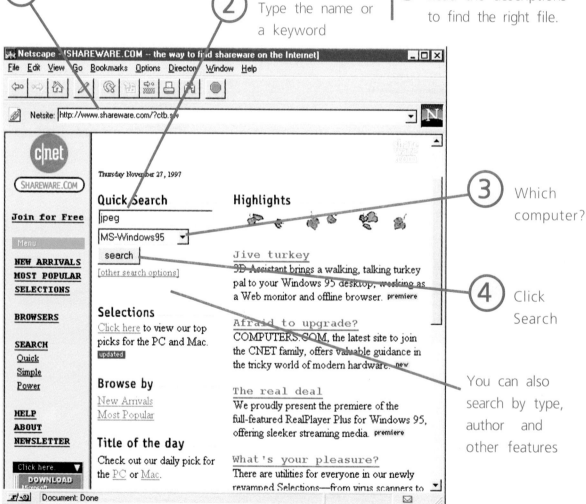

(3) Which computer?

(4) Click Search

You can also search by type, author and other features

6 Click on the filename to start the download – saving the file as usual.

⑥ Click to download

⑤ Read about the files

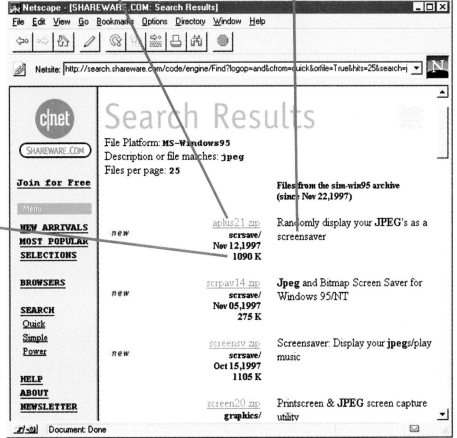

Check the size – is it worth the download time? Allow 1 minute for every 100Kb, or 10 for 1Mb. Even with the fastest modem, connections to busy sites rarely run at more than 2Kb per second.

Take note

c|net has more software at
http://www.gamecenter.com
and
http:// www.download.com

Tip

To be kept informed of new arrivals, click **Newsletter** and get on the list for *Shareware Dispatch*, their e-mail newsletter.

Shareware at Jumbo

Jumbo started up in mid-1995, with the aim of becoming the biggest and best shareware site on the Net. By early 1998, it had over 200,000 files at the tip of its trunk – and growing by nearly 10,000 a month. Despite this rate of growth, the files were well organised, though some links were incorrect or inactive.

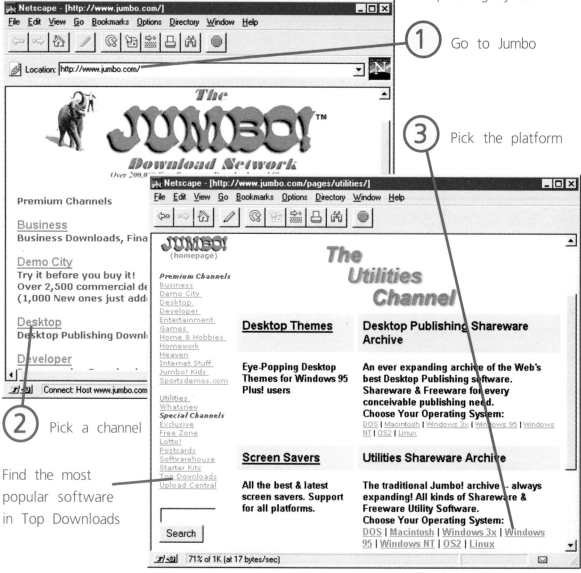

① Go to Jumbo

③ Pick the platform

② Pick a channel

Find the most popular software in Top Downloads

208

4 Select a category.

5 Scroll through the list – click  to find out more about the file.

6 Click 🐕 to download and pick a site – try the closest first.

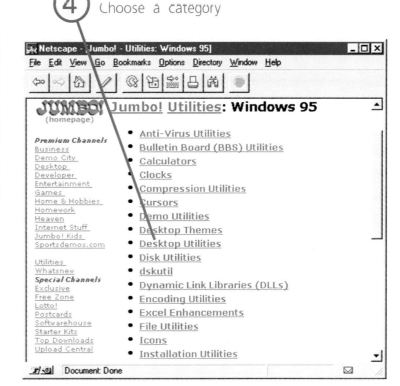

④ Choose a category

5 Read all about it

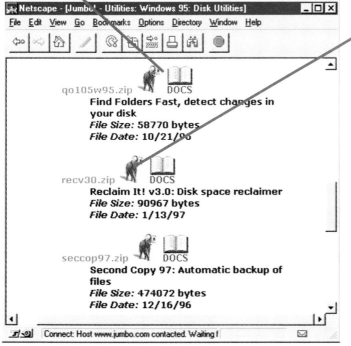

⑥ Click to download

Take note

Files are not stored at Jumbo. Instead, for each file there are links to FTP sites where it is stored. It adds an extra step, but speeds things up. As people only go to Jumbo to find links, not to download, the traffic is lighter than at other software sites.

Other shareware sites

Basic steps

New shareware sites are springing up all the time – and for fairly obvious reasons. It costs nothing, except a little research time, to put shareware links on your page, and shareware pulls in the surfers. Everyone likes to have visitors! And if you are a commercial site, the more visitors you get, the more you can charge for your advertising. The quality varies, but here are a two of the best.

Tucows

This is an entertaining and useful site, listing vast quantities of reviewed and rated shareware. Though the emphasis is on Winsock applications – i.e. those which are used while you are on-line to the Internet – it also includes HTML and graphics editors and utilities and much more besides. Each is shown with essential details, a review, a rating and – crucially – a link from which it can be downloaded.

1 Go to Tucows at: http://www.tucows.com

2 Select your region, then the closest site.

3 Click on the category.

4 Scroll through the list, reading the description and noting the rating.

5 Click **Download** when you find a suitable application.

Location: http://www.tucows.com/

Welcome to TUCOWS

The Ultimate Collection of Winsock Software

Please Choose:
To ensure faster and more reliable downloads, please choose a site within the continent or region closest to you.

- Africa
- Asia
- Australia
- Canada
- Caribbean
- Central America
- Europe
- United States

If you would like to learn more about the benefits of hosting a TUCOWS affiliate site, click here. Welcome to TUCOWS, the

Document: Done

① Go to Tucows

Tucows has been so successful that it is now has many 'mirror' sites – places that store the same sets of pages and files. Starting from the home page, find the site closest to you – and Bookmark it for future use.

② Select a region, then a site

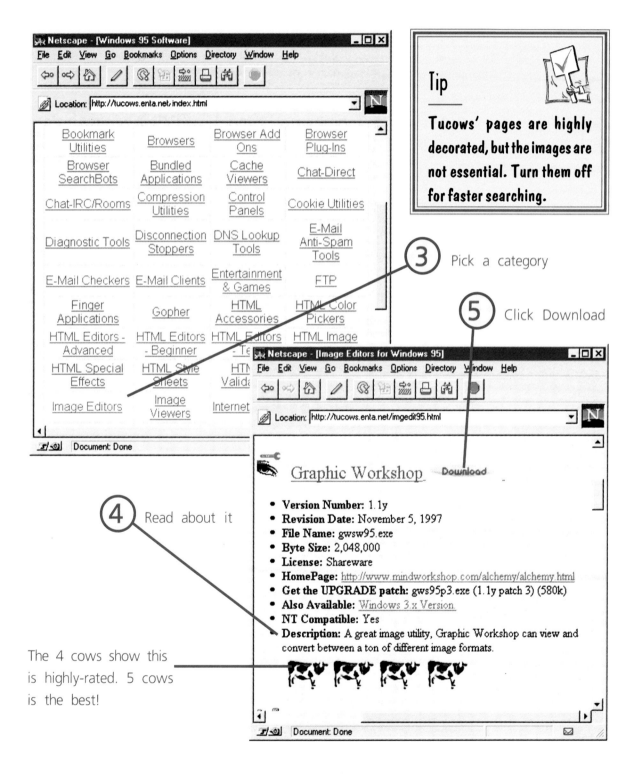

Netscape - [Windows 95 Software]

File   Edit   View   Go   Bookmarks   Options   Directory   Window   Help

Location: http://tucows.enta.net/index.html

Bookmark Utilities	Browsers	Browser Add Ons	Browser Plug-Ins
Browser SearchBots	Bundled Applications	Cache Viewers	Chat-Direct
Chat-IRC/Rooms	Compression Utilities	Control Panels	Cookie Utilities
Diagnostic Tools	Disconnection Stoppers	DNS Lookup Tools	E-Mail Anti-Spam Tools
E-Mail Checkers	E-Mail Clients	Entertainment & Games	FTP
Finger Applications	Gopher	HTML Accessories	HTML Color Pickers
HTML Editors - Advanced	HTML Editors - Beginner	HTML Editors - Te	HTML Image
HTML Special Effects	HTML Style Sheets	HTM	Valid
Image Editors	Image Viewers	Internet	

Document: Done

③ Pick a category

⑤ Click Download

Tip

Tucows' pages are highly decorated, but the images are not essential. Turn them off for faster searching.

Netscape - [Image Editors for Windows 95]

File   Edit   View   Go   Bookmarks   Options   Directory   Window   Help

Location: http://tucows.enta.net/imgedit95.html

Graphic Workshop   Download

- **Version Number:** 1.1y
- **Revision Date:** November 5, 1997
- **File Name:** gwsw95.exe
- **Byte Size:** 2,048,000
- **License:** Shareware
- **HomePage:** http://www.mindworkshop.com/alchemy/alchemy.html
- **Get the UPGRADE patch:** gws95p3.exe (1.1y patch 3) (580k)
- **Also Available:** Windows 3.x Version.
- **NT Compatible:** Yes
- **Description:** A great image utility, Graphic Workshop can view and convert between a ton of different image formats.

Document: Done

④ Read about it

The 4 cows show this is highly-rated. 5 cows is the best!

211

ZDNet Software Library

This is hosted by ZDNet, one of the Internet's great content providers. The site specialises in offering quality, rather than quantity, though over a wide area. It's a good place to look for kids' software and animated (or still) images, as well as the usual range of Internet and desktop tools and applications. The Software Library is at:

http://www.hotfiles.com

> **Take note**
>
> **ZD Net's main site is at:**
>
> http://www.zdnet.com

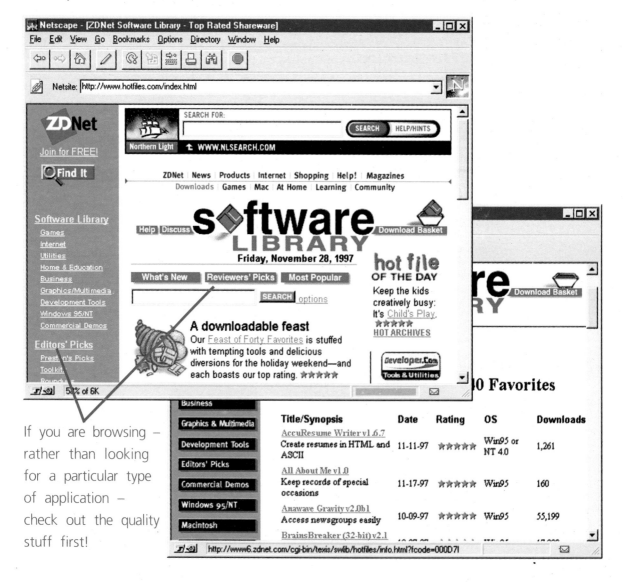

If you are browsing – rather than looking for a particular type of application – check out the quality stuff first!

clicked.com

Take note

Clicked is at:

www.clicked.com

This bills itself as an 'on-line superstore' and is included here for two reasons. First it has a Top 20 Shareware Gallery, with selected applications in each of a range of categories – making it a handy place to pick up some good stuff. Secondly, it hosts 'Baby Time', with a wealth of resources for the mother-to-be and young babies. Which goes to prove that the Internet is not just for nerds!

To go straight to the Top 20 Shareware, jump to: http://www.clicked.com/ shareware/index.html

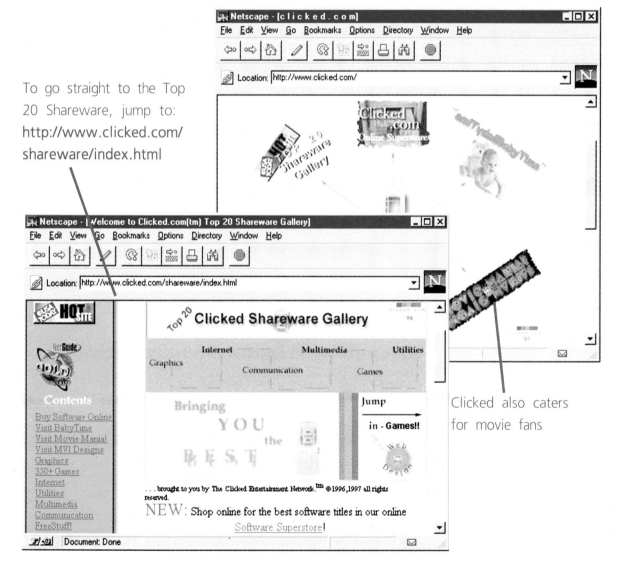

Clicked also caters for movie fans

Browsing the FTP sites

Basic steps

As you surf the Web with your browser, you may come across files that you would like to download. This can be done directly from within the browser. You can even browse through the directories at FTP sites and download from there – though this is done more efficiently with dedicated FTP software.

To find FTP sites from the Web, go to Yahoo and select *Computers and Internet – Internet – FTP sites*.

1 Click on a <u>link</u> to get to a site or go to its URL: http://*ftpsitename*

2 Enter a **directory** by clicking on its name.

3 When you find a file you want, click on it.

❑ If the browser has a suitable viewer, it will display the file. It can then be saved with **File – Save As** if wanted.

FTP icons

🔙 Parent directory – up one level

📁 Subdirectory

📄 Text – may be formatted

🗜 Compressed – usually ZIP for PCs

❓ Index or Help file

① Go an FTP site

③ Select a file

Open a directory ②

Netscape - [SUNET's Index of /ftp/pub/pc/Windows95/mirror-cica]

File   Edit   View   Go   Bookmarks   Options   Directory   Window   Help

Location: http://ftp.sunet.se/ftp/pub/pc/Windows95/mirror-cica/

Feedback   About   What's New   Search   Free Text Search

SUNET - Swedish University Network

WWW Catalog   Archie   X.500   Map   Universities

SUNET's Index of /ftp/pub/pc/Windows95/mirror-cica

Name	Last modified	Size	Description
🔙 Parent Directory	09-Mar-97 21:24	–	
❓ INDEX	26-Nov-97 11:48	417k	
🗜 INDEX.ZIP	26-Nov-97 11:48	158k	
🗜 LS-LTR.ZIP	26-Nov-97 11:48	86k	
📄 SOFTWARE.TXT	11-Mar-96 13:06	2k	
📁 access/	28-Nov-97 07:47	–	

Document: Done

❏ FTP direct

4 If you have the file's URL, you can jump straight to it with: **ftp://**_site/path/filename_

❏ Downloading

5 If the browser cannot display the file, it may go to the **Save As** dialog, or display the **Unknown File Type** dialog. Click [Save File...]

6 At the **Save As** dialog, select a folder.

7 The filename will be there already. Change it if it conflicts with an existing filename.

8 Click [Save] and wait while it downloads.

Tip

With large files, at busy times, it may be better to write down the URL and come back for it with WS_FTP. (See page 218.)

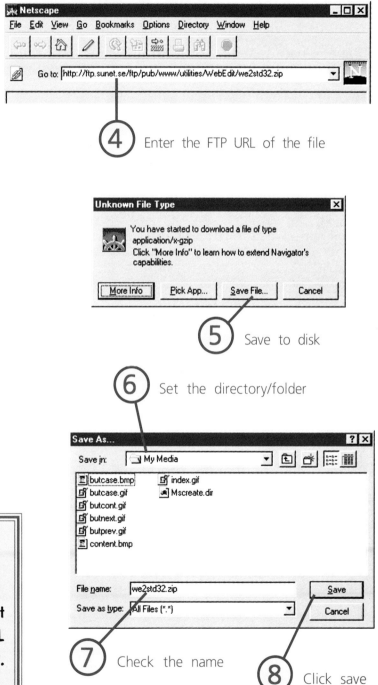

④ Enter the FTP URL of the file

⑤ Save to disk

⑥ Set the directory/folder

⑦ Check the name

⑧ Click save

215

Hypertext FTP

Some FTP sites now have proper Web pages for simpler access to their files. The big advantage here is that instead of having bare FTP directory listings, you can have an indexed system with descriptions of the files – this can save some wasted downloads!

Oakland University's Software Repository is a good example of an established FTP site that now offers an excellent Web interface. It is a mirror (identical copy) of the massive SimTel Coast to Coast Software Repository, hosts some specialist collections, has links to c|net's Virtual Software Library and has its own databanks.

1 Go to Oak at: http://ww.acs.oakland.edu/oak/oak.html

2 Select the collection (at Simtel.Net you will have to go down two more levels).

3 Pick a letter to get into the index.

4 Scroll through and select a category.

5 Browse the files and download as usual.

① Go to Oak   ② Select a collection

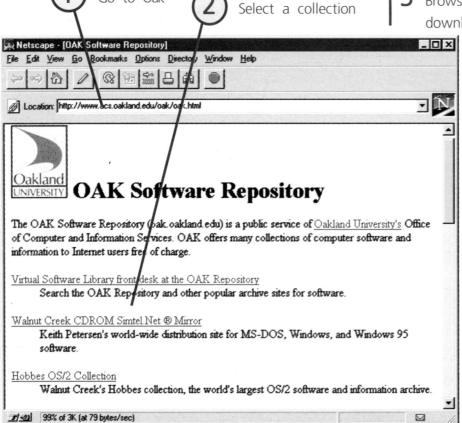

216

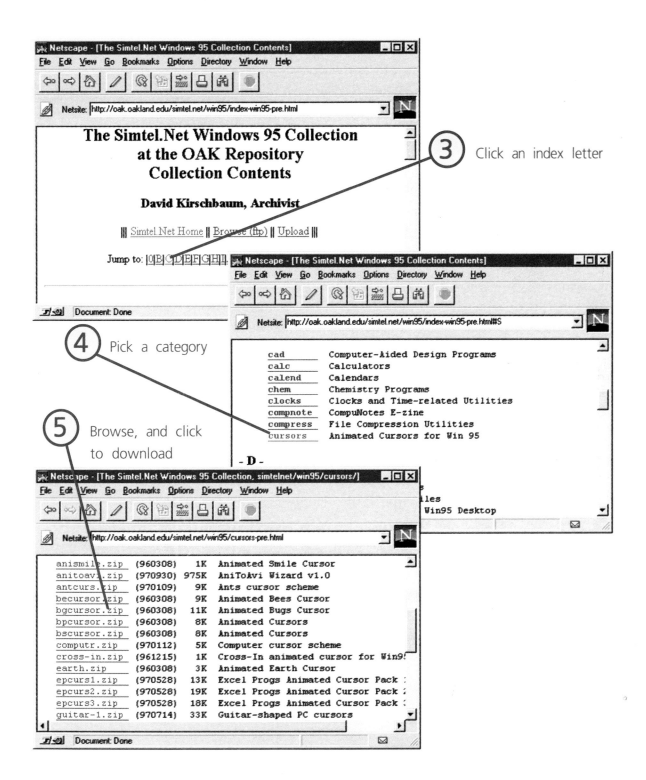

3 Click an index letter

4 Pick a category

5 Browse, and click to download

WS_FTP

If you use the FTP sites a lot, or you want to upload files, you should get some dedicated FTP software. WS_FTP is probably the best of these – and it's free. There are several versions of WS_FTP. The one illustrated here is for Windows 95. Get a copy from the author's (John Junod) home site at:

ftp://ftp2.ipswitch.com/pub/win32

or from any good shareware site. Amongst other places, you'll find it in the Internet section at:

http://www.shareware.com

WS_FTP is a *Winsock compliant* program, which means you must have Winsock running – and be logged on to your service provider before you can use it. If you have Windows 95, Winsock is built into the Dial-Up Networking.

Anonymous login

When connecting to an FTP site, you normally give 'anonymous' as the user name and your e-mail address as the password. This is known as **anonymous login**. The main exception is when you use FTP to upload your home page files to your access provider's site. Then, you will give the same User ID and password that you use when logging in at the start of a normal session.

With WS_FTP, you give your e-mail address during the installation process, so it is in place when needed in setting up a new connection.

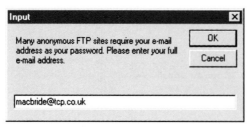

Tip

You can run **WS_FTP** alongside your browser, or by itself. The only essential is that you are logged onto the Internet.

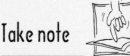

Take note

You must know the exact host name. If you also know the path to the directory, it speeds things up. If you do not give it, you will start at the top of the directory structure and have to work your way down.

218

Basic steps

1 Go on-line then run WS_FTP.

2 Pick a site from the **Profile** list – there are a dozen already set up.

or

3 Create a profile for a new site. Click ⏵New⏴ and enter a profile name and the exact **Host name**.

4 If this uses the (normal) anonymous login, tick **Anonymous**.

5 Switch to the **Startup** tab and enter the **Remote Host Directory**, if known.

6 Click ⏵Apply⏴ if you have set up a new profile, or made changes that you want to keep.

7 Click ⏵OK⏴ to start the connection.

Making the connection

WS_FTP is simple enough to use – just tell it where you want to go, and what directory to start at, then send it off to make the connection.

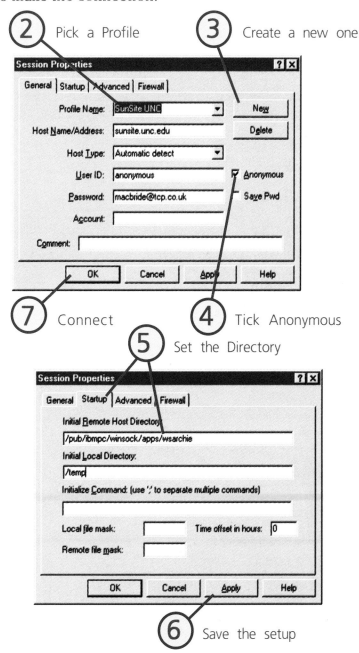

② Pick a Profile

③ Create a new one

⑦ Connect

④ Tick Anonymous

⑤ Set the Directory

⑥ Save the setup

Working at an FTP site

FTP gives you a two-way, interactive connection to the remote host. You can treat its directories and files as if they were in a drive in your own machine – almost.

● Downloading is like copying a file from another disk – but much slower. Be patient.

● If you want to upload a file, only do so into a directory that welcomes contributions – if you can't see one called UPLOADS, they probably don't want your files.

● Don't delete or edit files or directories on the Host – it shouldn't let you, but it might have let its guard slip.

WS_FTP options

There are a whole set of options that you can set to fine-tune WS_FTP to your way of working. Most can be safely left at their defaults until you have been using it for some time, but there is one that you should check.

It's very easy to double-click by mistake. What do you want to happen when you do this? Go to the **Advanced** tab, and select the **Double Click Action.**

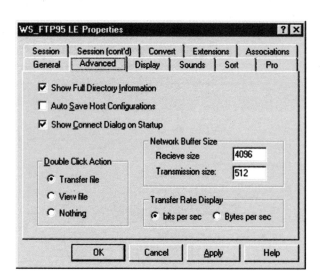

❏ **Downloading**

1 Change directory if need be – use the same techniques as in any File Manager.

2 Highlight a file that interests you.

3 Set the directory on your local system to receive a file.

4 Opt for **ASCII** to transfer text files, **Binary** for any others.

5 Click ← to download.

6 Use Close to return to the first panel and set up a new session.

7 Click Exit to end.

220

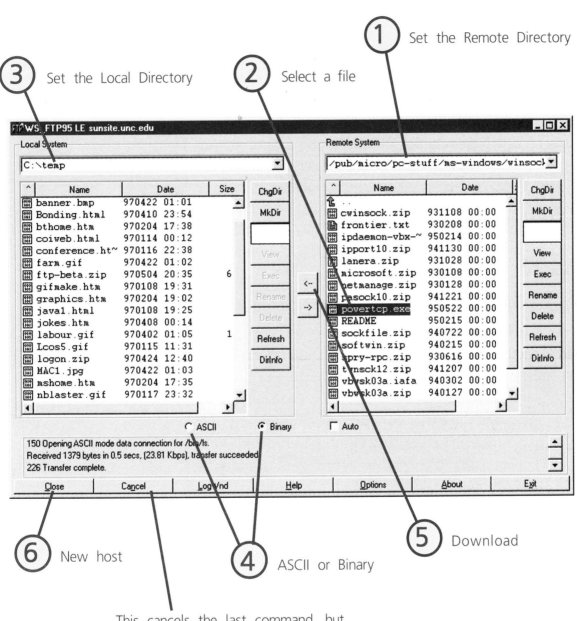

① Set the Remote Directory

③ Set the Local Directory

② Select a file

⑤ Download

⑥ New host

④ ASCII or Binary

This cancels the last command, but
leaves you still connected to the host

Archie

Browsing FTP sites is not an efficient way to find a file. You will find it far quicker if you know where to look, and for this you need Archie.

Scattered over the Internet are a number of hosts that act as Archie servers. Each of these has a database of the directory listings of major FTP sites, and a program for searching that database. The Archie servers know the names, locations, sizes and dates of last update of the files of those sites, though they do not know what is in the files, what type they are or what they do.

Search types

Archie can use one of four different matching methods as it searches its database.

Substring: Looks for the given string within the names of files and directories – and the more you can give, the better. For example, a search for Paint Shop Pro (graphics software) with '**psp**' produces nearly 100 hits, including 'crystalswa**psp**eedup.txt' and '**psp**lan.ps.Z'. Trying with '**pspro**' gets around 20 hits, including 'XD**PSpro**to.h', 's**pspro**g.txt' and '**pspro**41.zip' – the Paint Shop Pro package.

Substring (case sensitive): As substring, but matching lower/upper case characters exactly as given. '**pspro**' would not find 'XD**PSpro**to.h' (good), but equally, '**PSPRO**' would not find '**pspro**40.zip' (bad).

Exact: Looks for an exact match (including case). This gets results fastest, but you must know precisely what you want. If you are looking for shareware or beta-test software, this approach may miss the latest versions. For example, the latest beta of Netscape at

Take note

You can get dedicated software to run Archie searches — WsArchie is excellent — but unless you want to find an awful lot of files, it is much simpler to access Archie through the Web.

222

the time of writing was '**n32e40b4.exe**', but searching for this now will give you an out-of-date copy. A substring search for '**n32e**' will be more productive.

Regex: Use *regular expressions* when matching. These are similar to DOS wildcards. But not that similar – the differences are significant.

Regular expressions

The wildcard '.' (dot) stands for any single character. This was a rotten choice, as dot is an essential part of most filenames. If you want to use dot for its proper meaning – not as a wildcard – put a backslash in front of it '\.'

'winzip\.exe' will find the file 'winzip.exe'

'winzip.exe' will look for 'winzip**A**exe', 'winzip**B**exe', etc. and probably find nothing!

'*' is a repeater, standing for any number of whatever character was written before it. 'A*' means any number of A's. Use '.*' to stand for any set of any characters.

'babel**.***txt' will look for files that start with 'babel', end with 'txt' and have something (or nothing) in between.

You can specify a set of alternative single characters by enclosing them in square brackets – '[...]'

'babel97[**ab**]\.txt' will find 'babel97**a**.txt' and 'babel97**b**.txt'

● Ranges can be defined with '-', e.g. [**A-F**] is the same as [**ABCDEF**];

● '^' at the start of a range means match characters that are *not* in the list, e.g. [**^A-Z**] means ignore all capitals.

Archie through the Web

To run an Archie search from your browser, go to Yahoo and select *Computers and Internet – Internet – FTP Sites – Searching:Archie*. There you will find a number of links labelled Archie Request Form or Archie Gateway.

Basic steps

1 Go to an **Archie Request Form.**

2 Enter the search string.

3 Set the **Database** to Anonymous FTP.

4 Select the **Search Type.**

5 Set the **Case.**

6 Start the search.

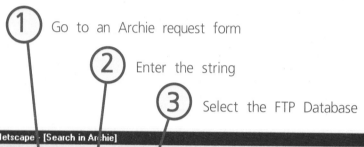

① Go to an Archie request form

② Enter the string

③ Select the FTP Database

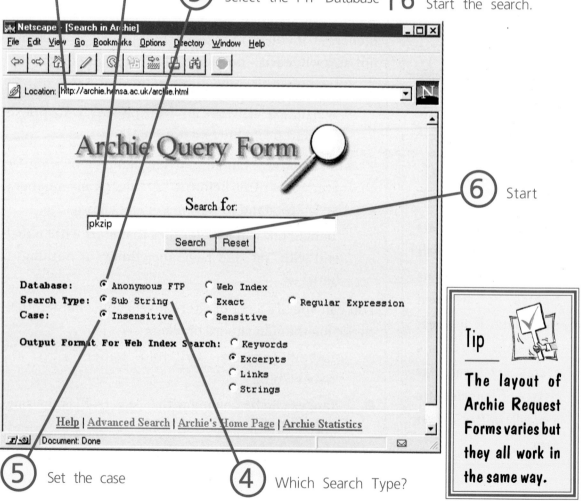

⑥ Start

⑤ Set the case

④ Which Search Type?

Tip

The layout of Archie Request Forms varies but they all work in the same way.

Files from an Archie Gateway

7 Scroll through the results to find the file.

8 Click on a filename to download the file.

❏ If the site or directory is linked, you can go to it to browse for files.

If your Archie search is productive, you will get a page or more listing the results. Here you will see the FTP sites, directories and name of the matching files. Sometimes all of these will be hyperlinked; sometimes there will only be a link to the file itself.

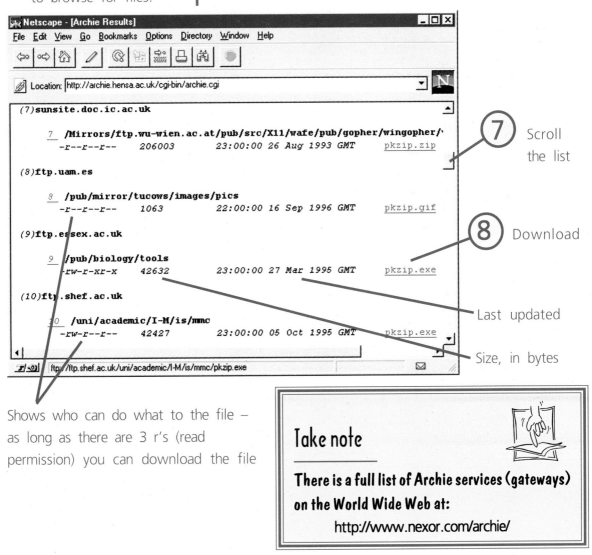

Scroll the list

Download

Last updated

Size, in bytes

Shows who can do what to the file – as long as there are 3 r's (read permission) you can download the file

Take note

There is a full list of Archie services (gateways) on the World Wide Web at:

http://www.nexor.com/archie/

Summary

- c|net runs **Software Central**, where it holds shareware, freeware, commercial software and updates.

- **shareware.com**, another c|net service, has a large collection of shareware – and an excellent search facility to help you find the programs you want.

- One of the biggest organised collections of shareware is at **Jumbo**.

- **Tucows** has the most complete collection of **Winsock applications**.

- **ZDnet** has a smaller collection of good software and other files, selected with the home user in mind.

- If you are starting to build a software collection, the **Top 20 Shareware Gallery** at **clicked.com** is a good place to start.

- You can reach the **FTP sites**, travel through their directories and download **through your Web browser**.

- If you want to download files regularly, it is worth getting and learning to use **WS_FTP**. With this you can download faster and more efficiently.

- **Archie** is a program for searching for files in the Internet's FTP archives. It lives, alongside its database, on **Archie servers**.

- Archie searches can be for **Exact** or **Substring** matches, or can use **regular expressions**.

- You can reach **Archie servers through the Web**, and run your searches there.

13 Viewers

Viewers and Helpers

Much of the material that is on the Web can be viewed directly through the browser without any special configuration. Both Netscape and Internet Explorer have built-in routines to handle GIF and JPG files – the graphics formats most commonly-used on the Web – and Media Player and other plug-ins for audio and video files.

There are interesting files on the Web that the browser cannot handle. TIF and BMP graphics, Word documents and PostScript files are all quite common. If you want to view these, you have to turn to other applications. If you have the programs, they can be linked into Netscape as Helper applications, so that they can be launched and used within the browser.

This linking can be done when you first come across a file of the right type.

Basic steps

❏ On-line configuring

1 Right click on the image icon.

2 Select **View** from the short menu.

3 At the **Unknown File Type**, click **Pick App...**

4 Type the path and file-name or click **Browse**.

5 Locate the program and click **Open**.

❏ The application will run and display the file. Next time it meets the same type, Netscape will know what to do.

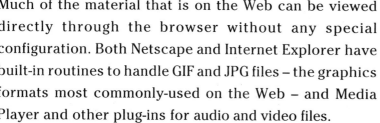

① Right click the icon

② Select View

③ Click Pick App

④ Browse for the program

Take note

With Internet Explorer, programs are linked in through the File Types of _Windows_ Explorer!

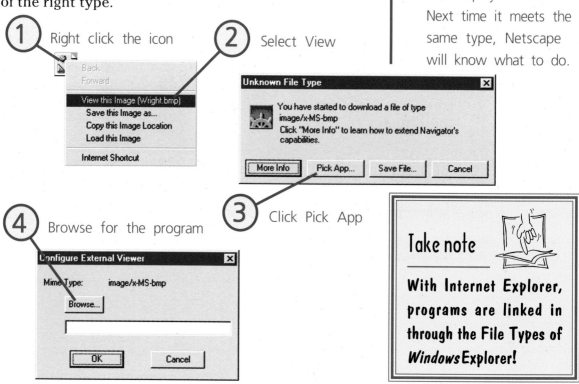

228

Basic steps

1 From the **Options** menu select **General Preferences**.

2 Switch to **Helpers**.

3 Select a file type marked **Ask User** for which you have suitable software.

4 Click **Browse**.

5 Switch to the application's folder.

6 Locate the program file and click **Open**.

Linking in Helpers

You may prefer to set up Helpers before you start browsing. Check through the file types listed in the **Helpers** panel (the Applications panel in Navigator 4.0). If you find any marked *Ask User*, that you can view with other applications on your system, link those applications in as Helpers.

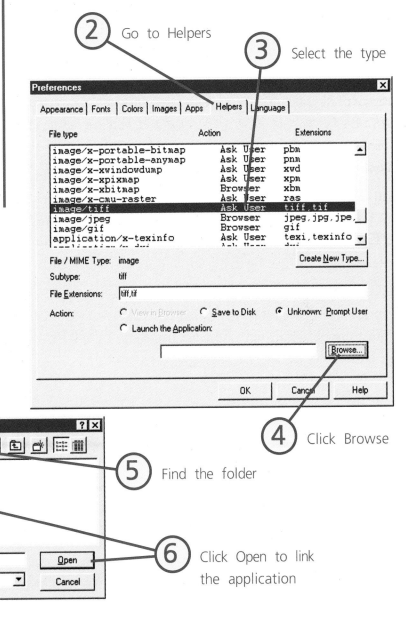

2 Go to Helpers

3 Select the type

4 Click Browse

5 Find the folder

6 Click Open to link the application

Viewers for graphics

If you need an application that can handle a wide range of graphic formats – viewing, converting between formats, resizing, enhancing and otherwise manipulating – here are a couple of packages that deserve a closer look, LView Pro and Paint Shop Pro.

LView Pro

This is the smaller of the two. It has a similar set of editing and retouching tools, but cannot cope with as wide a range of file formats. LView can read and save graphics in JPG, BMP, DIB, GIF, TGA, PCX, PPN and TIFF formats. This should be enough to cope with the majority of images that you will meet on the Web.

At the time of writing, it was available on the Net as LViewp1d2.zip, a 300Kb file. To install it, you simply set up a folder and unzip it. The whole lot takes less than 700Kb of disk space, with the program being just over 500Kb. By today's standards, that is compact.

If your main interest is in viewing files, and you would also like to experiment with editing graphics, LView Pro is a good choice.

Take note

LView Pro is shareware, but there is no charge if you only want to use it for personal, leisure purposes. You can find copies in the major shareware sites.

JPG and GIF

❑ The **JPG** extension identifies a file in JPEG (Joint Photographic Experts Group) format. A JPG file can handle graphics as 256 greyscales or 24-bit colour. If you start with a 16 or 256 colour bitmap, it will have to upgrade it to 16 million colours.

❑ **GIF** (Graphic Information Format) is a standard developed by CompuServe. It is limited to a maximum of 256 colours.

❑ Both have built-in compression, with JPGs being usually, but not always, more compact – typically half to one-fifth of the size of the equivalent GIF.

❑ At the end of the day, the quality of the viewed image depends mainly on the quality of the original file.

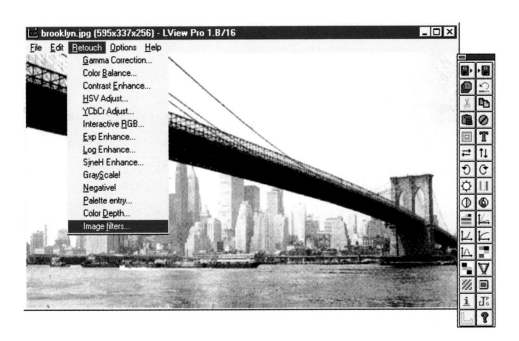

The image filters work by taking each point of colour and combining it in various ways with the surrounding points. It is a slow process – a picture the size of the one above will take several minutes, even on a fast machine – not something to be attempted on-line! 9 filters are pre-defined, and you can set the matrices for your own filters. It helps if you understand the maths, but trial and error will also get you there.

LView Pro has a full set of tools for adjusting colour, adding text, cropping, copying, rotating and mirroring. Most are fairly easy to use, and there is a brief but adequate Help system.

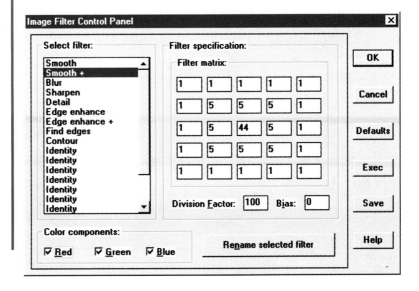

Paint Shop Pro

This is a much more substantial package than Lview Pro. The latest version (4.1) is on the Net as psp41.zip – a 2.7Mb file. This unzips to reveal a SETUP program and a further zipped file. SETUP will install it to its own directory, taking just under 7Mb of space. The EXE file and its DLLs add up to nearly 3Mb, making this slower to load than LView, and therefore less suitable for use as a viewer.

On the positive side, Paint Shop Pro has excellent editing facilities and is easier to use than Lview. Its approach to filters is a good example of this. Using the Filter Browser, you can preview the effect quickly and clearly, before applying a filter. Routines for defining filter matrices are also present, for more experienced users.

Take note

Paint Shop Pro can cope with just about every graphic format from WordPerfect graphics to Kodak PhotoCD.

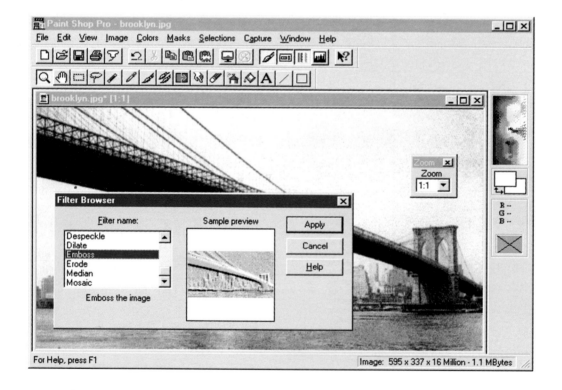

Basic steps

Batch conversion

1 Open the **File** menu and select **Batch Conversion**.

2 Set the **Input File Type**.

3 Set the **Output type**.

Either

4 Hold **[Control]** and click files to select them, then press **OK**.

or

5 Click **Select All**.

If you have a set of files in one format that you want to convert to another, they can be processed all at once through the batch conversion facility.

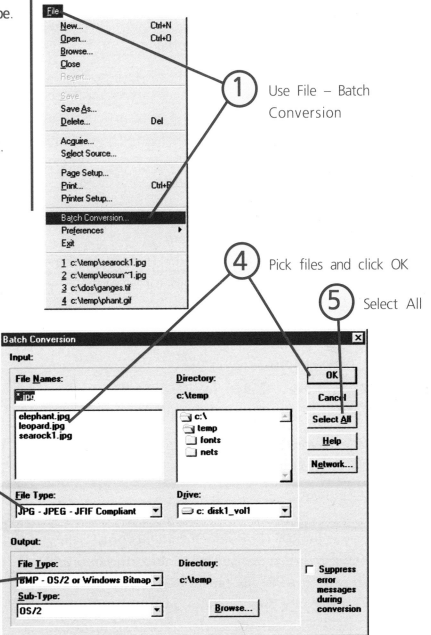

Use File – Batch Conversion

Set the Input File Type ...

and the Output File Type

Pick files and click OK

Select All

Text viewers

Much of the text that is on the Web is in HTML format – ideal for browsers; much of the text elsewhere on the Internet is plain ASCII text, that can be read with any editor or word-processor. However, there are also quite a few formatted text files out there, and the two most common formats are Word and Acrobat.

Microsoft Word

This is probably the most widely used word-processor at present, and you will find many Word-formatted documents on the Net. If you do not have Microsoft Word, you can read these using the free Word Viewer.

Get it through the Web at:

http://www.microsoft.com/MSWord

This is the Word page at Microsoft's site. Head for the **Free stuff**, or use the **Search** facility to look for 'Viewer'.

If you prefer, you can get it by FTP from:

ftp://ftp.microsoft.com/Softlib/Mslfiles

There are two versions:

wd95vw71.exe   (2.2Mb) for Windows 95

wordvu.exe   (1.2Mb) for DOS/Windows 3.1

These are self-extracting ZIP files. Run to open them up, then run SETUP.EXE to install them.

Acrobat

This is a viewer for PDF (Portable Document Format) files, a cross-platform format devised by Adobe – the Fonts and PageMaker people. A PDF file can be viewed on a Windows or DOS PC, a Mac or a Unix machine, and will always look the same – as long as suitable reader software is installed.

Take note

If you have an early version of Word, you may still need the Word Viewer to be able to read some files. Windows 95 users are moving over to Word 7.0 and Word 97, which have features that cannot be handled by earlier versions.

Tip

After you've been to the trouble of downloading your viewer, don't forget to link it into your browser as a Helper application!

Get your copy from the Web at:

http://www.adobe.com

and look for the Acrobat Reader for Windows; or by FTP:

ftp.adobe.com/pub/adobe/Applications/Acrobat/Windows

and download 'acroread.exe'. Run this to extract the files and install them into an Acrobat directory in one operation.

There is a set of control buttons for zooming in and out, changing pages, printing and searching for items.

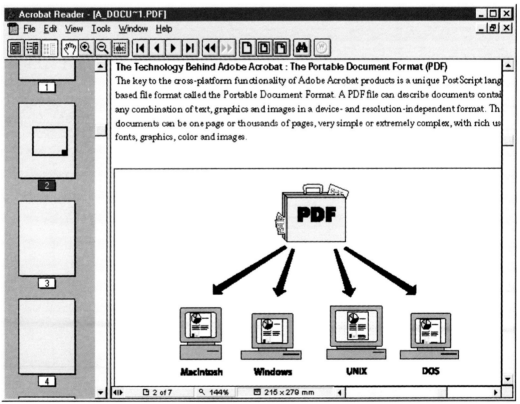

Use this panel to move through the pages, or turn it off for a larger viewing area.

PDF files are quite compact. This 7-page document, with three illustrations, was 127Kb.

Ghostview & Ghostscript

PostScript is another common document format. If you have access to a suitable printer, PostScript files present no problems. Simply download them, then pass them directly to the printer. You may not be able to view them on screen, but at least you can get paper copies.

If you do not have a PostScript printer, the answer lies in GhostScript. This can read PostScript files and convert them for screen display – and for output to other printers. Ghostview, its companion program, is a graphical interface to Ghostscript – making it far simpler to use.

Take note

PostScript files are often used for technical diagrams, music scores and other documents with a mixture of text and drawings.

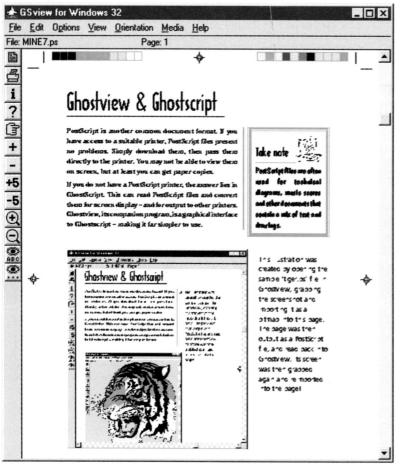

This illustration was created by opening the sample 'tiger.ps' file in Ghostview, grabbing the screenshot and importing it as a bitmap into this page. The page was then output as a PostScript file, and read back into Ghostview. Its screen was then grabbed again and reimported into the page!

Getting and setting up

At the time of writing, the latest versions were Ghostview 2.4, and Ghostscript 5.10. Updates are posted onto the Internet regularly, so check the numbering and the dates before you download. You will need the following ZIPped files – about 2Mb in total.

gsview24.zip	Ghostview for Windows
gs510ini.zip	the core Ghostscript routines
gs510fn1.zip	PostScript fonts

plus one of:

gs510dos.zip	(MS-DOS 32-bit)
gs510os2.zip	(OS/2)
gs510w32.zip	(Win32s, Win95, WinNT)

If you have a full set of Type 1 fonts, you do not need gs510fn1.zip.

The latest versions can be found at:

ftp://ftp.cs.wisc.edu/ghost/aladdin/   (Ghostscript)
ftp://ftp.cs.wisc.edu/ghost/rjl/   (Ghostview)

And check out their Web page at:

http://www.cs.wisc.edu/~ghost/index.html

There is a setup program in the 'gsview' file, plus detailed instructions in case the automatic installation doesn't work properly! When unpacked the files will take up around 6Mb of disk space, but this includes nearly 1Mb of samples and documentation which can be removed after viewing, leaving a core of just under 5Mb.

Take note

You can run Ghostscript without Ghostview, but not the other way round. Ghostscript uses complex command lines to load and interpret files; Ghostview gives you simple menu and icon controls and converts these into commands which it then passes to Ghostscript.

Multimedia

I do not think that multimedia is a particularly hot topic in the current state of Internet technology. You cannot view videos or listen to sound files in real time (though Netscape's Live Audio almost manages it), because the data simply cannot get down the line fast enough. Unless you are working for a company that has its own ISDN (high-speed, dedicated line) link into the Net, you cannot access it at faster than 56,600 baud. And this is at a quiet time on a good day!

Multimedia files have to be downloaded before they can be viewed. At present, download rates are typically around 1Kb a second. Sound files are rarely less than 100Kb, and video files rarely less than 1Mb – and ones worth viewing are often much larger. It means that it will take at best two minutes, and at worst over an hour, for the file to come in. You can browse elsewhere while this is happening, but that makes it take even longer to download.

However, if you really do want to browse in multimedia mode, you will need a viewer. Windows has *mplayer* for AVI files, but to see the more common MOV and MPG files you will need either *Vmpeg* or *Quicktime*. Both are regularly given away free on magazine-front CDs, and can be found at most Web shareware and ftp sites.

Take note

Quicktime installs itself as **PLAYER.EXE** (audio/video) and **VIEWER.EXE** (JPGs) in the **WINDOWS** directory, plus other files in **WINDOWS/SYSTEM**.

Tip

When you use an external viewer, the Web browser downloads the file into your temporary directory – /**DOS** or /**WINDOWS**/**TEMP**. Make this your viewer's startup directory, so that it can find the file!

Vmpeg is a compact package – around 350Kb installed – and can be configured to get the best out of both video and audio files.

Basic steps

1 Run Netscape.

2 Select **About Plug-ins** from the **Help** menu.

3 See what's there.

4 If you need more, get on-line and use the **click here** link to go to Netscape's plug-in page.

5 Download and install the missing plug-ins.

Plug-ins extend Netscape's ability to cope with different file formats. The full Netscape package has a core set, including Media Player, Shockwave, Live 3D and Live Audio. These should be enough for most purposes. If you come across a page that needs a plug-in that you do not have, you should get a message like this.

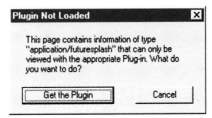

Click **Get the Plug-in** to download the software.

Run Netscape ④ Get more plug-ins

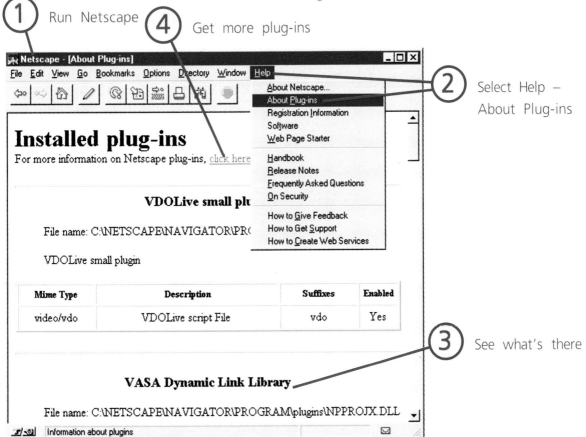

Select Help – About Plug-ins

See what's there

Summary

- **Viewers and helper** applications can be linked into your browser to enable you to view a greater variety of files.

- With **Internet Explorer**, applications are linked to file types using the standard Windows Explorer routines.

- **Lview Pro** is a compact and efficient viewer/editor that can handle the main graphics formats.

- **Paint Shop Pro** is probably the most comprehensive graphics shareware program available at present. It can cope with almost every graphics format and has an extensive set of easy-to-use editing tools.

- Though most text is plain ASCII, some documents are formatted.

- A **Word Viewer** will let you read Word documents, if you do not have Microsoft Word.

- The **Acrobat Reader** is needed to read PDF files.

- **Ghostview** and **Ghostscript** are needed to display and print **PostScript** files.

- **Multimedia** files tend to be large and take a long time to download. If you are keen on audio/video and have the patience to wait for them, you can link **Vmpeg** or **Quicktime** to view them.

- Netscape has **plug-ins** to extend the range of files that can be viewed.

240

14 Creating Web pages

HTML

Most access providers now offer to their customers the facilities to set up their own home pages. People use them to advertise their work, their products, their clubs, their hobbies – themselves!

HTML – HyperText Markup Language – is the system used to produce Web pages. Essentially, it is a set of tags (codes) that specify text styles, draw lines, display images, handle URL links and the other features that create Web pages. It is not difficult to use. There are only a limited number of tags and they follow fairly strict rules. All tags are enclosed in <angle brackets> to mark them off from the text, and they are normally used in pairs – one at the start and one at the end of the text that they affect. For example:

<H1> **This is a main heading** </H1>

Notice that the closing tag is the same as the opener, except that it has a forward slash at the start.

All pages have the same outline structure:

```
<HTML>
<HEAD>
    <TITLE>My Gnome Page</TITLE>
</HEAD>
<BODY>
    This page is under construction
</BODY>
</HTML>
```

> **Indenting is optional, but can make it easier to read**

The whole text is enclosed by <HTML> and </HTML> tags.

The <HEAD> area holds information about the page, and is not displayed – though the Title does appear in the browser's Title bar when loaded. This can be left blank.

The <BODY> area is where the main code goes.

Basic steps

1 Type your HTML text into NotePad (or any word-processor).

2 Save it with an '.HTM' extension, e.g. 'MYPAGE.HTM'.

3 Start your browser – don't go on-line – and use Open File to load in the document.

4 Check the display and return to NotePad to enhance and improve!

Take note

You can soon learn how to write Web pages using a word-processor, but it's even easier with an HTML editor. There is a good one in Netscape Gold – renamed as Composer in Communicator (Chapter 15) – and the Internet Explorer CD-ROM has FrontPage Express (Chapter 16).

242

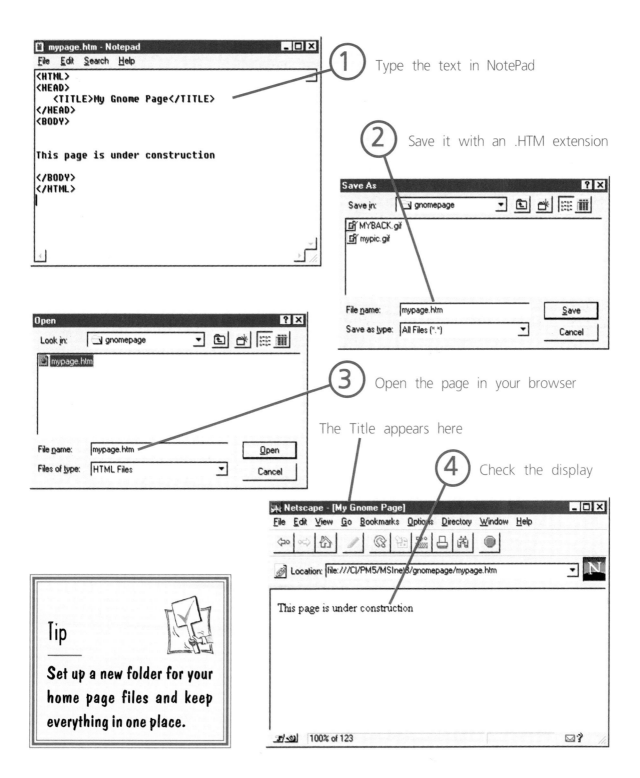

Type the text in NotePad

Save it with an .HTM extension

Open the page in your browser

The Title appears here

Check the display

Tip

Set up a new folder for your home page files and keep everything in one place.

Text tags

The simplest tags are the ones that format text. These will produce six levels of headings, a small, italicised style (mainly used for e-mail addresses), and bold and italic for emphasis.

<H1>	</H1>	# Heading 1
<H2>	</H2>	## Heading 2
<H3>	</H3>	### Heading 3
<H4>	</H4>	Heading 4
<H5>	</H5>	Heading 5
<H6>	</H6>	Heading 6
Untagged text		Plain
<B>	</B>	**Bold**
<I>	</I>	*Italic*
<Address>	</Address>	*Small italic style*

> Actual fonts and sizes depend on the browser, but the relative sizes stay the same.

The Heading and Address tags break the text up into separate lines, but untagged text appears as a continuous stream – no matter how you lay it out in NotePad. Create separate paragraphs with these tags:

<P>	Start a new paragaph
</P>	End of paragraph (optional)
 	Line break – use to create larger gaps

When a browser reads an HTML document, it ignores all spaces (apart from a single space between words), tabs and new lines. What this means is that it doesn't matter how you layout your HTML text. You can indent it, and add line breaks to make it easier for you to read, but it won't affect what your readers see – only the tags affect the layout of the page in the browser.

Tip

If you come across a great Web page and want to know how it was created, use the View Document Source command to see the HTML code.

If you want to use someone else's page as a model for your own, use File Save As to save it on your hard disk. You can then open it in NotePad and edit it. Any images in the page must be saved separately.

```
<HTML>
<HEAD>
  <TITLE>My Gnome Page</TITLE>
</HEAD>
<BODY>
  <H1>My Gnome Page</H1>
  <H3>Hello and welcome</H3>
  <H2>Gnomic sayings</H2>
  <P>Every gnome should have one.</P>
  <P>There's gno place like Gnome. (Old Alaskan proverb)</P>
  <P>Gnome is where the heart is.</P>
  <H2>Gnome computing</H2>
  Lots of links to go here!
  <BR>
  <H4>This page is under construction</H4>
  <ADDRESS>Ingrid Bottomlow </ADDRESS>
  <ADDRESS>Last Update: Mudday of this week</ADDRESS>
</BODY>
</HTML>
```

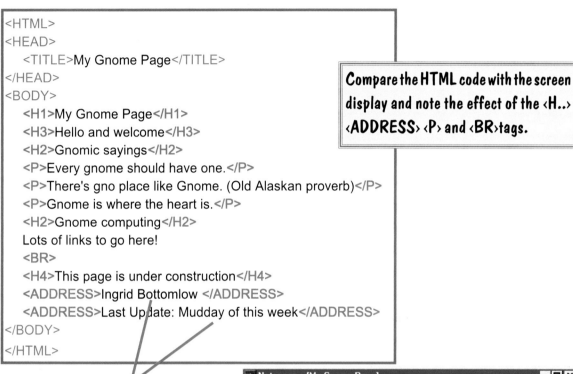

Compare the HTML code with the screen display and note the effect of the ‹H..› ‹ADDRESS› ‹P› and ‹BR›tags.

Why do each of these lines have to have tags at either end? What would happen if both were enclosed in a single set of <ADDRESS> </ADDRESS> tags?

Tip

Pages that consist only of text are fast to download — and sensible use of headings will make them attractive to your readers.

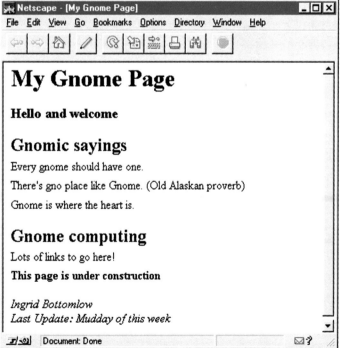

Netscape - [My Gnome Page]

File   Edit   View   Go   Bookmarks   Options   Directory   Window   Help

My Gnome Page

Hello and welcome

Gnomic sayings

Every gnome should have one.

There's gno place like Gnome. (Old Alaskan proverb)

Gnome is where the heart is.

Gnome computing

Lots of links to go here!

This page is under construction

Ingrid Bottomlow
Last Update: Mudday of this week

Document: Done

Colours

Text-only pages are fast to load, but can be a bit boring. Colour will add impact to your screens, without adding to the loading time.

Colours are defined by the values of their Red, Blue and Green components – given in that order and in hexadecimal digits. These values can be anything from 00 to FF, but are best set at 00 (off), 80 (half) or FF (full power), e.g.:

FFFF00

gives Red and Green at full, with no Blue, resulting in Yellow. Combinations of 00, 80 and FF values should come out true on all screens – other values may not.

BODY colors

The colours of the background and text of the page can be set by the BGCOLOR and TEXT options in the BODY tag.

`<BODY BGCOLOR = "#FFFFFF" TEXT = "#008000">`

This sets the background to White and the text to Dark Green.

Values are normally enclosed in "quotes" with a # at the start to show that they are hexadecimal. These can be omitted TEXT = **008000** works just as well.

FONT COLOR

At any point on the page, you can change the colour of the text with the tag:

`<FONT COLOR = "#Value" >`

The colour is used for all following text until it is reset with another <FONT COLOR = ... > tag. You can use it to pick out words within normal text – though you can get strange results if you use the tags inside Headings.

Simple colour values

R	G	B	Colour
00	00	00	Black
80	80	80	Grey
FF	FF	FF	White
00	00	80	Navy Blue
00	00	FF	Blue
00	80	00	Green
00	FF	00	Lime
80	00	00	Maroon
FF	00	00	Red
00	80	80	Turquoise
80	00	80	Purple
80	80	00	Olive
00	FF	FF	Aqua
FF	00	FF	Fuchsia
FF	FF	00	Yellow

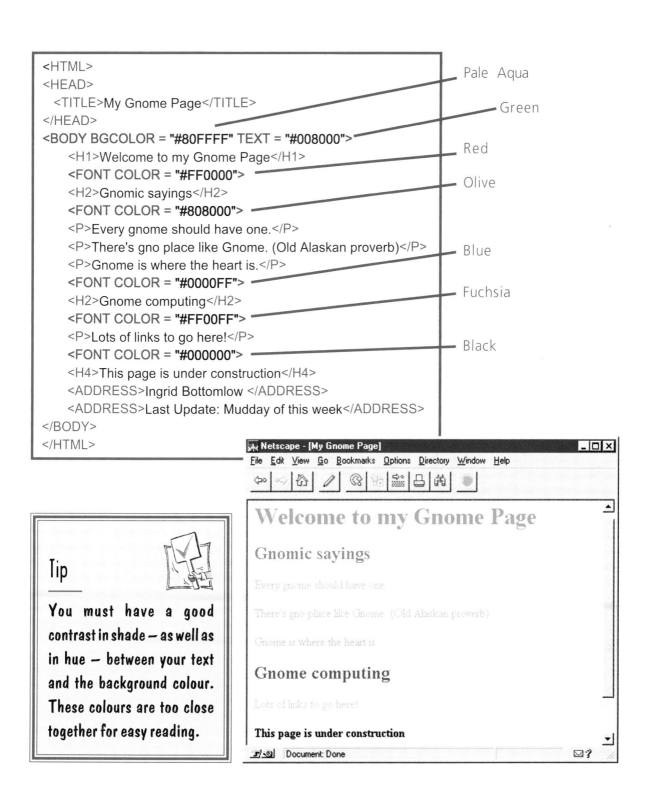

```
<HTML>
<HEAD>
  <TITLE>My Gnome Page</TITLE>
</HEAD>
<BODY BGCOLOR = "#80FFFF" TEXT = "#008000">
    <H1>Welcome to my Gnome Page</H1>
    <FONT COLOR = "#FF0000">
    <H2>Gnomic sayings</H2>
    <FONT COLOR = "#808000">
    <P>Every gnome should have one.</P>
    <P>There's gno place like Gnome. (Old Alaskan proverb)</P>
    <P>Gnome is where the heart is.</P>
    <FONT COLOR = "#0000FF">
    <H2>Gnome computing</H2>
    <FONT COLOR = "#FF00FF">
    <P>Lots of links to go here!</P>
    <FONT COLOR = "#000000">
    <H4>This page is under construction</H4>
    <ADDRESS>Ingrid Bottomlow </ADDRESS>
    <ADDRESS>Last Update: Mudday of this week</ADDRESS>
</BODY>
</HTML>
```

Pale Aqua

Green

Red

Olive

Blue

Fuchsia

Black

Tip

You must have a good contrast in shade — as well as in hue — between your text and the background colour. These colours are too close together for easy reading.

Netscape - [My Gnome Page]

File Edit View Go Bookmarks Options Directory Window Help

Welcome to my Gnome Page

Gnomic sayings

Every gnome should have one

There's gno place like Gnome. (Old Alaskan proverb)

Gnome is where the heart is

Gnome computing

Lots of links to go here!

This page is under construction

Document: Done

247

Lists and lines

Here are two more ways to enhance the appearance of your pages, without adding to download time.

Lists

These come in two varieties – bulleted and numbered. Both types are constructed in the same way.

- <UL> </UL> (unordered/bulleted) or <OL> </OL> (ordered/numbered) enclose the whole list.

- Each item in the list is enclosed by <LI> </LI> tags,

e.g.

```
<UL>
 <LI> List item </LI>
 <LI> List item </LI>
 <LI> List item </LI>
</UL>
```

Lines

Also called Horizontal Rules, these are created with the tag <HR>. This is a single tag – there is no </HR> to end it. A simple <HR> produces a thin line with an indented effect. For variety, use the options:

SIZE to set the thickness. This is measured in pixels.

WIDTH can also be set in pixels, but is best given as a percentage of the width of the window – you don't know how wide your readers' windows will be.

NOSHADE makes the line solid.

You can see examples of all of these opposite.

Take note

Bullets are normally round. You can set the style to SQUARE, DISK or ROUND with the TYPE option, e.g.

<UL TYPE = DISK>

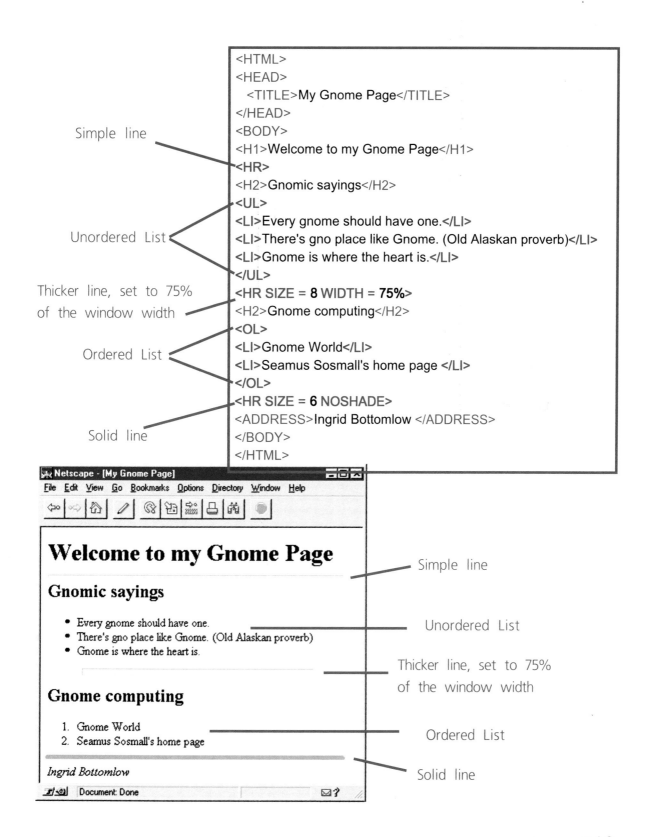

Simple line

Unordered List

Thicker line, set to 75% of the window width

Ordered List

Solid line

```
<HTML>
<HEAD>
  <TITLE>My Gnome Page</TITLE>
</HEAD>
<BODY>
<H1>Welcome to my Gnome Page</H1>
<HR>
<H2>Gnomic sayings</H2>
<UL>
<LI>Every gnome should have one.</LI>
<LI>There's gno place like Gnome. (Old Alaskan proverb)</LI>
<LI>Gnome is where the heart is.</LI>
</UL>
<HR SIZE = 8 WIDTH = 75%>
<H2>Gnome computing</H2>
<OL>
<LI>Gnome World</LI>
<LI>Seamus Sosmall's home page </LI>
</OL>
<HR SIZE = 6 NOSHADE>
<ADDRESS>Ingrid Bottomlow </ADDRESS>
</BODY>
</HTML>
```

Netscape - [My Gnome Page]

File Edit View Go Bookmarks Options Directory Window Help

Welcome to my Gnome Page

Gnomic sayings

- Every gnome should have one.
- There's gno place like Gnome. (Old Alaskan proverb)
- Gnome is where the heart is.

Gnome computing

1. Gnome World
2. Seamus Sosmall's home page

Ingrid Bottomlow

Document: Done

Simple line

Unordered List

Thicker line, set to 75% of the window width

Ordered List

Solid line

249

Images

There's no doubt that images add greatly to a page, but there is a cost. Image files are very large compared to text files, and even small images will significantly increase the downloading time for a page. In the example opposite, the text takes 600 bytes – almost instant downloading – while the picture is over 30Kb and will take 10 seconds or more to come in. So, include images, but keep your visitors happy by following these rules:

● Keep the images as small as possible;

● If you want to display large images – perhaps your own photo gallery, put them on separate (linked) pages and tell your visitors how big they will be.

● Include text describing the image, for the benefit of those who browse with AutoLoad Images turned off.

The basic image tag is:

    <IMG SRC = "filename">

You can also use these options:

    ALIGN = "left/center/right"
    ALT = "description"

ALIGN sets the position of the image acros the page.

ALT is the text to display if the image is not loaded into a browser. In the example opposite, if image loading was turned off, you would see this: A picture of me - 32Kb

Background images

You can tile a page with the BACKGROUND = "filename" option in the <BODY> tag. The image is repeated across and down to fill the window.

Tip

Images must be in GIF or JPG format for browsers to be able to display them. When you are preparing your images, try both formats and use the smallest.

Take note

Paint can only produce BMP images. To convert these to GIF or JPG you will need PaintShop Pro, LView or similar graphics software. Head for a shareware site and look for graphics software.

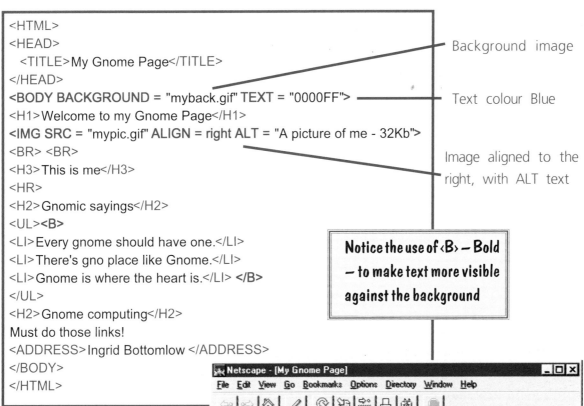

```
<HTML>
<HEAD>
   <TITLE>My Gnome Page</TITLE>
</HEAD>
<BODY BACKGROUND = "myback.gif" TEXT = "0000FF">
<H1>Welcome to my Gnome Page</H1>
<IMG SRC = "mypic.gif" ALIGN = right ALT = "A picture of me - 32Kb">
<BR> <BR>
<H3>This is me</H3>
<HR>
<H2>Gnomic sayings</H2>
<UL><B>
<LI>Every gnome should have one.</LI>
<LI>There's gno place like Gnome.</LI>
<LI>Gnome is where the heart is.</LI> </B>
</UL>
<H2>Gnome computing</H2>
Must do those links!
<ADDRESS>Ingrid Bottomlow </ADDRESS>
</BODY>
</HTML>
```

Background image

Text colour Blue

Image aligned to the right, with ALT text

Notice the use of <B> – Bold – to make text more visible against the background

The trick with background images is to use one which doesn't clash too much with the text. Very pale or bright images and black text work well. In this example, the background image is the same as the main picture, but smaller and with fewer, paler colours – and if it was even simpler and paler, the text would be more readable.

Links

A link is created with a pair of tags. The first contains the URL of the page or file to be linked, and takes the form:

<A HREF=*URL*>

The second is a simple closing tag </A>. The two enclose the image or text that becomes the clickable link, e.g.

<A HREF="http://www.gnomeworld.gn">Gnome World </A>

As you can see from the example opposite, the link can be embedded within a larger item of text – only '**here**' is clickable in the *IT's Made Simple* line. You can also use an image with, or instead of, text to make the link.

The example only has Web URLs, but you can equally well create links to FTP files and newsgroups. You can also add a link to give readers an easy way to contact you. This line:

<A HREF = "mailto:me@my.e-mail.address"> Mail me </A>

will open a new mail message window, with your e-mail address in the To: slot.

Links within the page

If you have a page that runs over several screens, you might want to include links within the page, so that your readers can jump from one part to another. The clickable link follows the same pattern as above, but you must first define a named place, or *anchor*, to jump to.

<A NAME = "Top">**This is the start of something big** </A>

This defines the place as 'Top'. The anchor tags can fit round any text or image.

The HREF tag is slightly different for a jump.

<A HREF = #Top> **Return to top of page** </A>

Notice the # before the anchor name. This is essential.

Take note

There's more to links than is shown here. In fact there is a lot more to HTML than can be covered in this book. If this has whetted your appetite and you want to know more, read *Designing Internet Home Pages Made Simple*.

Tip

At some point, contact your access provider to find out what to call the home page file and where to store it and its images.

Anchor created on the heading

```
<HTML>
<HEAD>
  <TITLE>My Gnome Page</TITLE>
</HEAD>
<BODY>
<A NAME = "Top"><H1>Welcome to my Gnome Page</H1>  </A>
<IMG SRC = "mypic.gif" ALIGN = right ALT = "A picture of me">
<H2>Gnomic sayings</H2>
<UL>
<LI>Every gnome should have one.</LI>
<LI>There's gno place like Gnome.</LI>
<LI>Gnome is where the heart is.</LI>
</UL>
<H2>Gnome computing</H2>
<P><A HREF="http://www.gnomeworld.gn"> <IMG SRC = "world.gif"> Gnome World  </A>
<P><A HREF="http://www.gnome.net/~seamus"> Seamus Sosmall's home page </A>
<P>IT's Made Simple  <A HREF="http://www.bh.co.uk/MadeSimple.htm"> here</A>
<P><A HREF = #Top> Return to top of page </A>
<ADDRESS>Ingrid Bottomlow </ADDRESS>
</BODY>
</HTML>
```

Link with an image and text

Link on one word only

Link to jump to the top

Linked images are outlined

Linked text is underlined

Netscape - [My Gnome Page]

File Edit View Go Bookmarks Options Directory Window Help

Welcome to my Gnome Page

Gnomic sayings

- Every gnome should have one.
- There's gno place like Gnome.
- Gnome is where the heart is.

Gnome computing

Gnome World

Seamus Sosmall's home page

IT's Made Simple here

Return to top of page

Document: Done

253

Summary

- **HTML** stands for HyperText Markup Language, and is a set of tags and instructions that tells browsers how to display a page.

- **Text can be formatted** to appear as headings, bulletted or numbered lists, or in the *address* style.

- The background and the text can be set in the **colours** of your choice.

- Plain text pages can be improved by the use of **bulleted** or **numbered lists** and of **lines**.

- **Images** can be inserted anywhere on the page, and aligned to the left, centre or right of the display.

- Include **ALTernative text** in your image tags, for readers who have their image loading turned off.

- An image can be set to form a **background**, and will be repeated across and down to fill the window.

- You can add **links** to your other pages, to pages on remote sites or to a targeted point within a page.

15 Netscape's editor

The HTML editor

Netscape Gold's editor (Composer in Communicator) is easy to use and handles most aspects of HTML. It has no tools for creating forms or frames (sub-divided windows) – areas where many HTML editors also struggle. However, it is very good for handling text, images, links and tables. It also provides an easy way to upload files to your access provider when you are ready to publish your home page.

If you want a hand in designing your pages, Netscape has templates and wizards available on-line.

Basic steps

1 If you want to use a **Template** or **Wizard**, go on-line first.

2 Open the **File** menu, and point to **New Document**.

3 Select **Blank** to start from scratch.

or

4 Select **Template** or **Wizard** and follow its instructions.

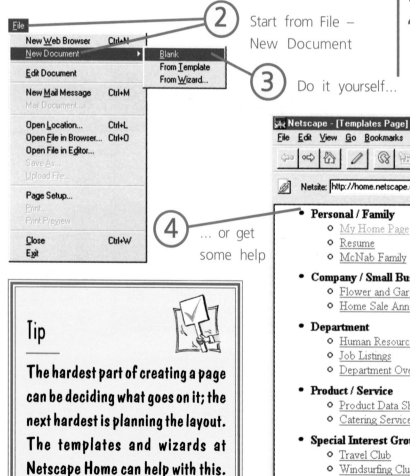

Start from File – New Document

Do it yourself...

... or get some help

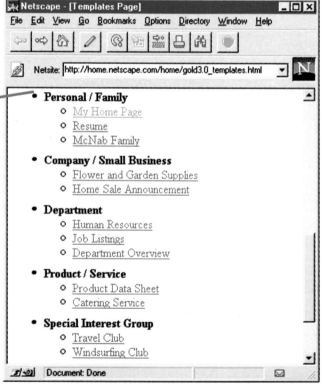

Tip

The hardest part of creating a page can be deciding what goes on it; the next hardest is planning the layout. The templates and wizards at Netscape Home can help with this.

The editor window

Use the editor as you would any word-processor. Style, alignment and indents can be set from the Paragraph Format Toolbar; font size, emphasis and colour settings can be set from the Character Format Toolbar.

Images, links, lines and tables can be inserted where required in the text.

File and Edit tools

Character Format tools

Paragraph Format tools

Insert objects

View in Browser   Link   Anchor   Line

Image   Table

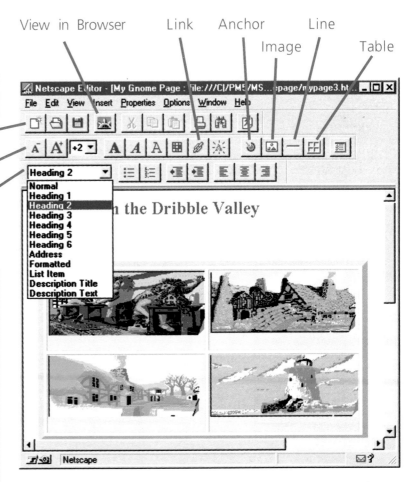

Text-only tables are easy to construct. Those containing images need some tweaking to make them work well.

Editor Preferences

These can, of course, be set to changed at any time, but it is as well to get a few of the key ones sorted out at the very start. But before going to the panels, you should arm yourself with some information:

- If you may ever want to edit the HTML code directly – perhaps to add tags that the editor cannot handle – you will need to take the text into Notepad or a word processor. Decide which you will use, and locate its .EXE file in your folders. (NotePad should be in the Windows folder.)

- If you want to be able to edit images, you will need to link in a graphics program such as Paint Shop Pro or Lview. Paint will not do, as the images should be in <u>JPG or GIF format</u> (page 230).

- If you are creating your own home page, to be published on the Web, you need to know where the files should be stored on your access provider's site, and the URL of your page. Talk to your access provider.

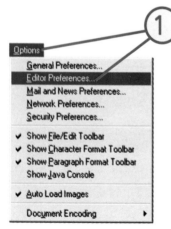

Select Options – Editor Preferences…

Tip

Leave the Appearance options alone, unless you want all your pages to have a common appearance.

1 Open the **Options** menu (**Edit – Preferences** in Composer) and select Editor Preferences…

2 On the **General** panel, enter your **name** – this is written into your pages (see page 264).

3 **Browse** through your folders to locate text and image editors if you need them.

4 Turn **Auto save** on.

5 On the **Publish** panel, leave the **Maintain links** and **Keep images with documents** options checked.

6 Enter the **FTP** URL of your space at your access provider's site.

7 Enter the HTTP URL for your home page.

8 Enter your **user name** and **password** – these will be needed when you upload your files.

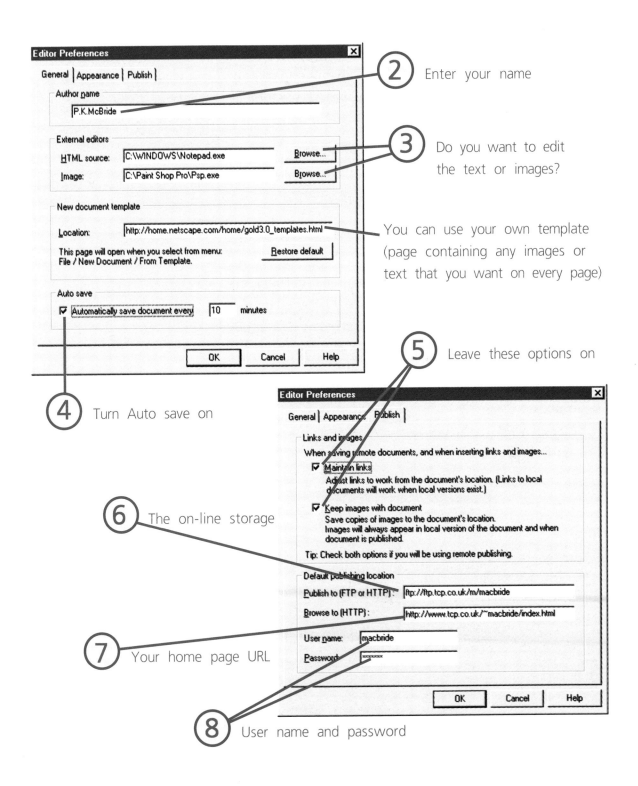

Enter your name

Do you want to edit the text or images?

You can use your own template (page containing any images or text that you want on every page)

Leave these options on

Turn Auto save on

The on-line storage

Your home page URL

User name and password

Tables

Tables are very fiddly things to construct when you are writing the HTML code directly in NotePad, but remarkably easy in the Editor. If you don't believe me, have a look at the Document Source after you have made a table!

Before you start, sketch out the table on paper – it saves having to adjust it later.

Made Simple Books	Out Now	1998
Applications	28	6
Internet	8	4
Programming	8	3

This needs a table of 4 Rows and 3 Columns. Initially, all the text will have the Normal style. Once it is typed in, the top row and left column text can be restyled as Headings.

The overall size of the table can be fixed pixels, or set as a percentage of the window. Percentages are better – you cannot know how large your readers' windows will be.

1 Use **Insert** – **Table** or click FF to open the New Table Properties.

2 Set the number of **Rows** and **Columns**.

3 Set the display options as required.

4 Click **OK** to create the blank table.

5 Move through the cells entering your text.

❑ **Fine tuning**

6 Select the cell(s) and right click to open the short menu.

7 Select **Table Properties** and adjust settings as desired.

① Open New Table Properties

② Set the Rows and Columns

③ Set display options

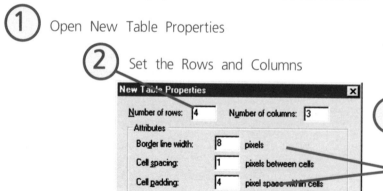

See screenshot opposite

Background colour

Heading text works just as well

④ Click OK

Alignment of table across the screen

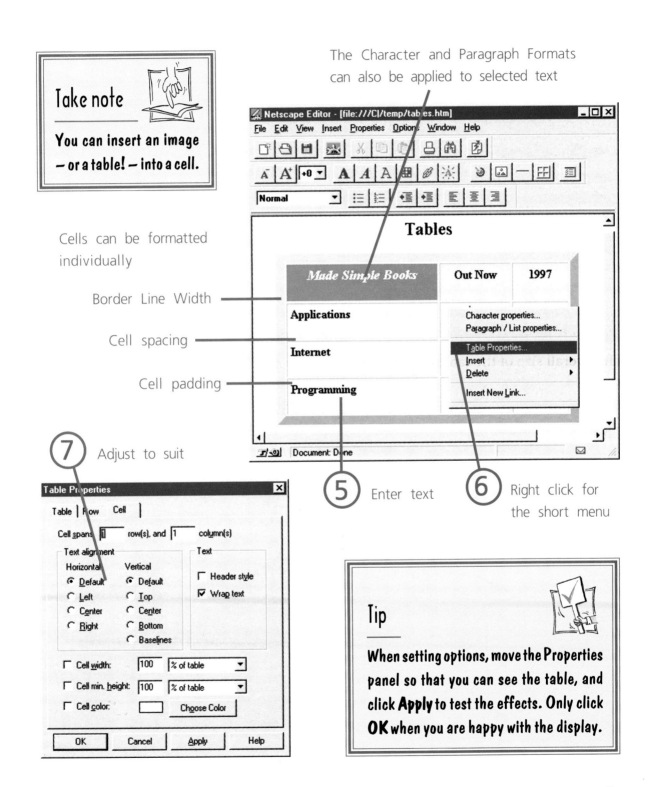

Take note

You can insert an image
— or a table! — into a cell.

Cells can be formatted
individually

Border Line Width

Cell spacing

Cell padding

Netscape Editor - [file:///C|/temp/tables.htm]

File Edit View Insert Properties Options Window Help

Normal

Tables

Made Simple Books	**Out Now**	**1997**
Applications		
Internet		
Programming		

Character properties...
Paragraph / List properties...

Table Properties...
Insert
Delete

Insert New Link...

Document: Done

⑦ Adjust to suit

Table Properties

Table | Row | Cell |

Cell spans 1 row(s), and 1 column(s)

Text alignment

Horizontal
- ● Default
- ○ Left
- ○ Center
- ○ Right

Vertical
- ● Default
- ○ Top
- ○ Center
- ○ Bottom
- ○ Baselines

Text
- ☐ Header style
- ☑ Wrap text

☐ Cell width: 100 % of table
☐ Cell min. height: 100 % of table
☐ Cell color: ▢ Choose Color

OK   Cancel   Apply   Help

⑤ Enter text

⑥ Right click for
the short menu

Tip

When setting options, move the Properties
panel so that you can see the table, and
click **Apply** to test the effects. Only click
OK when you are happy with the display.

261

Forms

Forms are an excellent way to get feedback from your visitors. Unfortunately Netscape's HTML editor cannot handle them, though they can be written in NotePad (or any other word-processor) without too much trouble.

The simple example given here shows some of the main features of forms. You might like to copy it, then adapt it and extend it to fit your needs.

The text at the bottom of this page should be typed into a new page, between the <BODY> and </BODY> tags. When viewed in the editor you will see the torn 'tag' icon in place of each of the <FORM> and <INPUT> tags in your text. View the page in your browser, and the tags will turn into text slots, radio buttons and a "Send Now" button.

Basic steps

1 Click 🗋 to start a new document.

2 Use View – Edit Document to take it into NotePad.

3 Type in the code shown below.

4 Save the file and return to the HTML editor.

5 Click 🖼 to view it in the Browse window.

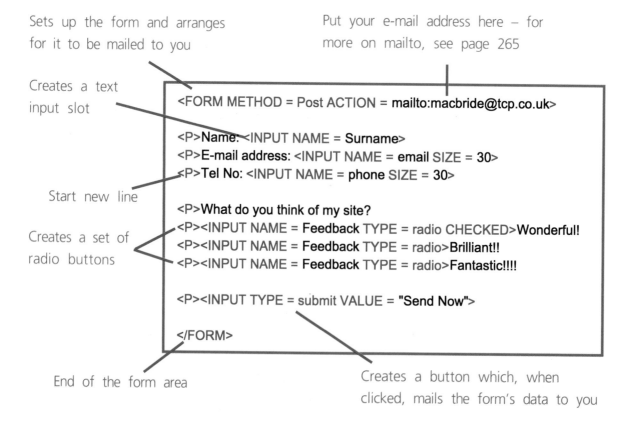

Sets up the form and arranges for it to be mailed to you

Put your e-mail address here – for more on mailto, see page 265

Creates a text input slot

Start new line

Creates a set of radio buttons

```
<FORM METHOD = Post ACTION = mailto:macbride@tcp.co.uk>

<P>Name: <INPUT NAME = Surname>
<P>E-mail address: <INPUT NAME = email SIZE = 30>
<P>Tel No: <INPUT NAME = phone SIZE = 30>

<P>What do you think of my site?
<P><INPUT NAME = Feedback TYPE = radio CHECKED>Wonderful!
<P><INPUT NAME = Feedback TYPE = radio>Brilliant!!
<P><INPUT NAME = Feedback TYPE = radio>Fantastic!!!!

<P><INPUT TYPE = submit VALUE = "Send Now">

</FORM>
```

End of the form area

Creates a button which, when clicked, mails the form's data to you

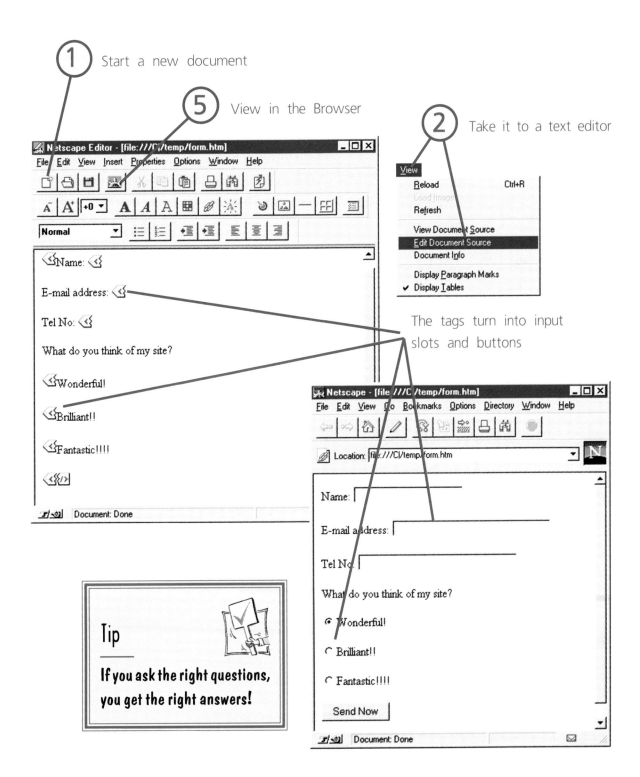

① Start a new document

⑤ View in the Browser

② Take it to a text editor

The tags turn into input slots and buttons

Tip

If you ask the right questions, you get the right answers!

263

Finishing touches

Headers and keywords

The <HEAD> area is invisible unless you view the document source, but it is important. This is the part that holds the page's title, its author's name, and the keywords that search engines will use for classifying – and for finding – the page. These can all be entered through the Document Properties panel, and should be done for any page that you want people to be able to find.

Basic steps

1 Open the **Properties** menu and select **Document**.

2 Enter the **Title**, **Author** and a **Description**.

3 Enter keywords to describe your home page into both the **Keywords** and **Classification** slots.

4 Click **OK**.

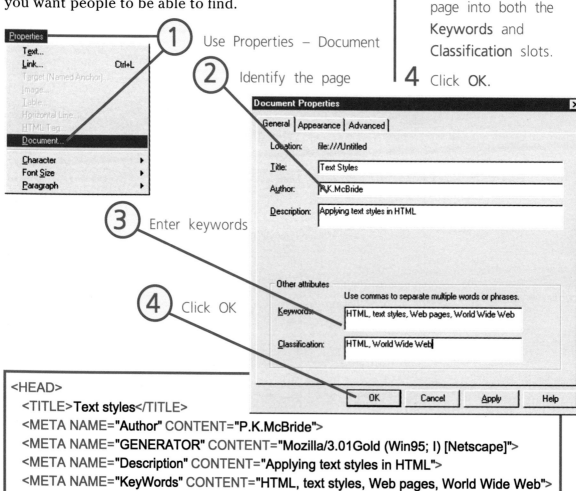

Use Properties – Document

Identify the page

Enter keywords

Click OK

```
<HEAD>
  <TITLE>Text styles</TITLE>
  <META NAME="Author" CONTENT="P.K.McBride">
  <META NAME="GENERATOR" CONTENT="Mozilla/3.01Gold (Win95; I) [Netscape]">
  <META NAME="Description" CONTENT="Applying text styles in HTML">
  <META NAME="KeyWords" CONTENT="HTML, text styles, Web pages, World Wide Web">
  <META NAME="Classification" CONTENT="HTML, World Wide Web">
</HEAD>
```

Mail from the page

1 Type in some suitable text, such as *Mail to me* and select all or part of it.

2 Click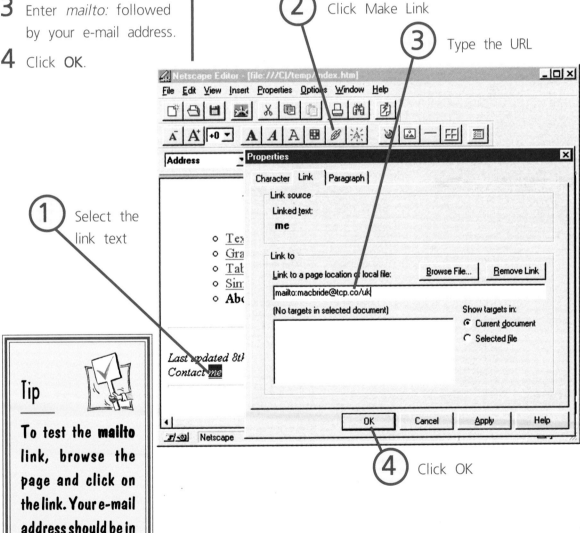

3 Enter *mailto:* followed by your e-mail address.

4 Click **OK**.

If you want readers to be able to get in touch with you, include a mailing link in your page. This should have *mailto:* followed by your e-mail address as the URL. When a reader clicks on this link, the Mail Composition window will open, with your address already in the Mail To slot.

Click Make Link

Type the URL

Select the link text

Tip

To test the **mailto** link, browse the page and click on the link. Your e-mail address should be in the **Mail To** slot.

Click OK

Publishing your page

To publish your page(s) on the World Wide Web, you must upload all the necessary files to the appropriate place at your access provider's site. Before doing this, check your files, and check your links.

Organising the files

When you upload your files to your access provider's site, they will be copied to one folder, with the links automatically adjusted to match their location. If they are not there already, move the files for your pages and images into one folder – then edit each page containing links and adjust the URLs if necessary.

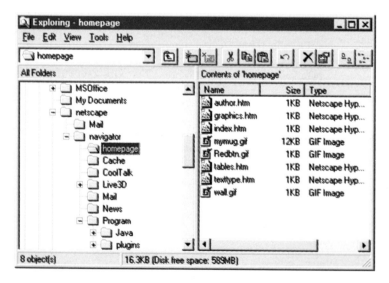

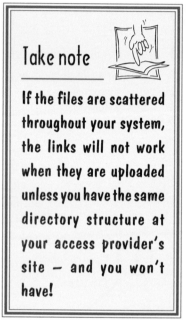

Take note

If the files are scattered throughout your system, the links will not work when they are uploaded unless you have the same directory structure at your access provider's site – and you won't have!

Final testing

Double check the links by loading the home page (the top page of the set) into the Browser window. Visit every linked page and make sure that every image is displayed. If you have links to remote sites, go on-line and check those links.

Basic steps

Uploading

1 Connect to your on-line service.

2 Open the home page in the HTML editor.

3 Select **File** – **Publish** or click 📄

4 Set the **All files** option.

5 Enter your **Password**.

6 Click **OK**.

7 Wait while the files upload.

8 Click **Yes** and browse your new on-line pages, checking their links carefully.

Netscape makes uploading very simple. If you do have trouble, check the FTP address with your access provider – that is the most likely cause of problems.

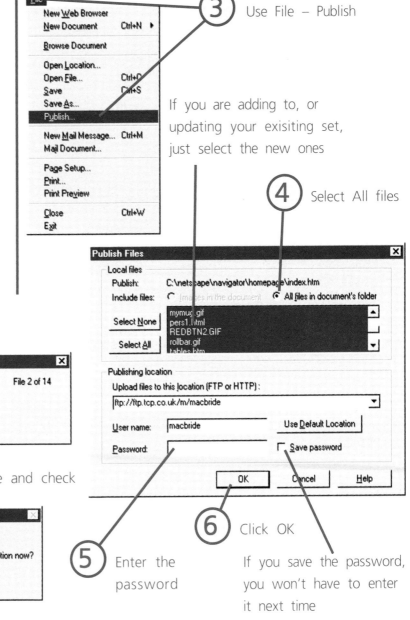

③ Use File – Publish

If you are adding to, or updating your exisiting set, just select the new ones

④ Select All files

⑤ Enter the password

⑥ Click OK

If you save the password, you won't have to enter it next time

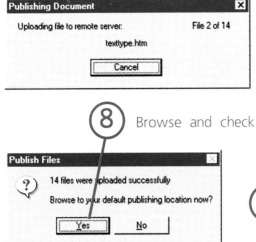

⑦ Watch and wait

⑧ Browse and check

267

Summary

- **Netscape's HTML editor** makes Web page creation much easier. It is used just like a word-processor, and can handle text formatting, lines, images, links and tables.

- If you want to **edit the source code** directly, you should link a text editor in the Preferences panel.

- If you **write your name** into the Preferences panel, it will be automatically entered into your pages to identify you as the author.

- You must give the **FTP address** of your Web space, and the **URL** of your **home page**.

- **Tables** can be constructed easily in the editor, but if you want forms, you have to write the source code!

- If you add **keywords**, search engines will be able to index your site.

- Before uploading your pages, **assemble all the files** into one folder.

- **After publishing** your page, check it thoroughly.

16 FrontPage Express

Introducing FrontPage

FrontPage Express is supplied as part of the full Internet Explorer package. It is a cut-down version of FrontPage, a comprehensive Web page creation and site administration package (with additional graphics software). FrontPage Express lacks the administration and graphics software but has almost identical page editing facilities. The good set of tools, wizards and WebBots (see page 280) greatly simplify page creation.

Basic steps

1 Open the **File** menu, and select **New**.

2 Select **Normal Page** to start from scratch.

or

3 Select a **Wizard** and follow its instructions.

4 Click **OK**.

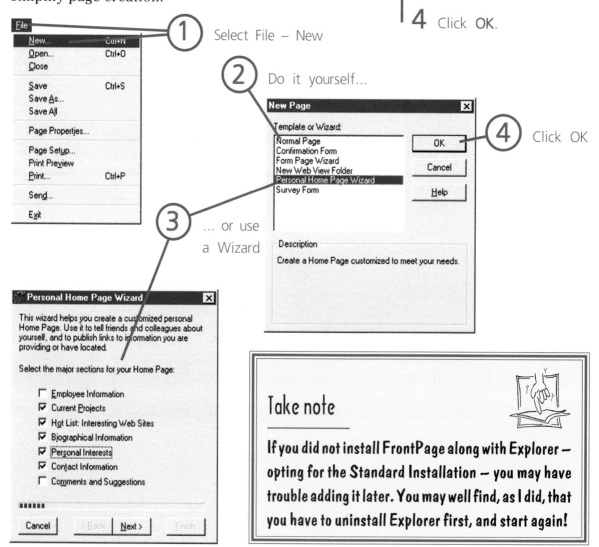

Select File – New

Do it yourself...

... or use a Wizard

Click OK

Take note

If you did not install FrontPage along with Explorer – opting for the Standard Installation – you may have trouble adding it later. You may well find, as I did, that you have to uninstall Explorer first, and start again!

The editing tools

The main toolbar is identical to that of Word. Use these tools to set styles, fonts, alignment, bulleted or numbered lists, idents, emphasis and colour.

The second toolbar has the usual file and cut-and-paste facilities, plus tools for inserting tables, images, links, and WebBot componets.

The Form Fields toolbar can be docked in the window frame or set to float anywhere on the window.

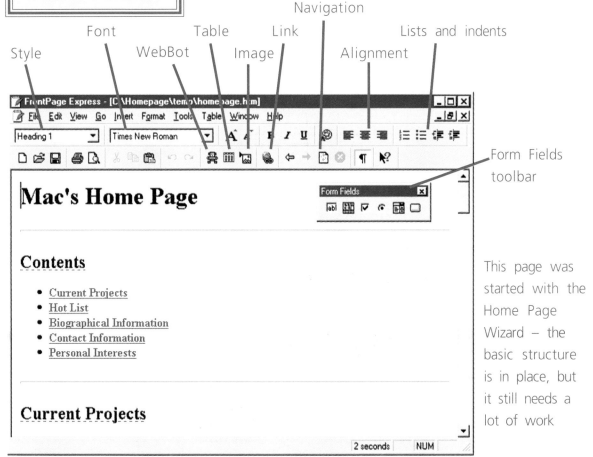

Navigation

Style Font WebBot Table Image Link Alignment Lists and indents

Form Fields toolbar

This page was started with the Home Page Wizard – the basic structure is in place, but it still needs a lot of work

Tables

Like Netscape's editor, FrontPage makes light work of the chore of setting up tables. The Insert table tool will give you the basic structure. You can then work your way round the cells, inserting text, images – or even other tables. Formats can be applied to the whole table, or to selected rows, columns or individual cells. The overall size of the table can be fixed in pixels, or set as a percentage of the window.

Basic steps

1 Place the cursor where the table is to go.

2 Click .

3 Drag the highlight to set the size.

4 Enter and format your text and images.

5 Right click on the table to get the short menu.

6 Select **Table Properties**

7 Adjust settings as required.

8 Click **OK**.

② Click Insert Table

③ Drag to size

2 by 4 Table

④ Enter and format contents

① Position the cursor

⑤ Right click on the table

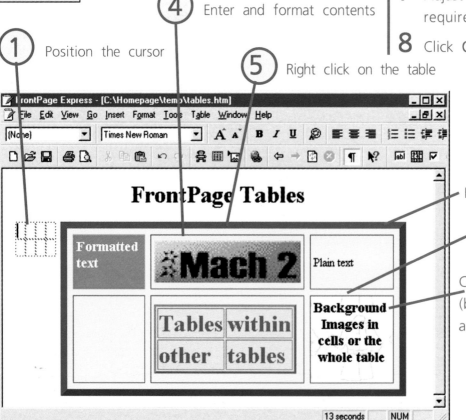

Border Line Width

Cell spacing (between cells)

Cell padding (between contents and frame)

Cells can be formatted individually

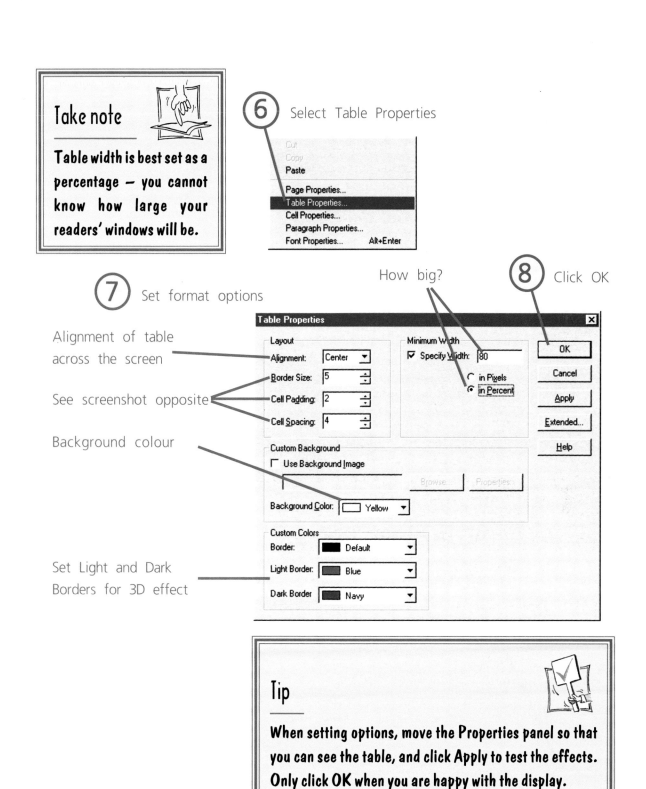

Take note

Table width is best set as a percentage – you cannot know how large your readers' windows will be.

(6) Select Table Properties

Cut
Copy
Paste

Page Properties...
Table Properties...
Cell Properties...
Paragraph Properties...
Font Properties...   Alt+Enter

How big?

(8) Click OK

(7) Set format options

Alignment of table across the screen

See screenshot opposite

Background colour

Set Light and Dark Borders for 3D effect

Table Properties

Layout
Alignment: Center
Border Size: 5
Cell Padding: 2
Cell Spacing: 4

Minimum Width
☑ Specify Width: 80
  ○ in Pixels
  ● in Percent

OK
Cancel
Apply
Extended...
Help

Custom Background
☐ Use Background Image

Browse   Properties

Background Color: ☐ Yellow

Custom Colors
Border: ■ Default
Light Border: ■ Blue
Dark Border: ■ Navy

Tip

When setting options, move the Properties panel so that you can see the table, and click Apply to test the effects. Only click OK when you are happy with the display.

273

Forms

Writing your own HTML code to create a form can take time. The Form Fields toolbar in FrontPage simplifies the job, though you still have to do some work to ensure that when the form is sent back to you, you can identify the items your visitor entered and the selections s/he made.

● Every Form Field must have a name.

● Text boxes can have sample text in them.

● Check boxes can be set on or off and need labels to tell the visitor what they're for.

● Radio buttons must have a Value (for feedback) and a text prompt.

● Drop-down menus need Choices (menu items) and Values (for feedback).

1 Place the cursor (type a label if needed) where you want the first field.

2 Select the field from the Form Field toolbar.

3 Right click on the field and select **Form Field Properties**.

4 Set the **Name** and **Value** as required.

5 Click **OK**.

6 Repeat to add more fields.

Keep all the fields within the outline – unless you want to have several separate forms on the page.

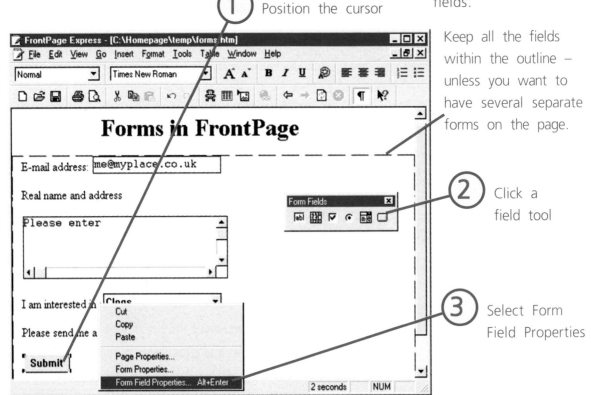

Position the cursor

Click a field tool

Select Form Field Properties

274

The Form Fields

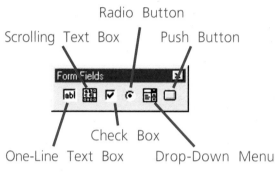

Scrolling Text Box

Radio Button

Push Button

One-Line Text Box

Check Box

Drop-Down Menu

Buttons are simple – use Submit for one to send the form, or Reset to clear the values.

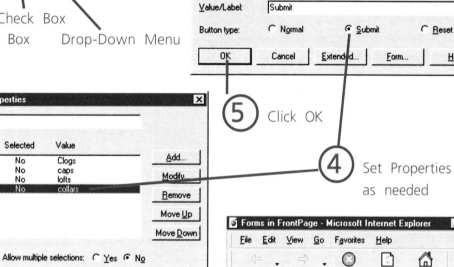

⑤ Click OK

④ Set Properties as needed

Menus are more complicated. To create each item, click **Add** and type in the **Choice** (which appears on the menu). This will also be used as the feedback Value, unless you select **Specify Value** and enter your own word.

The Form as it appears in the browser

Images

Images are not difficult to manage in HTML, but FrontPage offers a few nice extra touches. It has a small, but well designed, set of Clip Art images – the Backgrounds and Lines are particularly good.

Basic steps

1 Open the **Insert** menu and select **Image**.

2 Switch to the **Clip Art** panel.

3 Select a **Category**.

4 Pick an image and click **OK**.

5 Right click on the image for its menu and select **Image Properties**.

6 Add a link if wanted.

7 Use the **Appearance** panel to set its size and position, if necessary.

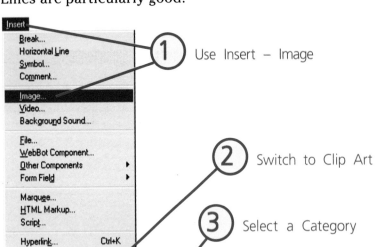

Use Insert – Image ①

Switch to Clip Art ②

Select a Category ③

Pick an image ④

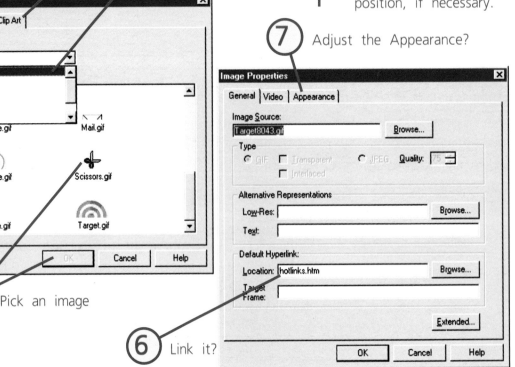

Adjust the Appearance? ⑦

Link it? ⑥

Basic steps

1 Open the **Format** menu and select **Background**.

2 Click **Browse**.

3 Select a background from the **Insert Image** dialog box.

4 Turn on Watermark if wanted.

5 Click **OK**.

You'll find this image in the Icons set

Backgrounds

A Background image can be easily added. If wanted, it can be set as a **Watermark**, so that when the screen is scrolled the background stays in place while the text and any other images move over it.

① Use Format – Background

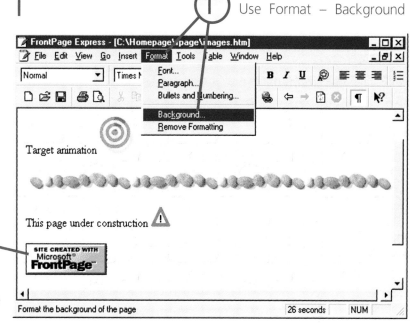

④ Set as Watermark?

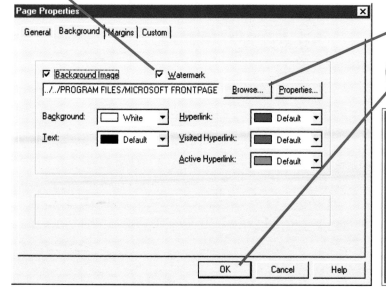

② Browse for an image

⑤ Click OK

Take note

The Watermark effect only works when the page is viewed with Internet Explorer 4.0.

277

Marquees

If you want scrolling text on your page, you can do it two ways – write a program in Java, JavaScript or ActiveX (hard work), or use a marquee. This will let you scroll text in either direction at a chosen speed.

You can only set the background colour from the Marquee Properties panel. If you want coloured text, or a different font or size, use the standard formatting tools.

- To select the marquee's text for formatting, click to the left – the whole text will be highlighted.

- To select the marquee itself (for moving or deleting), click anywhere within its border – the select handles will appear at the corners and mid-frame.

Key options

Delay   milliseconds between moves

Amount number of pixels to move

Scroll the text moves across and off before repeating

Slide   the repeat starts once the last character has been brought into view

Basic steps

1 Place the cursor where you want the marquee.

2 Type in the **Text**.

3 Select the options to define how the text scrolls.

4 In **Repeat**, select **Continuously** or set the number of **Times**.

5 Set a **Background Color** if wanted.

6 Click **OK**.

7 Select the text.

8 Set font styles and colour as required.

9 Save the page and view it in Explorer.

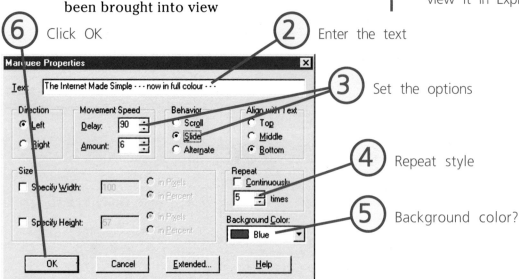

⑥ Click OK

② Enter the text

③ Set the options

④ Repeat style

⑤ Background color?

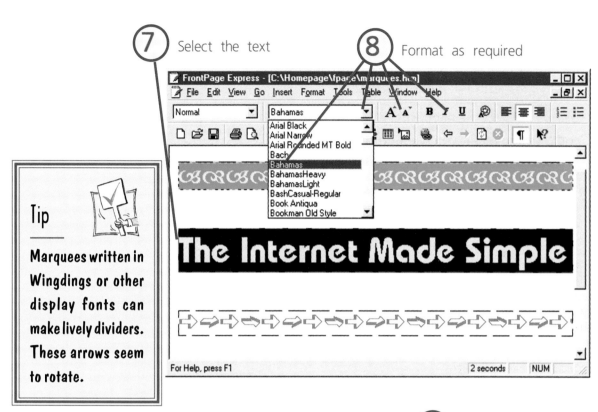

⑦ Select the text

⑧ Format as required

⑨ Check the effect

Tip

Marquees written in Wingdings or other display fonts can make lively dividers. These arrows seem to rotate.

Take note

Marquees only work when viewed through Internet Explorer. A visitor using Netscape will see plain text.

279

WebBots

WebBots are unique to FrontPage. They are ready-written routines that can add an extra level of interactivity to your page. There are three in the FrontPage Express package:

- **Include** imports an existing HTML file into the page;

- **Search** sets up a form to let visitors search for stuff at your site;

- **Timestamp** records the time and date of edits.

Basic steps

1 Place the cursor where you want the WebBot.

2 Open the **Insert** menu and select **WebBot Component**.

3 Select a WebBot.

4 Click **OK**.

5 Complete the options as required.

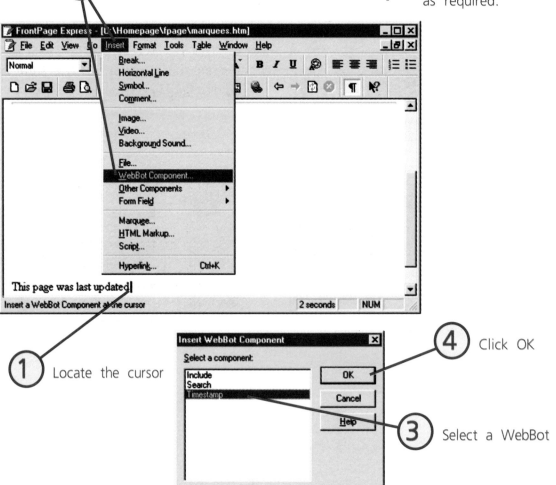

Use Insert – WebBot Component

1 Locate the cursor

3 Select a WebBot

4 Click OK

Include

Use this if you want the same headers or logos on every page. The included file can also have a background image and colour settings.

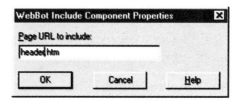

Search

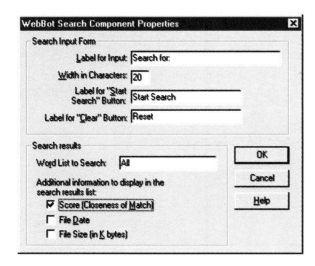

This produces a small form with a text box for the search item and buttons to start or reset the search. The Search WebBot will only work if your Internet Service Provider has FrontPage Extensions installed and running on their server. At the time of writing, few seemed to be offering this.

Timestamp

This should be set to record the time you edit and save the page. The automatic update only applies if the page has advanced WebBot, ActiveX or other components at work on it.

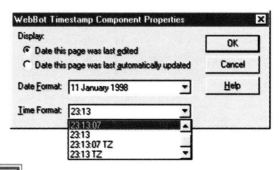

Take note

There's more on WebBots — and the other features of FrontPage Express (as well as the full FrontPage package) in *FrontPage Made Simple.*

Saving and publishing

The full version of FrontPage contains site management facilities, and could be used for running an intranet (within an organisation) or an extensive Web site. Aspects of this show through in FrontPage Express – you'll notice it in the saving routines.

Saving

Where most applications assume that you will save your files onto your hard disks, FrontPage assumes that they will be saved – as pages – directly to your Web site. While you are still developing your pages, you are better saving them as files on your hard disk.

1 Open the **File** menu and select **Save As...**

2 Edit the **Page Title** if required.

3 Click **As File...**

4 Select the folder.

5 Edit the **File name** if required.

6 Click **Save**.

7 If the page contains images, you will be asked if you want to save them to the same folder – click Yes.

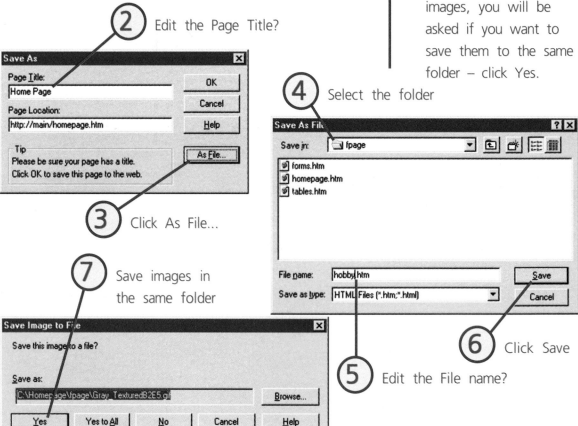

② Edit the Page Title?

③ Click As File...

⑦ Save images in the same folder

④ Select the folder

⑥ Click Save

⑤ Edit the File name?

Basic steps

Publishing

1 Open the **File** menu and select **Save As**.

2 Click **OK** and save any images if asked.

❑ The Web Publishing Wizard will start. Get on-line now.

3 Browse for the folder containing your files.

4 Select your server if you have set one up, otherwise click **New**.

5 Give the URL for your home page – your provider will tell you it.

6 Complete the Wizard.

The Web Publishing Wizard handles most of this. Before you run it, make sure that all the files – including any images and sounds – are all in one folder, and that this folder does not contain any other files.

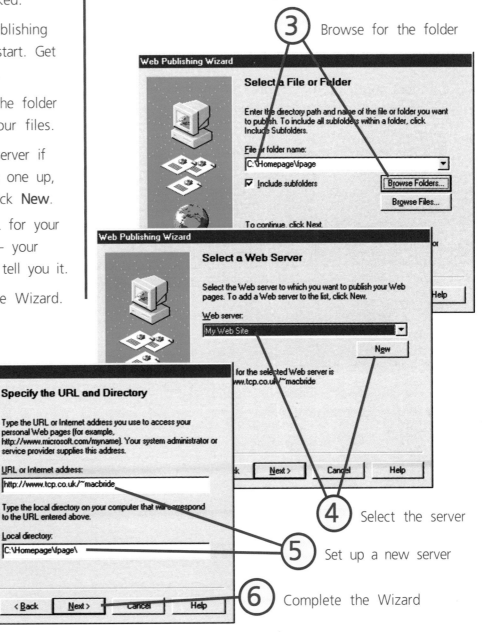

③ Browse for the folder

④ Select the server

⑤ Set up a new server

⑥ Complete the Wizard

Summary

- FrontPage Express is a cut-down version of Microsoft FrontPage. It has the same **excellent HTML editor**, but lacks the site management software.

- **Tables** are easily constructed. The table, selected cells or the contents of cells can be formatted separately.

- The **Form Fields** toolbar simplifies the creation of forms, but you will have to do some work – and you will need some understanding of forms – to set them up properly.

- There are sets of **Clip Art images** which can be incorporated into your pages.

- **Backgrounds** can be set as **Watermarks** to create an interesting effect.

- The simplest way to get scrolling text is to use a **marquee**, though these can only be enjoyed by visitors using Internet Explorer 4.0.

- **WebBots components** can add some extra interactivity to your pages.

- Page files should be **saved to your hard disk** at first. When you want to upload them to your home page directory at your service provider's site, use the **Web Publishing Wizard**.

Appendices

Access providers

Most of the big access providers, and some of the smaller ones, offer free trial membership. Take one of them up on the offer – but with care! There will be a limit to how many hours you can spend on-line for free. Once you are set up and on-line, you can look around to see who is providing services in your area and what their rates are.

Decision factors

- How much time a month will you spend on-line? You will get some hours 'free' in the membership charge, then pay for any additional time. Work out a total membership plus extra hours cost per month.

- How much will you pay for your phone calls? Is there a dial-in point within your local area? If you have a cable phone, can you call free in the evening?

- If you need to contact them, how good is their Help line (ring them!), and what do calls to it cost?

- How busy is their system – unfortunately you won't find this out until you start to use them regularly.

- Do they offer Web space for home pages? And help in creating them?

- Do they offer any additional services that you would want to use?

Provider lists

UK readers can find a comprehensive list of links to access providers at the **UK Directory**. Browse to:

http://www.ukdirectory.co.uk

select **Computers** from the top menu, then **Internet Service Providers**. You will find national and regional lists.

Take note

With most free trial membership offers, you will have to give your credit card details at the start, and will be debited for any hours you use over the free limit. Access providers may also set additional charges for premium services. These are typically financial and other commercial reference sources, but some on-line games incur extra costs.

Wherever you live, you can find a list of access providers in your area through **Yahoo**. Browse to:

http://www.yahoo.com

Work through these menu selections: **Regional > Countries** and pick your country, then continue: **Business > Companies > Internet Services > Access Providers.**

Type in the name of your home town or county and search for it *only in Access Providers* – with any luck it will narrow the field.

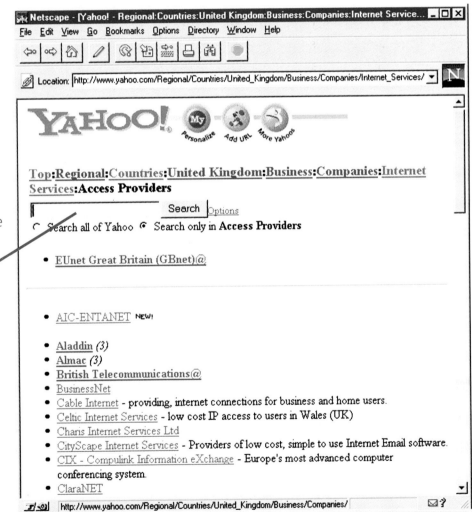

Shareware sites

www.clicked.com

Clicked offers the 'top 20 applications' in each of these areas. Internet applications, graphics, communications, multimedia, games and utilities.

www.download.net

This is a searchable archive for games, graphics, Internet, Winsock and desktop applications.

home.pi.net/~tuur

Quality, not quantity is the watchword here. The shareware listed at the Internet Top 20 is all reviewed and tested before inclusion.

www.jumbo.com

Jumbo takes a different approach – it will take everything it can find. Jumbo had over 200,000 programs on offer at the time of writing.

www.q-d.com/wsc.htm

Shareware Central runs an interactive catalog, welcoming submissions from shareware authors.

www.softsite.com

The Software Site is primarily for games enthusiasts. Its shareware is all tested and reviewed.

www.ukshareware.com

UK Shareware offers a good range of Internet applications and utilities.

www.hotfiles.com/index.html

The Software Library is just one of the Internet services run by ZDNet – and well worth a visit. A good source of graphics and software for the home user.

❑ Shareware can be tried out for free. If you want to use it after the trial period, you are asked to pay a (small) fee to its authors. The program's Help menu will tell you how to register your copy.

Some programs are **freeware** – and some of this is excellent!

Tip

CNET (www.cnet.com), one of the most active Internet 'broadcasters' runs several excellent shareware sites at:

ww.browsers.com/
www.gamecenter.com/
www.download.com/
www.shareware.com/

Tip

Pick your time carefully and you can download files faster. Avoid 7-11 in the evening, when you will be sharing your service provider's bandwidth with many other users. Avoid the working day at the FTP site, when you will be competing for the host computer's time with its local users — and remember that US sites will be anything from 5 to 10 hours behind UK time!

ftp.demon.co.uk (Demon Internet)

An excellent source of Internet tools and information – and while you're there you might look at what they have to offer as a service provider.

ftp.eff.org

The Electronic Frontier Foundation archives – if you are interested in Unix or Linux, this is where to go for software and source code.

ftp.uwp.edu

Its **/pub/msdos/games** directory is a major store of games – and it is frequently so crowded you can't get in.

ftp.microsoft.com

Microsoft's FTP base. Search it for information and software they have released into the public domain.

micros.hensa.ac.uk

Lots of Windows stuff in **/mirrors/cica/win3/desktop**. This is a mirror (copy) of the main cica site in the States.

src.doc.ic.ac.uk (Sunsite UK)

A miror of the major Sun FTP archive with huge range of DOS, Windows and other stuff, but a very busy site. Start from the **/pub** directory.

Take note

This is a very limited selection of a huge number of sites, with the focus on those in or closest to the UK. A full list can be found at:

ftp://scitsc.wlv.ac.uk/pub/netinfo/ftpsites

Parity and other bits

If you have ever played Chinese whispers, you will know that messages get garbled when you cannot hear clearly. The problem is worse with data communications, for computers cannot guess meanings. Over time a number of different **protocols** have been developed to ensure that data gets through. One of the earliest methods, still in use today, was based on the *parity* bit.

If you look at an **ASCII** table, you will see that the codes for all the normal text characters are less than 128. Now you can represent any numbers from 0 to 127 in binary using only 7 bits. As there are 8 bits to a byte, this leaves the leftmost bit available for checking purposes – enter the parity bit.

Even parity

With even parity checking, the '1's in each byte are counted, before transmission, and if there are an odd number, the eighth bit is set to '1'. When the byte reaches the other end of the line, if there are not an even number of '1's, the system knows that an error has occurred, and a message is sent out. If the byte gets through intact, the eighth bit is reset to '0' to restore the original character.

Character	ASCII	Binary	Even?	Parity bit set
S	83	01100011	Y	01100011
I	73	01001001	N	11001001
M	77	01001101	Y	01001101
P	80	01100000	Y	01100000
L	76	01001100	N	11001100
E	69	01000101	N	11000101

Take note

Parity checking is not foolproof. If two bits are corrupted in the same byte, it will still be even, and the error will not be detected. Parity checking is only the first line of defence against error.

Definitions

Binary files – programs, graphics, sounds, ZIP files and the like. If it isn't simple ASCII text, it's binary. If necessary binary files can be converted to a 7-bit form for transmission over connections that use 7 Data bits. One of the first Internet tools that you may need is a decoder to convert these files back to their proper 8-bit form. Don't worry – there are decoders out there, and they are free, and easy to find.

Odd parity

This is the same as even parity, except that the parity bit is adjusted so that every transmitted byte has an odd number of '1' bits. Either method will serve just as well, as long as the systems at both ends of the line use the same one.

Data bits

This refers to the bits in each byte that are used for holding data – typically 7 for ASCII text with parity checking, or 8 for **binary files**.

Stop bits

Some systems mark the end of each character by adding 1, 1.5 or 2 extra bits. (Yes, you can have half a bit as an electrical signal.) The extra bits do increase the length of signal for each character, but if they cut down errors – and retransmissions – then the overall volume of traffic on the line is reduced.

Common patterns

Parity, data bits and stop bits can be combined in many different ways. The two you are most likely to meet are:

8-N-1   8 Data bits, No Parity and 1 Stop bit.

7-E-1   7 Data bits, Even Parity and 1 Stop bit.

8-N-1 is the most common.

Data transfer protocols

These protocols come into use when you are downloading binary and text files. They control the flow of data, checking for errors and retransmitting corrupted parts of the file. The basic technique is to chop the data flow into blocks, and perform a calculation on the bytes to get a **checksum**. The block and its checksum are then sent off together. The same calculations are performed on the bytes at the other end, and if the result does not agree with the checksum, the receiving system asks for retransmission of that block.

Common data transfer protocols

Kermit — one of the oldest and slowest protocols, but also a reliable one. If all else fails, try Kermit.

Xmodem — another old one, but reliable and in regular use. This works equally well with binary and text files. You will sometimes see it labelled **Xmodem/CRC**. CRC stands for Cyclical Redundancy Check, a mathematically complex, but very effective form of error-checking.

Ymodem — a development of Xmodem, offering slightly faster data transfer.

Zmodem — the main difference here is that Zmodem gives faster throughput and can cope with a total connection failure. With the others, if the line goes down during the transmission of a file, you have to start again from scratch next time you try to download it. With Zmodem, the transfer can pick up where it left off, adding the new data to the part-finished file from the previous session.

Checksums

- The simplest technique adds up the values of the bytes, subtracting 256 every time the total goes over that. This results in a single byte checksum, e.g.

Char	Code	Sum
S	83	83
i	105	188
m	109	297
		−256
		41
p	112	153
l	108	261
		−256
		5
e	101	106
Checksum	=	106

Tip

Don't bother to try to understand the workings of Cyclical Redundancy Checks, unless you are a mathematician or a masochist.

Handshaking

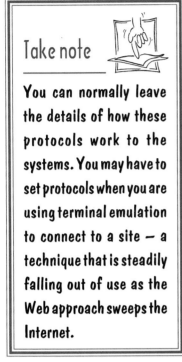

Take note

You can normally leave the details of how these protocols work to the systems. You may have to set protocols when you are using terminal emulation to connect to a site – a technique that is steadily falling out of use as the Web approach sweeps the Internet.

Handshaking is used to control the flow of data during the normal run of the session. It is needed because data may well be sent down the line faster than the receiving computer can cope with it.

There are three alternatives:

Hardware   where it is left to the hardware of the systems at both ends.

XON/XOFF   where the handshaking is managed by software. If the computer at the receiving end wants to halt the flow for a moment while it stores received data on disk, it will send an XOFF. An XON restarts the flow.

None   to be used where the other system does not use handshaking. You will rarely meet this.

If necessary you can set the protocols on the **Connection** and **Advanced Connection** panels of the **Modem Properties** dialog box

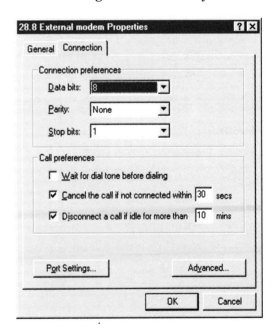

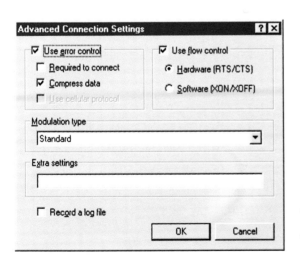

The **Call Preferences** are the only settings you will normally want to adjust for yourself

293

Data compression

The same kind of data compression techniques that allow Stacker to cram twice as much data on your hard disk, allow modems to push data through faster. On modems, they are usually merged with error correction techniques. There are two standards – MNP and V.42bis, offering compression from 2:1 up to 4:1. Both are widely used, and many current modems support both standards.

Data compression does not always give faster throughput. It basically works by replacing repeated bytes (or patterns of bytes) by one copy of the byte plus a count of the repetitions. It therefore works best with text files, where blocks of spaces and repeated patterns are common. It does not work well with executable files, where repetition is rare, and if the file is already compressed then further 'compression' can actually make it bigger! Most picture formats have some sort of compression built into them, and many of the text files available for downloading over the Internet are ZIPped.

If you want to test the effects of compression, get a copy of WinZIP (from any shareware site), and try ZIPping files of different types. You should find that compression ranges from 90% or more, down to 5% – you may even find that some small files produce larger 'compressed' files!

Definitions

MNP – Microcom Network Protocol. Microcom is one of the leading data communications companies.

ZIP – extension given to files that have been compressed by PKZIP or WINZIP. You need WINZIP to restore these to their proper state.

Index

K

Kermit 292
Keywords 88, 264

L

LAN 2
Lines, in HTML 248
Links, in HTML 252
Lists, in HTML 248
Live 3D 68
Local Area Network 2
Location, Netscape 34
Log on 148
Logical operators 111, 115, 122
Lurk 192
LView Pro 230
Lycos
  Personal Guide 98
  Searches 121
  Top 5% 96

M

Magellan
  Searching 122
Mail and News Preferences, Netscape 40
MailCity 169
Mailing lists 6
mailto, in HTML 265
Major TFPsites 289
MapEdit 67
Marquees, FrontPage 278
Match styles, Yahoo 90
Member directories 178
Memory cache, Netscape 39

Menus, Yahoo 87
Messages, Sending 154
Microcom Network Protocol 294
Microsoft Home Page 62
MicroSoft Network
  Directory 179
MIME 198
Minus sign 111, 122
MNP 294
Modem 15
  Commands 30
  Properties, Windows 95 28
  Settings 28
Modifiers 111
mpack 198
Multi-part binaries 200
Multimedia 238
munpack 198
My Channel, Excite 94

N

Naming conventions 10
Navigator 4.0 36
Navigator Preferences 44
NEAR operator 115
Net Nanny 81
NetGuide 170
Netiquette 192
Netscape 34
  HTML editor 256
  Home 46
  Mail 150
  Network Preferences 39
  Plug-ins 239
  Search 130

FRONTPAGE, Nat McBride, ISBN 0 7506 2941 X

FrontPage is the choice of professionals – and enthusiastic amateurs – for creating attractive, interactive Web pages and maintaining Web sites. Clearly explained, with lively examples, this book will show you how to use FrontPage to design and build professional quality Web sites.

DESIGNING INTERNET HOME PAGES, Lilian Hobbs, ISBN 0 7506 2941 X

Like to have your own home page on the World Wide Web? This book tells you how! Most Internet providers allow subscribers their own Web page, where they can tell people about themselves, show pictures and video clips, and get feedback through forms. With the help of this book, you'll soon have your own Web page designed and running.

COMPUSERVE, Keith Brindley, ISBN 0 7506 3512 6

CompuServe is the UK's largest Internet service provider with over 500,000 members. Want to shop on-line, get educational resources for the kids, send and receive email, join forums, and chat over the Internet? This book will tell you how in clear Made Simple style. Learn how to get the best out of CompuServe, or read it to get a flavour of the service before you subscribe,.

For more on the Internet try these best selling Made Simple books:

NETSCAPE, Sam Kennington, ISBN 0 7506 3514 2

INTERNET EXPLORER, Sam Kennington, ISBN 0 7506 3523 4

A Web browsers is the one essential tool for searching and browsing the Internet, and knowing how to use your browser is the key to working efficiently on the Internet. We have two books in the *Made Simple* series which cover the most popular browsers in use today.

Netscape's Navigator browser software has now reached an installed base of more than 38 million users, becoming the world's most popular personal computer application.

Internet Explorer, from Microsoft, is challenging Navigator's No. 1 position. In the newer versions this browser offers the same combination of power and ease of use.

Let these Made Simple books show you how to:

- set up your browser to suit the way you like to work
- surf the Web efficiently and find things quickly
- download files from the Internet
- use e-mail and read Newsgroup articles from within Internet Explorer
- create your own Web pages

All of these books, and the rest of the Made Simple Series, are available in your local bookshop, or in case of difficulty, direct from: Heinemann Publishers, Oxford, OX2 8EJ. Tel 01865 314300; Fax 01865 314091; Credit Card Sales, Tel 01865 314627.

COMPUTING
MADE SIMPLE

ONLY £8.99 · 160 PAGES · PAPERBACK

Access 97 for Windows
Moira Stephen
0 7506 3800 1   1997

Access for Windows 95 (Version 7)
Moira Stephen
0 7506 2818 9   1996

Access for Windows 3.1 (Version 2)
Moira Stephen
0 7506 2309 8   1995

NEW
Compuserve
Keith Brindley
0 7506 3512 6   1998

Designing Internet Home Pages
Lilian Hobbs
0 7506 2941 X   1996

Excel 97 for Windows
Stephen Morris
0 7506 3802 8   1997

Excel for Windows 95 (Version 7)
Stephen Morris
0 7506 2816 2   1996

Excel for Windows 3.1 (Version 5)
Stephen Morris
0 7506 2070 6   1994

NEW
Explorer (Version 4.0)
Sam Kennington
0 7506 3796 X   1998

NEW
FrontPage 97
Nat McBride
0 7506 3941 5   1998

Hard Drives
Ian Sinclair
0 7506 2313 6   1995

Internet Explorer
Sam Kennington
0 7506 3513 4   1997

Internet Resources
P. K. McBride
0 7506 2836 7   1996

NEW
Internet (Colour Edition)
P. K. McBride 0 7506 3944 X   1998   £14.99

The Internet for Windows 95 (Second Edition)
P. K. McBride
0 7506 3846 X   1997

Internet for Windows 3.1
P. K. McBride
0 7506 2311 X   1995

Lotus 1-2-3 for Windows 3.1 (Version 5)
Stephen Morris
0 7506 2307 1   1995

MS DOS   (Up To Version 6.22)
Ian Sinclair
0 7506 2069 2   1994

Microsoft Networking
P. K. McBride
0 7506 2837 5   1996

Multimedia for Windows 95
Simon Collin
0 7506 3397 2   1997

Multimedia for Windows 3.1
Simon Collin
0 7506 2314 4   1995

Netscape
Sam Kennington
0 7506 3514 2   1997

NEW
Netscape Communicator (Version 4.0)
Sam Kennington
0 7506 4040 5   1998

Office 97 for Windows
P. K. McBride
0 7506 3798 6   1997

Office 95
P. K. McBride
0 7506 2625 9   1995

NEW
Pagemaker
Steve Heath
0 7506 4050 2   1998

Powerpoint 97 for Windows
Moira Stephen
0 7506 3799 4   1997

Powerpoint for Windows 95 (Version 7)
Moira Stephen
0 7506 2817 0   1996

Powerpoint for Windows 3.1 (Version 4.0)
Moira Stephen
0 7506 2420 5   1995

NEW
Publisher 97
Moira Stephen
0 7506 3943 1   1998

NEW
Searching The Internet
P. K. McBride
0 7506 3794 3   1998

NEW
Windows 98
P. K. McBride
0 7506 4039 1   1998

Windows 95
P. K. McBride
0 7506 2306 3   1995

Windows 3.1
P. K. McBride
0 7506 2072 2   1994

Windows NT (Version 4.0)
Lilian Hobbs
0 7506 3511 8   1997

Word 97 for Windows
Keith Brindley
0 7506 3801 X   1997

Word for Windows 95 (Version 7)
Keith Brindley
0 7506 2815 4   1996

Word for Windows 3.1 (Version 6)
Keith Brindley
0 7506 2071 4   1994

Word Pro for Windows 3.1 (Version 4.0)
Moira Stephen
0 7506 2626 7   1995

Works for Windows 95 (Version 4.0)
P. K. McBride
0 7506 3396 4   1996

Works for Windows 3.1 (Version 3)
P. K. McBride
0 7506 2065 X   1994